THE
COMPLEAT
COOK

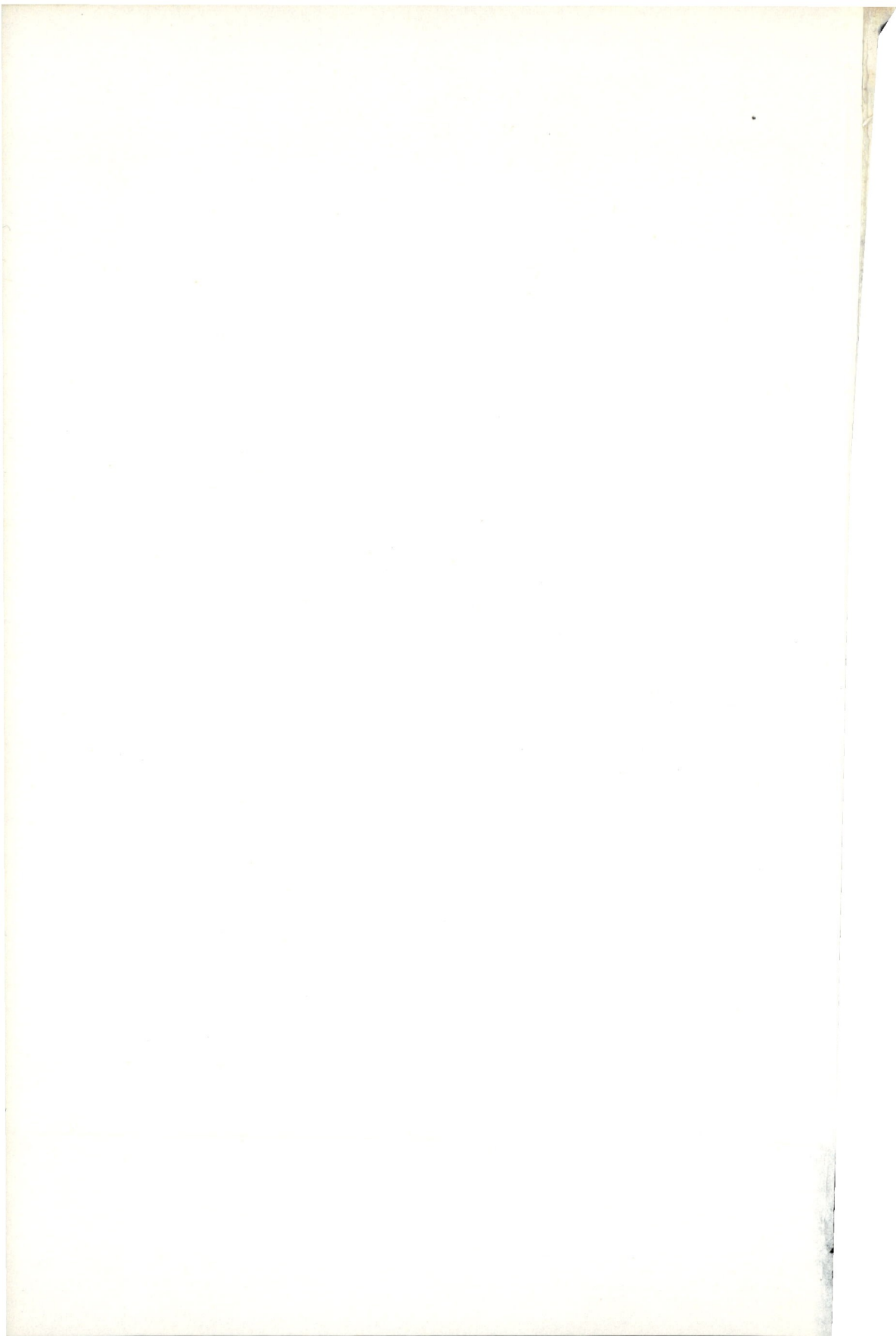

THE COMPLEAT COOK

or
the Secrets of a
Seventeenth-Century Housewife

by

REBECCA PRICE

compiled and introduced by
MADELEINE MASSON

original research material by
Anthony Vaughan

illustrated by
Pamela Lander

Routledge & Kegan Paul
LONDON

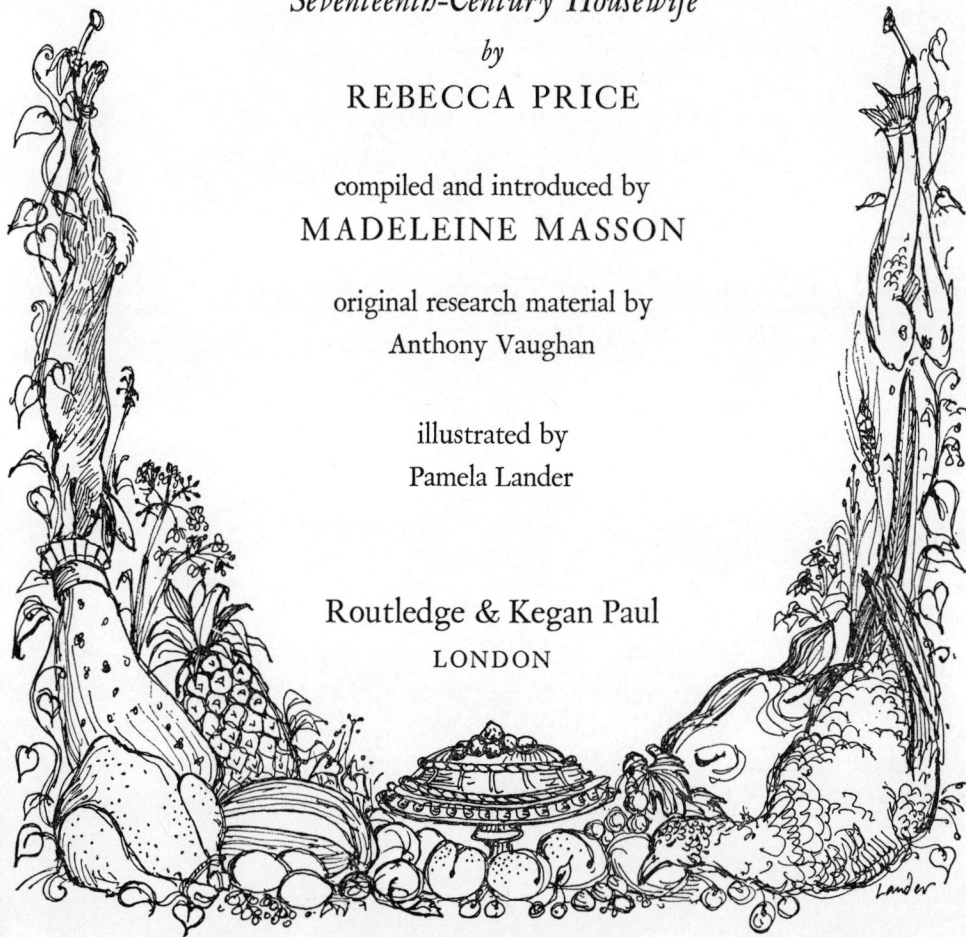

First published in 1974
by Routledge & Kegan Paul Ltd
Broadway House, 68-74 Carter Lane,
London EC4V 5EL
Printed in Great Britain by
W & J Mackay Limited, Chatham
© *Madeleine Masson 1974*

ISBN 0 7100 7444 1

This book is dedicated to
Merrick, Sarah, David, Diana
and Jeremy

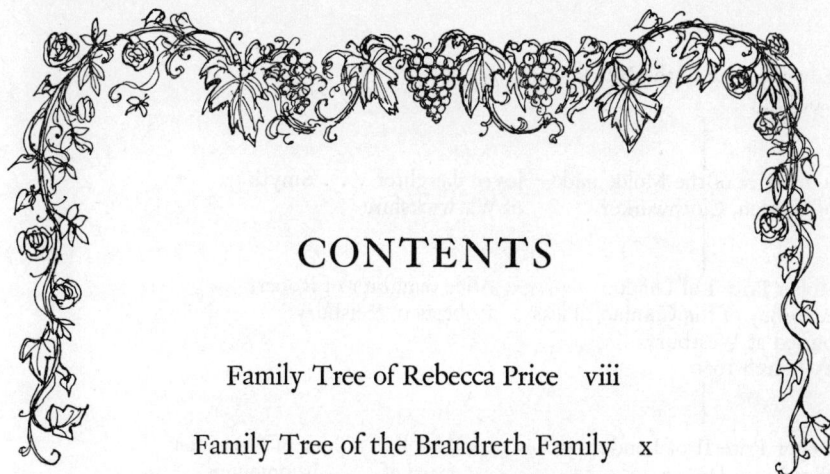

CONTENTS

Edward Price of the Molde =
Co. Flint

John Price of the Molde and = Joyce daughter . . . Smyth
of London, Clothworker   of Warwickshire

Roger Price I of London   = Alice daughter of Robert
Attorney of the Common Pleas   Roberts of Salisbury
buried at Westbury
25 March 1660

Roger Price II of London and   = Izraell daughter of Nathaniel
Westbury, Draper 1601–58   Love of . . . Ironmonger

Roger Price III of Westbury = Ann Ingham   George
died Bilbao 1677/8   daughter of . . .

Roger Price IV   = Elizabeth   Thomas   Edward
(M.P. Buckingham   buried 10 April   buried 4 June
1702)   1689   1702
1653–1705

                                                    Charles   Ingham
                                                    buried   1666–1729
John Price   Thomas Price = Mary . . .   9 September
Gentleman   died 1733   1683
Commoner
St John's College   Campbell Price
Oxford   died 1749
1683–1706

                                      George = . . .

                          Anna Maria = John Warner II
                                 (nephew of John Warner I)

                         John Warner III

FAMILY TREE
OF REBECCA PRICE

Joseph | REBECCA 1660–1740 = Nehemiah Brandreth of Houghton Regis (*see* Brandreth pedigree)

Anne died 12 May 1728 = 1. John Warner I Citizen of London 2. William Kersteman

Dorothy = . . . Wase

Edward

Henry Brandreth I of St Stephen Walbrook = Alice Bruch All Hallows the Less
purchased Houghton Regis Estate 1654   died 2 March 1683
1610–73

Solomon   Nehemiah I = REBECCA 2nd daughter of
1642–85   1652–1719   Roger Price Esq. of Westbury
                                        Bucks 1660–1740

                    Henry II = Mary Chibbald
                    died 1739   daughter of Wm Chibbald
                    aged 39   Deptford, Kent

            Ann   = Wm Duncombe   Mary   = Samuel Doddington
            1721 –fl.1772 | of Chalgrave   baptised   of Eastbury
                            Attorney   1731   Somerset
                                                               Esq.
                        Issue

Henry III = Rebecca Beech   Alice   = Thos Newton
1723–52   died 1779   baptised   Lombard St
            aged 55   1722   Goldsmith

FAMILY TREE OF THE BRANDRETH FAMILY

Alice = (1) Thos Smythe (2) William Milard
1649–1729   of Binderton   of London Knight
             Sussex Esq.   1653–1710

Nehemiah II = Isabella   Alice II   Rebecca = Thos Beech
died 1746   died 1717   died unmarried   of Redbourne
aged 58   aged 29   1772 aged 88   Herts

Thoswihan M.D. = Mary daughter   Isabella = Thos. Baskerfield
1712–52   of Banbrigg   baptised   Oilman
                 Buckeridge   1715
                 died 1784
                 aged 74

                 Nehemiah III = Frances Alston
                 1713–53
                 Attorney of
                 Dunstable
                            Issue
                                        Rebecca = Henry   Anne
                                                  Brandreth III

        Henry IV = Dionisia Turner
        1770–1846 died 1836

Henry V   Sarah Prosser = Thos Gibbs
1797–1840   1779–1858   1771–1849
unmarried

               Humphrey = Emma Jemima
               (took name   Barbara Smith
               Brandreth)   died 1867 aged 60
               1807–58

               Henry Chernocke Gibbs = Evelyn Frances
               Brandreth 1856–1908   Christabel Lawton

                            Issue
                            but the estate at this time
                            passed out of the family

ACKNOWLEDGMENTS

This work compiled from Rebecca Price's Receipt Book would never have been published in its present form without the teamwork which would certainly have appealed to the family-loving Rebecca.

Jenny and Tony Vaughan not only sustained and encouraged me to persevere with my self-imposed task but fed me continuously with information, notes and valuable data.

I must also thank The Public Record Office; the Society of Genealogists; Mr E. J. Davis, Buckinghamshire County Archivist; Miss Patricia Bell, the Bedfordshire County Archivist; Mr P. I. King, Northamptonshire County Archivist; the Brotherton Library at the University of Leeds; Messrs Connells of Bedford; Mr James Stewart of the University of London who made the whole project possible; the Rev. R. T. Brandreth and his mother, Mrs Brandreth, who visited Houghton Regis and remembered it as it must have been in Rebecca's time; the Rev. Leslie Blackburn, vicar of Houghton Regis; the Rev. R. J. W. Hill, vicar of Brackley and Westbury; Mr E. Sprawson of Beechborough School, Westbury, for the loan of the print of Westbury Manor; Mr R. H. Monier Williams, clerk to the Tallow Chandlers' Company; Mr K. W. Dickens of the Sussex Archaeological Society; Mr G. V. M. Heap of The Bookshop, Wells, from whom the original manuscript was bought; Mr H. O. White, secretary of the Bedfordshire Historical Record Society; Miss Ruth Hurst, assistant curator of the Pilkington Glass Museum; the Guildhall Library; and the British Sugar Bureau.

I am also indebted to Mrs Hazel Thurston, Mrs Ruth Bellord, and Mrs Sylvia Huxtable who typed and re-typed the manuscript, and to Miss Auriol Hyde Parker who helped correct the proofs.

INTRODUCTION

Nearly three hundred years ago, in 1681, a young woman living in West-bury in the county of Buckingham, compiled a unique document which posterity would know as *Rebecca Price's Receipt Book*.

This lady who has been my invisible companion and task-master for a long time entered my life in a curious way. A telephone call from my son-in-law, Anthony Vaughan, who is something of an antiquarian, and who, like myself, collects ancient cookery books, informed me that according to a catalogue a country bookseller near to his home was offering for sale a most unusual manuscript of receipts and asked whether I should like to become joint owner of so rare an acquisition.

Some days later, Tony appeared, staggering under the weight of a vast calf-bound folio volume which contained an important collection of seventeenth-century receipts. The manuscript was in good condition, and it was obvious that the recipes contributed by members of the writer's family, friends and servants throughout an unusually long life were the distillation of her experience and knowledge as mistress of a large and wealthy household.

This book was a rare find. The recipes were fascinating, for they complemented many of the account books of the period, which, while giving current prices, are merely a list of tantalizing and unrelated figures. Rebecca's long and detailed receipts gave a picture of the social and economic conditions of a comfortable and well-ordered household of the period. Also her manuscript had a uniquely personal touch which is inevitably absent from the few contemporary cookery books of the time.

The young Rebecca's writing was firm and legible, remaining so until well into her old age. It was evident that this receipt book was a labour of pride and love. A meticulous and methodical index listed every type of dish and confection known to the well-to-do seventeenth-century housewife, and it was obvious from changes in the handwriting that this was the dedicated opus of a lifetime.

But who, we wondered, was the industrious Rebecca Price? Such was our curiosity that long before we thought of publishing the manuscript we began the search that was ultimately to bring Rebecca to life for us.

At that time our only clues were the names T. A. Brandreth written inside the back cover, and the inscription:

This Booke was written by me: Rebecca Price in the Yare 1681

No record of the Price family was available to us until, in the records of the Society of Genealogists,[1] Tony discovered a collection of printed marriage licences for the second half of the seventeenth century which contained the following entry:

Nehemiah Brandreth of Houghton Regis, in the County of Beds, Esq., Bachelor and Rebecca Price of St. Paul's Covent Garden, Spinster, aged 23, at St. Paul's Covent Garden, 19th September, 1683.

The chase was on! The next step was to locate the Brandreth family tree. Once this was in our hands, the pieces of the puzzle began to fall into place. But there were still great *lacunae*. We discovered that *two* scrapbooks containing contemporary inventories, receipts and other Brandreth papers had been in the bookseller's possession, but had, alas, been sold to a casual buyer, as at that time the connection between the author of the cookery

[1] The Library is at 37 Harrington Gardens, London SW7.

manuscript and the Brandreth family was not known. All subsequent efforts to trace the buyer of these documents have so far been unsuccessful.

After many months during which I toiled over Rebecca's receipts, Tony pulled another dazzling rabbit from the hat, for he came up with a copy of Rebecca's will (and some of the wills made by her family), and I was allowed an intimate glimpse into the life and times of a woman who, born in the year of the Restoration of Charles II, lived on through the reigns of James II, William and Mary, Queen Anne and George I, and died when George II was on the throne.

Suddenly the cold ashes of history began to glow with meaning as I read and re-read Rebecca's words:

> Item I give and Bequeath to my said Daughter Alice Brandreth and her Executors and Administrators, the Picture of my late ffather set in Gold and my two receipt Books in folio written by myself one of which said Books being for Surgery and physick and the other for Cookery and Preserves both of the said Books being bound with Leather and on the inside of the Lidds of each of them is mentioned that they were written in the year 1681 by Rebecca Price (that being my Maiden name) . . .

The book dealing with 'Surgery and Physick' has vanished, and is, in all probability, lying in some attic coated with dust, waiting to be discovered, as was its companion volume, the receipt book.

On 10 April 1740, three days before her death, Rebecca wrote her will.[1] It is a remarkably clear and detailed document, and it is obvious from its length, clarity and precision that not only was the old lady in full possession of her faculties, but that the indomitable qualities which had made her such a formidable personage in the family circle were much in evidence at the close of her life.

Apart from being an excellent guide to Rebecca's character and relations with her family, the will is an important document for it highlights, not only her favourite possessions and describes their provenance, but also gives an accurate picture of the decor and *modus vivendi* of a lady who, though not a member of the nobility, was the daughter of one country squire and the widow of another; both men of wealth and standing.

Rebecca lived in considerable comfort and style surrounded by furniture and bibelots which would today fetch astronomic prices in the saleroom. From 'the Mohair Bed wherein I now lye with the feather Bed Bolster pillows and all the quilts and Blankets belonging to it' the old

[1] See Appendix I.

[3]

woman looked around her familiar room, checking each item and marking it down to be given to those she cherished. Nobody was forgotten: the poor of the parish of Houghton Regis received ten pounds; her servant, Richard Arnott, was left twenty pounds. As for daughter Alice, apart from money, china, linen and silver, she was left many personal mementoes such as 'my inlaid dressing Box lined with Silk'. Rebecca's grandson, Henry Brandreth, was left the precious receipt book and a watch and seal 'when he shall attain his age of one and Twenty years'.

So vividly and accurately did Rebecca describe her bedchamber and dressing-room that we can clearly see her in 'the thirteenth yeare of the Reigne of Our Sovereigne Lord George the Second by the Grace of God of Great Britain ffrance and Ireland King Defender of the faith . . .' moving about, albeit a trifle wearily and stiffly in the large rooms whose windows, framed by 'Six yellow Stuff Window Curtains with Valence and Rods to them', looked out over the well-tended grounds and across to the village green.

The bedchamber must have been a pretty room. Rebecca's 'Great easy Chair' was covered with a 'blew Gold and Silver Stuff' with matching cushion, and a 'Peir or Long Looking Glass in a Gilt fframe' stood between the windows. There were a 'Buroe and Wallnutree Dressing Table' and a 'Wallnutree Card Table'. There is also mention of 'one peice of Tapestry Hangings' and a 'Gilt leather Screen with two leaves'.

Each item in the dressing-room is carefully inventoried, and these include 'a Comb box two Powder boxes two Patch boxes and two small Brushes all inlaid'.

Every piece of silver, each jug, dish and humble kitchen crock is itemized. Rebecca loved her home and it may well be that in this spring which was to be her last, her mind might have been occupied with memories of a long life, which, though not dramatic or different from that of her friends and neighbours, was none the less filled with colour and incident, with the love of a good man and the laughter of many children.

So far as we can judge at this remove in time, Rebecca led a blameless life. From the cradle to the grave she lived according to the tenets of her time and circumstances; but we who look upon her from almost three centuries away can clothe the skeleton that lies in Houghton Regis church and we can trace, even in her few writings and memoranda, a woman of exceptionally strong character, a creature of determination with an excellent head for figures, a flair for organization and a passion for order and detail.

Though Rebecca was no culinary genius tossing off flashes of gastro-

[4]

nomic inspiration, her book, the fore-runner of Mrs Beeton, was meticulously accurate, and her receipts, many of which are extremely long and complicated, are presented with clarity and punctiliousness.

Rebecca, like most women of her time, would have read and been impressed by *Country Contentments, or the English Housewife*. This was written by a *man*, Gervase Markham. The following appears upon its title page:

> The English housewife containing the inwards and outwards vertues which ought to be in a compleat woman. As her skill in Physick, chirogery, cookery, extraction of oils, banquetting stuff, ordering of great feasts, preserving of all sorts of wines, conceited secret distillations of perfumes, ordering of wool, hemp or flax, making cloth and dying; the knowledge of dairies, the office of malting of oats, their excellent uses in families, of brewing, baking and all other things belonging to a household.

Published in 1613, it was to be the most important of early English cookbooks. In it Markham gives a number of receipts for apple pie, a dessert so favoured by the Elizabethans that Robert Green could think of no greater compliment in praise of a lovely lady than to liken her breath to 'the steame of apple pyes'.

There was nothing very inspiring about English cookery according to French visitors to Britain in the early part of the seventeenth century, although their own *cuisine* at home was anything but *haute*, for it was not until the publication of *Le Cuisiner Français* in 1651 by François Pierre de la Varenne that cookery standards in France and throughout the civilized world were revolutionized. Monsieur de la Varenne did away with the spices and oils dear to the medieval cook, and in their place he used truffles, mushrooms and subtle and delicate sauces.

One of de la Varenne's most splendid dishes is *Poulet en ragout dans une bouteille*. This is made with a boned chicken stuffed with a forcemeat of mushrooms, truffles, sweetbreads, pigeons, egg yolks and seasonings—the whole inserted (like a ship) into a bottle. The mouth of the bottle is then sealed with a cork made of pastry. When the ragout is nearly ready, a diamond is used to cut the bottle so as to extract the contents whole.

Rebecca Price was born in London on 10 April 1660. Her family had long associations with the City, though originally they came from the Molde in Flintshire. Her great-grandfather, Roger Price I, was a famous clerk of the Tallow Chandlers' Company from 1608–35, and master of the company in 1638. He has been described as 'a perfect Elizabethan Gentleman'.

His coat of arms (three Cornish choughs) appears on the charter granted to the company in 1602–3 to which he was one of the signatories.

At first he lived in Fryer Alley on the north side of the Tallow Chandlers' Hall. Later he moved to Sweet Apple Court in Bishopsgate where he became tenant of the house, garden and alley first called Sopehouse Alley. Liverpool Street Station is now on the site. He was Attorney of the Common Pleas, and evidently a skilful lawyer for he resolved the eighty-year-old dispute over Alderman John Steward's bequest to the Tallow Chandlers' Company made in 1481. In recognition of his services the Tallow Chandlers awarded him £10.

Roger I must have lived on to a great age as he is mentioned in his son's will of 15 February 1657. This is also borne out by the bishop's transcripts of Westbury which record the burial of Roger Price Sen. on 25 March 1660.

His son, Roger II, born in March 1601, was described in the *Visitation of London* in 1634 as a draper and it is known he was educated at Merchant Taylors' School in 1614–15. He must also have been a member of the Tallow Chandlers' Company as he was master of the company in 1646. He was married on 25 June 1627. As early as 1641 he was mentioned in a census as one of the City of London's wealthiest and most influential men. His election as alderman of Walbrook Ward was reported to the aldermen of the City of London on 8 September 1651. On 9 September he was elected one of the sheriffs in Common Hall (a number of persons elected in succession since 24 June having refused to serve). On 12 September he appeared in the Court of Aldermen and was sworn in as alderman, but he then asked to be discharged of the offices of both alderman and sheriff. This was agreed on payment of a fine of £800, and he was exempted from holding either office for ever. He died in 1658.

It was to this second Roger Price, Rebecca's grandfather, that Sir Joseph Sheldon was apprenticed in May 1647. Sir Joseph rose to become alderman of the City from 1666 to 1681, and it was he who was in charge of rebuilding the Tallow Chandlers' Hall after the Great Fire. The panelled parlour there he had built at his own expense. Later he was translated to the Drapers' Company and his portrait by Zoest hangs in the hall there. He was to become Lord Mayor of London. One suspects that Rebecca must have stayed with the Sheldons in London for her father, Roger III, was godfather to Sir Joseph's daughter, Elizabeth, and left her his silver warming-pan.

Roger II, Rebecca's grandfather, owned a town house in old St Paul's Churchyard, where no doubt he carried on his expanding business. Presumably this would have remained the Prices' London home until it was burned down in the Great Fire.

In 1650 he bought the estate of Westbury. It is likely that he had Royalist sympathies—certainly the Sheldons were Royalists—and he may have felt it prudent to have a country retreat after the murder of Charles I. Here he settled to become sheriff of Buckinghamshire in 1655 so that by the time Roger III, Rebecca's father, inherited the estate in 1658, Roger II could with justification describe himself in his will as 'Esquire'.

His will (dated 15 February 1657), like that of his granddaughter, is concise, and like hers it is interesting because of the light it throws on family affairs. The Prices were, it seems, keenly interested in making certain that their funerals were well organized.

> as for my body [writes old Roger Price in his will] I desire it may be buried in the church at Westbury under my seat without any pompe or funeral and that some of my servants do not go out of the church until they see the grave quite finished and the seat of my pew set up again over my grave before they depart . . .

Roger Price I was still alive when his son died, and Roger II, in *his* will, asked that 'my executor [his son, Roger III] *be very careful* of my dear and aged father if he demand the money upon bond that I owe him'.

Another Price trait was their care for their servants. Roger Price II, like his son and granddaughter, mentions many family servants such as Samuel the ploughman, Judith the chambermaid, his man Philip Pool, his footboy, and Simon Chapman, his woodward, who twenty years later was still the Prices' woodward, and was also remembered in Rebecca's father's will.

Roger Price III, Rebecca's father, travelled extensively abroad. He no doubt carried on the flourishing family business in London and he increased his fortunes so that he was able to leave each of his nine younger children in his will portions of £1,500 each—an astronomical figure in those days. He died in Bilbao in 1677, and was buried at Westbury. His will, dated 26 August 1676, was proved in the Prerogative Court of Canterbury on 13 March 1677.

Rebecca's mother, Ann *née* Ingham, died in 1670 when Rebecca was ten years old, leaving her husband to cope with seven son (Roger, George, Thomas, Charles, Edward, Ingham and Joseph) and three daughters (Anne, Rebecca and Dorothy—a fourth daughter, Herel, died in infancy). But Rebecca, it seems, though motherless, was in no sense a lonely child. She belonged to a close-knit and clannish family, all of whom cherished and spoilt the little girl.

The London of Rebecca's childhood was still the London of Elizabethan houses with Tudor beams and overhanging upper storeys. It was
a bustling, lusty city, crowded beyond belief. Roger Price, like most
wealthy merchants of his ilk, lived and worked in his town house. In these
houses servants, apprentices, business staff, porters and messengers slept
in whatever corner was available.

The heart of the city and Roger Price's stamping ground was the
Royal Exchange founded by Sir Thomas Gresham. A Hollar engraving of
the period shows that it must have been the meeting place for merchants
and visitors from all over the world. Men are variously dressed and
coiffed in ruffs and turbans and high fur caps which speak of the icy winds
of Russia.

Rebecca's childhood years were pleasant and sheltered though she
must have heard reports from the family and servants of the three major
disasters which shook England when she was very young. In three suc-
cessive years the country was to be tried by the Great Plague; the Fire of
London; and the terrible night of June 1667 when the Dutch, having
stormed Sheerness, sailed up the Medway and fired the English Fleet
which lay at its moorings. Piling Pelion on Ossa they towed away as a
prize *The Royal Charles*, the ship in which the King had sailed home.

In spite of pestilence and fire, the Price family continued to prosper
and to make good investments in property, furniture, jewellery and plate.
During the Civil War much fine English plate, both sacred and secular,
had been cast into the melting pot to help the King's cause, and now,
under his son, goldsmiths and silversmiths were once again ready to
design and execute good pieces for those who could afford them. Rebecca's
father wisely ordered many fine pieces, some of which would be left to
Rebecca, who, in her turn, left them to her grandchildren.

Much of Rebecca's childhood was spent at Westbury, the place which
held her happiest memories. The village of Westbury forms, with its
parish, the north-west angle of Buckinghamshire, being bounded on the
north by the parish of Biddlesden, on the west by that of Mixbury, and
on the east by the parish of Water Stratford. The acquisition of Westbury
Manor had been an important step in the life of her grandfather, Roger
Price II, for by purchasing this property he had established himself as a
country squire.

Luck was with Roger Price II when he first went a-hunting for a
country estate, for Westbury Manor fell into his hands at a knockdown
price. According to a letter dated 16 February 1750, written by Henry
Purefoy, a neighbour of the Prices, to the antiquarian Browne Willis, his

close friend, the manor of Westbury had been sold to Roger Price by the grief-stricken widow of its owner, one Sir Thomas Lyttleton.

As to the owners of the Mannor of Westbury by my writings I cannot trace it higher than Sr L'Estrange Mordaunt who was Lord thereof in Charles 1st, his time, and passed his right therein to one Sr Laurent Washington,[1] then of Chancery Office and Sr Laurence's executors (being legally empowered) sold the said mannor (which had a numerous parcell of about twenty petty freeholders in it) to Sir Thomas Littleton of Worcestersh Barn't; but it was a woeful purchase to him, for chancing to bring 5 or six hundred pounds more than the occasion required to the Mannor House at Westbury, where the deeds were executed; as hee returned to his own home in his coach and six, over Mixbury Warren (then thick with trees and a nest of Robbers) he was assaulted there by a noted Rogue who was called Colonell Downs and his Gang, and tho he and his servants made a brave resistance they were overpowered and Sr Thomas Lyttleton was shot in his coach and they went off with their prize; but his servants raised the countrey and pursued Downs so closely that hee, venturing to leap his horse thru' a live quick hedge, his horse was catched in ye hedge and hee was taken prisoner, and was conveyed to Oxford Jayell where he was tried, condemned and executed and very much by the interest of my great-grandfather George Purefoy who, on this occassion stook close to his skirts.

This Sr Thomas Lyttleton's widow built the present Mannor House at Westbury, but on the losse of her favourite and eldest son grew beside herself, and hating Westbury, thereupon sold the estate to the present Price's family without any consideration for the timber growing thereon, so that after the writings were executed, the steward asking her ladyship what consideration was allowed for the timber then growing on the estate, she said, 'None at all.' 'Why then Madam', said hee, 'you have fairly given away the estate to the Prices' for there is now growing more timber on the estate than the Estate is worth.' . . .

This account of Sr Thomas Littleton's being shot I had from old Wm May of Warwick Castle in Biddlesden Parish lately deceased

[1] Purefoy refers to Sir Lawrence Washington. This was an error: he was never knighted and actually purchased Westbury Manor in the reign of James I. He was the younger son of Lawrence Washington of Sulgrave Manor Northants., thereby becoming great-great-great-uncle to America's glory, George Washington. Browne Willis says that Lawrence's son sold it in 1639 to Sir Thomas Lyttleton, an ardent Royalist. Lipscombe in his *History of Bucks*. Vol. III records that in 1643 Lyttleton 'suffered much for his loyalty being plundered to a great extent at his seat in this village'. His widow sold it to Roger Price in 1650.

upward of 80 years of age; and the other, of Lady Littleton's selling the estate to the Prices' on disadvantageous terms I had from Mary Hobcraft of Shalstone who nursed me when I was a child, and she was daughter to *Chapman*, Mr. Price's Steward.

Letter written from Shalstone by 'H. P.' (Henry Purefoy) to Browne Willis, 16 February 1750. Letter No. 583, *Purefoy Letters*, vol. II, pp. 400–1.

It is evident that by the time Rebecca was born, the Price family was well established and well esteemed in Buckinghamshire. They owned a good deal of property in and around Westbury, for Browne Willis mentions the demolition of houses owned by 'Mr. Price of Westbury' which were in the High Street of Fenny Stratford, 'opposite the Great House'.

It is clear from family papers and letters of the period that Roger Price and his children were on excellent terms with their neighbours and that there was much social intercourse with the first families in the county. Among these were the Verneys of Claydon, the Wentworths of Lillingstone Lovell, the Pollards of Finmere, and the Purefoys of Shalstone, whose letters and diaries contain mentions of Roger Price and his descendants, particularly of his son Roger IV, Rebecca's eldest brother, who became MP for Buckinghamshire and was a contemporary of Henry Purefoy.

It is known that the Westbury manor house was formerly the rectorial household which before 1540 had belonged to Elstow Priory. Little of the old manor house remains today, the present manor house of Cotswold stone having been completely rebuilt on the site of it.

The beautiful manor gardens which existed in Rebecca's day were known as the Butts, where the villagers practised with bow and arrow. The target must have been fixed below the bank which runs along the south side of the church. The gardens reached down in terraces to the river where the Price children and their friends would have fished and played by the old mill and the thatched stone cottages.

From 1650 for two hundred years the Westbury estate was held by the Price family whose devotion to the village was expressed in many practical ways, not the least being the charming stone bridge which crosses the infant Ouse in front of the present manor house. According to the inscription, the bridge was built by 'Thos Price, Esq. 1739'.

Owing to financial reverses of one sort and another the Price family were obliged to sell Westbury manor, and, in the nineteenth century, their beloved country house passed into the hands of strangers.

Rebecca was born into one of the most exciting and colourful periods in English history—the Restoration—an epoch rich in drama, whose monarch, Charles II, returning from exile to claim the throne of his murdered father, was to be one of the most endearing and extravagant of England's kings.

Rebecca was one month old, a dolly swaddled in her nurse's arms, when Charles II came home. John Evelyn recorded the event in his *Diary*.

> He [Charles II] with his brothers, landed at Dover on 23rd of May [1660] and entered London in triumph on the 29th, his birthday— with above 20,000 horse and foot, brandishing their swords and shout- ing with inexpressible joy; the ways strewed with flowers, the bells ringing, the streets hung with tapestry, fountains running with wine; the Mayor, Aldermen, all the companies in their liveries, chains of gold, banners; lords and nobles, cloth of silver, gold and velvet everybody clad in, the windows and balconies all set with ladies. Trumpets, music and myriads of people flocking in the streets, and was as far as Rochester, so they were seven hours in passing the city, even from two in the afternoon till nine at night. I stood in the Strand, and beheld it, and blessed God!

The drabness of Cromwell's rule gave way to the gaiety and frivolity of court life. Charles II had learned much in exile, and in France he had taken good note of the way in which Louis XIV conducted his court. He brought back with him a taste for luxury, for splendid clothes and beautiful women. The sad colours of Cromwell's regime soon gave way to hues and materials approved by that fop, Monsieur, husband of Minette, Charles II's beloved sister, Henrietta of England.

Rebecca lived in an era in which literature, the arts and the sciences flourished. The Restoration scene was rich in playwrights, poets and writers of every description. John Milton wrote his *Paradise Lost* after 1660. For the delight of posterity, John Evelyn and Samuel Pepys re- corded their daily lives. Christopher Wren was dreaming of the topless towers of Ilium, and architects of his ilk were Hugh May and Nicholas Hawksmoor. Isaac Newton was musing on a pippin, Grinling Gibbons was well on in his labours, and the music of Henry Purcell sweetened the air.

Britain was about to enter an era of prosperity. Roger Price took good note of industries that were to be profitable. Among these were copper, lead and coal-mining, fishing and the making of cloth. Even a minor in- dustry like lace-making seemed to have a bright future since it had been introduced into Buckinghamshire by Catherine of Aragon whose dowry was derived from the revenues of Steeple Claydon.

While still a small child Rebecca must have developed the keen interest in cookery which was to remain with her throughout her long life, for many of the entries in her book are prefaced with the words, 'My mother's receipt'. Mrs Price had died when Rebecca was ten, yet it is clear that as a little girl Rebecca had watched her preparing certain dishes and had no doubt eagerly helped her brothers and sisters when it was necessary to gather flowers, fruit or herbs from the garden or countryside. Mrs Price's receipt for cowslip wine which requires half a peck of *picked* cowslips to every gallon of water suggests that every available child was sent out into the fields to collect the flowers with the morning dew still upon them.

Later, at school, it is apparent that cookery played an important part in Rebecca's curriculum because she records many receipts 'given me at School' or 'given me at Hackney'. Most of these are of a nature to delight little girls; for instance, in one of them mussel shells are used for 'Shell-Bread'. A great favourite was 'egg and bacon rashers' made from marzipan.

The education of women in the seventeenth century was inferior to that of the time of Elizabeth I, yet Rebecca's handwriting, spelling and general knowledge was certainly better than that of many of her contemporaries. In general, the more gently bred the lady, the more execrable their writing, and nearly always their spelling was phonetic. Lady Sussex, a remarkably intelligent and cultivated woman, had no qualms about spelling Yorkshire as Oyskecher, St Albans as Sentarbones and Lincolns-Inn-Fields as Lingeslinds fildes.[1]

In the neighbourhood of London there were many schools where girls could be boarded, though families that still clung to the old religion occasionally smuggled their children out of England and put them into a French or Spanish convent to be educated.

Hackney was among the most popular centres for girls' schools. In fact there were so many that they were collectively known as 'the ladies' university'. The charms of the students were not unknown to Pepys. On a visit to Hackney church on 21 April 1667 he admitted in his *Diary* 'that which I went chiefly to see was the young ladies of the schools whereof there is a great store, very pretty!'

One of the most fashionable of these schools was the establishment run by Mrs Hannah Woolley, the author of a well-known seventeenth-century

[1] See *Memoirs of the Verney Family during the Civil War*, Longmans Green, 1892, vol. iii. Letter from Lady Sussex to Sir Edmund Verney and his son in 1641: 'The unexpected sade neuse gave me a harty soro, most for your lose of such a mother and for myselfe of soe deare a friend.'

cookery book. Mrs Bathsua Makin, once a governess in the royal family, had a school at Tottenham High Cross on the way to Ware. Her prospectus included preserving, pastry and cookery. At Mrs Salmon's school at Hackney, French and Italian were taught, as well as book-keeping and verse-making.

Roger Price's business often took him to Europe. It is reasonable to suppose that he might from time to time have been accompanied by one or other of his daughters for it is obvious from some of Rebecca's 'foreign' receipts that they had been obtained *in situ*. Several such receipts were given her at Montpelier, a place much favoured by the British on account of its 'pure ayre and fayre women'.

As a merchant, Rebecca's father had contacts all over the world, some of whom would have tried to please the motherless little girl by bringing her gifts of exotic sweetmeats and eastern delicacies. Among Roger Price's closest friends in London were Sir William Dolben, Recorder of the City of London, and Sir Joseph Sheldon, one time Lord Mayor of London and his father's old apprentice.

Sir Joseph was a collector of rare and valuable objects. He had his portrait and that of his daughter painted by Lely. At his death, he left his sister, Ellen Mohun, a number of paintings, among them 'the picture of King Charles the ffirst in my withdrawing Roome'. This brief sentence states clearly his political affiliations which one surmises may well have been shared by Roger Price.

So the young Rebecca led a pleasant and ordered life, spending some of her time in London and all the summer months at Westbury. Though Westbury manor cannot be compared with the great family houses in the neighbourhood, the Prices were a large family employing a big staff, all of whom in the course of time became family retainers.

A seventeenth-century home was a manner of agricultural and domestic factory for nearly everything needed for sustaining the needs of daily life was made on the premises. Food was grown and processed; wool and hides were produced as raw material for the making of textiles and clothing; flax and hemp were grown and processed, and no great house was without its builders, harness-makers, and tool- and implement-makers.

It is fairly certain that one of Rebecca's sisters gave her *Country Contentments* by Gervase Markham in which this knowledgeable gentleman had laid down the rules by which a lady might best govern, not only her household, but her mind. Markham, in his first chapter heading, includes the following:

[13]

INTRODUCTION

Of the inward vertues of the minde which ought to be in every housewife. And first of her generall knowledge both in Physick and Surgerie, with plaine approued medicynes for the health of the Household, also the extraction of excellent oyles fit for those purposes . . .

Rebecca must have given as much thought and care to the preparation of the 'approued medicynes for health of the Household' as she did to the compilation of her cookery book. Though Rebecca's manuscript has vanished, Markham's receipts remain. They were an ever-present help in time of trouble. There is no malady he cannot treat, from 'pestilent fever' to 'infection of the Plague', and those suffering from symptoms attributable to either of these two dread scourges must have run to his pages for advice. Whether Rebecca ever had to have recourse to Markham's treatment for 'Frenzie' or inflammation of the brain is not known, but, if she did, one can only hope that the patient was healthy and had a strong desire to live. The exact treatment was as follows:

> You shall cause the Juice of Beets to be with a surridge [syringe] squirted up into the patients' nostrils, which will purge and cleanse his head exceedingly; then give him to drinke posset ale, in which violet leaves and lettuce hath been boyled, and it will suddenly bring him to a very temperate mildness and make the passion of '*Frenzie*' forsake him.

A seventeenth-century housewife learned to cook, distil, pickle and preserve. She had to see to it that her store-rooms were filled with smoked and cured ham and bacon, and with fish and meats pickled or salted down for use in the long winter months. She must be prepared for all emergencies, for no traveller was ever turned away without a meal to sustain him on his way. The summer was her busiest time. Fruit and vegetables had to be picked, pickled or candied. Wines and syrups had to be brewed.

Herbs and flowers played an important role, not only for their colour and scent, which were, in fact, less appreciated than their other 'vertues', but because they were the basis of the medicines, perfumes, pomatums, washes and pastilles used in the home. The use of herbs is the oldest form of medicine. The word 'drug' is derived from an Anglo-Saxon word meaning 'to dry', the reference being to dried herbs—the first drugs. Centuries later the Arabians made medicinal herbs more palatable by concocting them into various forms of syrups. These juleps and robs and electuaries are still part of all European pharmacopoeias. Juleps were prepared for immediate use and did not keep. Electuaries were a composition of powdered herbs blended with honey. Proper syrups were a more elaborate affair altogether, and were made to keep: a loloch was thicker than a syrup but not as thick as an electuary. It was eaten off the end of a stick of liquorice.[1] Roses and lavender had to be picked and dried along with other blooms to ensure a good supply of potpourri and sachets to perfume closets and linen presses.

Macaulay has said in his *History of England* that after 1685, a century after the apogee of Elizabeth's reign, England was turned into a garden and leaves and flowers played their part in the household economy. Girls were taught to use angelica oil in musk to perfume their gloves and dresses, and with the help of Sir Hugh Platt's book, *Delightes for Ladies*, many a young bride was able to seek perfection in her married life. He gives numerous receipts and hints for the making of jams and jellies for invalids. One of his suggestions was to gild pills to make them less objectionable to the patient; another was to preserve fruits in vegetable 'pitch' (coating), and he gives the recipe for a special syrup of roses which, when used for candying 'must be hard and glitter like diamonds'.

All the time Rebecca was absorbing knowledge of the household arts she was keeping up her receipt book. She already had a basis of excellent recipes from her late mother and new donors appeared each time she dined abroad.

Her donors fall into three well-defined groups: her family, her servants, and her friends and acquaintances. She appears to have written down the recipes exactly as told to her, for her spelling often shows evidence of their pronunciation; for example, Mrs Brown, a countrywoman, gave her a recipe in which 'a rowne ole'—a round hole—was mentioned; whereas Lady Sheldon invariably said 'garther' for gather, employing the fashionable long 'a'.

Two contrasting characters who come through to us most strongly are Aunt Rye and Lady Sheldon. Aunt Rye's receipts are full of warnings not to let things boil too long, and her words tumble over each other in their breathless enthusiasm which sometimes leads her to muddle the ingredients. This is clear in the receipt in which Aunt Rye states 'Then put in the whites of eggs redy beaten . . .' only to correct herself by saying that 'it was a mistake to say they must be put in before . . .'

Rebecca was severe with her donors. One unfortunate lady who had given her recipe for 'Almond Bisquittes' had obviously not done her homework, for having tried out the recipe Rebecca wrote 'I having made

[1] See H. W. W. Leyel, *Herbal Delights*, London, Faber, 1937.

them did not approve of them' and the recipe was heavily scored through.

A different type of woman was my Lady Sheldon. A great London hostess, holding court at 'The Drum', Drury Lane—her husband was Lord Mayor—she was used to retinues of servants and relays of kitchen maids, so that one of her recipes contains the imperious direction 'stir for 10 hours'. Her recipes are often exotic and elaborate.

Another such donor was my Lady Howe, though it is obvious that she was not so experienced a cook as my Lady Sheldon. She has an affected style; fruits to be gathered were always 'the fairest' and nothing less than silver is suitable for their preparation. She was not above cheating a little. Her recipe for pike is lifted entire, without acknowledgment, from *The Queen's Closet Open'd*, a popular cookery book of the period which ran to many editions.

Leech, the Westbury housekeeper, and Newton, the cook at Houghton Regis, were sound practical cooks; their instructions were clear, precise and to the point as one would expect from professionals.

Not very far from Westbury, a neighbour, Henry Brandreth, was having long deliberations with his son, Nehemiah, over whom he should choose as a bride. Henry Brandreth, a stern religious man, was devoted to his family and it was his ambition to settle them all well in life before he departed this earth.

He had bought the manor, Houghton Regis, in 1669 from John, Earl of Bridgwater. His family consisted of his wife, Alice, two sons, Solomon and Nehemiah, and an only daughter, Alice. Solomon was simple, or at least 'unstable', and his future was a great anxiety to his parents. Eventually his father left him an annuity in trust, which made detailed provision for his comfort with an honest and discreet servant to 'look to him the said Solomon to keepe him out of ill company'. Henry Brandreth's main ambition was to keep his daughter at home as long as he possibly could. In fact, so reluctant was he to part with her that in the end all his prolonged negotiations with landowners all over the country came to nothing. There are letters about possible matches from the year 1668 when Alice was nineteen to 1671. One rather embittered father wrote, 'My son is free enough, but if you refuse a Northamptonshire gentleman of £1,100 per annum in possession because of the remoteness thoe the next county to yours, you give me smale hopes of accepting my poore son, thoe I could give him the Revenue in possession which you mention.'

Henry Brandreth died in 1673 leaving a widow and the three children. Of these Solomon died unmarried, so that the Houghton Regis property went to the second son, Nehemiah, who thus acquired the manor of Houghton Regis, the land and the advowson.

An estate in Hertfordshire had been settled on Alice in her father's life-time, and she was to receive a marriage portion of £3,000. Later on, her widowed mother released to her the reversion, on the death of Solomon without issue, of the fee farm rent of £41 charged on the Rectory. This is the property which Alice later acquired in Houghton Regis and left to Nehemiah and Rebecca's younger son, another Nehemiah.

We know nothing of the courtship of Rebecca and Nehemiah. Our first positive piece of information about their union is the record of their marriage in London at St Paul's, Covent Garden, on 29 September 1683.

Nehemiah's mother, the widowed Mrs Brandreth, had died six months earlier and, except for the mentally-defective Solomon and the amiable Alice who was to become a lifelong friend, Rebecca began her married life without being hemmed in by too many relations. The following extract from the will of the widow Brandreth shows that she left to her daughter, Alice, her jewellery and some silver and linen; to her son she had sensibly left furniture and kitchen utensils so that the young couple could begin married life with a varied and important assortment of household goods and chattels.

> Item I give and bequeathe unto my daughter Alice Brandreth her Executors and Administrators and Assigns to her and thier owne use one Necklace of Orientall pearles one Jewell of Diamonds one great Silver Flagon one Silver Chaffendish; one great silver Bason and one full and equall third part of all my linnen and Nappery, the whole into three equall parts to be divided by indifferent Appraisers and I will direct that when the same is divided into three parts my said daughter or her Assigns shall choose which of the same shee or they shall think fitting.
>
> Item I give and bequeathe unto my son Nehemiah all his Executors and Assigns to his and their own use and behoove all the brewing vessels being in and out of the Messuage at Houghton wherein I live and now belonging to me and all the furnaces with Brewhouse of the said Messuage and all the Household goods implements and things usually standing and being in the kitchen the Hall next the kitchen and Parlour next that Hall of the said Messuage and the Bedsteads and Bedding in the Men's chamber over the last mentioned chamber and the bed and bedding in the same Chamber on the same floor where the Maid usually lyeth.

From Mrs Brandreth's will, it is obvious that the newly-married couple lived in the typical sixteenth- or early seventeenth-century yeoman long

[17]

house with kitchen, parlour and hall on the ground floor, with three chambers above and attic rooms in the roof space for servants.[1]

We know exactly what Rebecca's kitchen at Houghton Regis was like as fortunately a detailed inventory taken on her death has survived.[2] Though devastatingly unpractical to the modern woman, it was in fact carefully planned. Wide fire openings under four centred arches contained the hearths before which a variety of spits and other contraptions afforded a means of roasting and grilling, while large brick ovens were available for baking. The buttery and pantry had, for a long time been integrated in the service quarters of a dwelling-house, though it may well be that the 'pastry' a new-fangled innovation had been built on. Subsequently, this room was to become the stillroom and in it were one or two ovens used both for baking and for the drying out of herbs and flowers.

In large establishments the service quarters would include a squillry, a game larder,[3] a meal house and a bottling-house. Rebecca became a most efficient bottler. Her method of bottling sound fruit whole in glass jars in the warmth of an oven after the bread has been baked could hardly be bettered today. Her attention to the dryness and cleanliness of both jars and fruit, and the importance of not allowing the fruit to split and so be spoilt in appearance contrasts strongly with later eighteenth- and nine-teenth-century cookbooks in which cooks were instructed to 'boil the fruit to a mash'.

Sometimes the sealed jars were buried in sand or earth, or placed in damp cellars. There are instructions to 'wipe off' the 'mould' from the glass, as indicated by Rebecca's recipe for bottling plums. She had discovered that by sealing the jars whilst hot by waxing the corks and then storing them in a cool dry place they kept 'a yare or more'. Her own observations had taught her the importance of sterilization for good bottling.

Even a young country squire like Nehemiah Brandreth might have a retinue of well over fifty servants, and it is more than probable that Rebecca, like her contemporaries, had as many maids and men as she needed to help with the chores around the house and gardens.

The furnishings of the seventeenth-century kitchen consisted in the main of a stout table of oak or elm with oak benches or stools. But there were, then as now, a plethora of kitchen utensils and gadgets to gladden

[1] See: Brandreth Family and Estate, from the County Record Office, Shire Hall, Bedford. Brandreth MSS. Acc. Nos Brandreth 71. Baker 2 and 9.

[2] Public Record Office PROB 3/42/35. See Appendix II.

[3] One of the finest examples is at Uppark, West Sussex.

the heart of the housewife and to help her in her labours. Even in humble cottages, dredgers, nutmeg graters, sieves, rolling-pins, funnels, ladles and skimmers, choppers, jars, filters and stills were used.[1]

In larger households there would have been a wide range of bowls and basins, pestles and mortars, knives, cleavers, dishes, pots and pans and a variety of tubs and troughs.

Over the kitchen fire hung a large iron or bronze cooking pot. This was attached to a bar in the chimney. The skillets and posnets of bronze were fitted with short legs which enabled them to stand in the embers of an open fire. Roasting was done by fastening the joint to a slim iron bar (or to a number of iron bars forming a central cage but tapering to a single bar at the ends) known as a spit. Beneath the spit was a pan to catch the meat juices. Spits were supported by andirons, jacks or spit-jacks which made the spit revolve automatically. These were worked by an elaborate mechanical device worked by a weight and system of gears. Such an elaborate gadget would only have been used in the most up-to-date household, much as a deep freeze today is still considered a luxury.

Other interesting additions to the hearth were bellows made of wood or metal, fire-tongs, pokers, trivets, frying-pans and kettles. Fire-forks served as pokers and tongs and toasting irons were used for bread or bacon.

Wood was the fuel in general use. Coal was exorbitantly expensive and was measured in bushels and chaldrons. In 1684 a chaldron (36 bushels or $25\frac{1}{2}$ cwts) cost fifteen shillings.

Rebecca enjoyed making cakes and biscuits and all manner of bread and pies. Her bread and pastry-making equipment would have consisted of kneading troughs and moulding boards. The brick ovens were heated with faggots. Later the ashes were raked out by means of a 'slice'—a long-handled instrument like a spade. Another aid to baking was the 'peel' (often spelled 'peeler' or 'pelle', from the French *pelle*, a spade). This resembled the utensil from which it took its name. The peel was used to withdraw loaves from the ovens.

Most kitchens were equipped with moulding boards on which the loaves were shaped while the flour was usually contained in troughs. Troughs were also used to house salted and pickled meat for winter use.

Ale and beer were the usual drinks of the period, though Rebecca alludes to wine and sack. Until the end of the fifteenth century little beer was brewed in Britain, and the practice of adding bitter herbs, particu-

[1] See Francis W. Steer, *Farm and Cottage Inventories of Mid-Essex 1635–1749*, Phillimore, Shopwyke Hall, Chichester, 1969.

larly hops which were introduced from Flanders early in the century, was at first regarded with some misgiving. Sir Hugh Platt advised those who wished 'to brew good and wholesome Beere, without any hoppes at al' to use an extract of wormwood!

Imported wine was drunk at sophisticated tables and then, as now, inferior wines were doctored and passed off as products of better quality. Rebecca's cellar certainly contained white French and German table wines, sweet wines from the Levant, ale, beer and cider. It is evident from her recipes that cider and ale were brewed and enjoyed in vast quantities. In one of the receipts for cider she says 'The best Receipt for Sider that I know off is this and by which I used to make my sider which always prov'd good and mightily liked off.'

The thirsts of the day were heavy and were usually assuaged in taverns which, besides providing the usual beers and wines, also offered specialities such as 'Buttered Ale', which contained no butter, but was warm ale, sweetened with sugar and spiced with cinnamon. Another favourite was 'Lambs' Wool', a drink made from the pulp of roasted apples, white wine, spice and sugar. 'Cock Ale', too, was much esteemed by country squires. Its ingredients sound extremely nasty. It was composed of a parboiled ancient cock whose remains were ground and tied up in a canvas bag with certain quantities of sack, raisins, mace and cloves, the whole mass being left suspended for seven days in a vessel holding ten gallons of ale. The ale was subsequently bottled and left to mature.

Although 'Usquebaugh', a kind of whisky, was brewed in Ireland, spirits did not feature so much in the kind of household of which Rebecca Brandreth was mistress. Though there are constant references to *Acqua Vitae* in the seventeenth century, it seems that this name was applied to any strong spirit distilled from fruit, wine leaves or fermented grain.

Rebecca does not refer in detail to her glass but it is certain that she possessed some British flint glass which was introduced during the period of seal glasses—probably before 1680 when the glass-makers of Liège first tried to work in the English fashion.

Her receipt book comes at an interesting transitional period in the history of glass, for until the fourth quarter of the seventeenth century and the advent of Ravenscroft crystal, glass was little used at table. Up till that date in wealthy households, such as those of the Price family and their friends and relations, expensive silver and oriental porcelain would have been used almost exclusively, apart from imported Venetian glass.[1]

[1] From a Catalogue issued in 1677:
Quart ribbed bottles 16 oz cost   3. 0. 0.

Throughout the receipts there are many references to silver bowls, por-ringers, salvers, chaffing-dishes, 'cheney cups' (china cups) and basins. It is, however, clear from the manuscript that syllabub glasses, jelly glasses, sweetmeat glasses and glass plates, all different in shape and function, were already in general use by the 1680s[1] as were glass gallipots or jars for cooking, which must incidentally have had a considerable degree of resistance to heat. At the time of her death Rebecca's heirs would have inherited a collection of glasses used for drinking beer, claret, sack, 'sullibub' and brandy. But the greatest revolution in the drinking habits of the British was due to three non-alcoholic beverages. These were chocolate, coffee and tea.

Europe was introduced to the drinking of chocolate by Spain in 1600, but it was not drunk in Britain until it was exported for the home market from the West Indies. In 1657 an enterprising Frenchman opened a choco-late shop in Queen's Head Alley, Bishopsgate. His blocks of chocolate sold from ten to fifteen shillings a pound, so it was a long time before ordinary folk could buy this exotic brew. In 1685 the wealthy merchant, Sir John Bankes, paid five shillings for a 'Chockalet pot'. As this commodity came in chunks it had to be grated, so a grater was often part of the equipment needed to drink chocolate, as were the pretty cups set in their silver holders in the Spanish manner.

Oxford claims the distinction of opening the first coffee house, but coffee made its appearance in London in 1652 when a coffee house was opened in St Michael's Alley by a Turkish merchant who launched a 'strong, bitter brew' upon a willing public. Soon, coffee was all the rage, and no household of any standing could afford to be without it.

China was the original home of the tea-bush known botanically as *Camelia sinensis*. According to legend and tradition, China tea has been grown and drunk for 4,000 years, since the time of the Emperor Shen Nung, said to be the discoverer of the tea-bush. Until the time of the Ming Emperors (1368–1644), tea dust was boiled in a kettle, or the leaves were whipped in an open bowl of boiling water.

Portuguese, Venetian and other explorers brought back tales of tea

---

Pint bottles of the same	10 oz	2.	0.	0.
Half pint bottle ditto	8 oz	1.	6.	0.
¼ pint bottles ditto	5 oz	1.	0.	0.
Quartern bottles all over nipt diamond waies	16 oz	4s.	0.	

[1] The Vauxhall glassworks were opened in 1670. Here, workmen brought from Venice blew glass and made mirrors.

from the Far East, and a Venetian, Gianbatista Remusio, wrote after a visit to China in 1559 that 'they doe take this herb and boil it well in water. One or two cups of this decoction taken on an empty stomach removes fever, headache, stomachache pain in the side or in the joints, and is good also for gout.'

It was the East India Company which first brought tea to Europe in the beginning of the seventeenth century. The British East India Company made its first trip to China in 1601 and was later granted a monopoly of trade between the Cape of Good Hope and the Straits of Magellan, but silk was its main cargo.

China tea found its way to England from Holland, and in 1658 a coffee-house proprietor by the name of Thomas Garvey is thought to have been the first man to serve tea to the public at his coffee shop near the Royal Exchange, together with a list of all the ills the new drink was supposed to cure. Eight years later, the East India Company, which had a well-developed sense of public relations, made a presentation of gifts which included tea, bought in Holland, to Charles II, whose wife, Catharine of Braganza, was known to like her cup of *tscha*. Tea rapidly became popular in court circles and elsewhere, and when the Emperor Kang Hai opened the China ports to European vessels, the acute East India Company made its first direct shipment of tea to England from Amoy in 1689.

The sailing ships let water into the holds, so suitable cargo had to be found to store below the tea-chests to keep them dry. Among these cargoes were teapots of Yi-hsing stoneware. The first European-made teapots were copies from Chinese models in Holland. Early Chinese vessels that look like teapots were, in fact, used to contain wine. When they took to infusing their tea, the Chinese seem to have preferred tea-pots of unglazed red or brown stoneware made at Yi-hsing near Shanghai. These were thought to give a better flavour than teapots of white porcelain.

A Dutch potter, John Philip Elers, started making unglazed redware teapots in Staffordshire in 1693. His was the first of a series of Staffordshire experiments in clay that lasted all through the eighteenth century.

Chocolate- and coffee-pots were at first so similar that it was only possible to distinguish a chocolate-pot from a coffee-pot by the lid finial which could be swivelled round or slipped forward, or entirely removed to expose the opening for the 'moliquet' (or swizzle-stick) with which the chocolate was stirred.

In the early days when they were so alike, coffee-pots and teapots were plain, conical, with hinged dunce-caps, lids, finials, straight spouts and loop handles like the chocolate-pot. The earliest example of a silver tea-pot known in England was made in 1670–1. It is a more severe and rather clumsy elder sister to a slightly raffish-looking coffee-pot made ten years later, and is 3½ inches taller. Sir Joseph Sheldon in his will dated 1681 left '. . . my silver Tea pott' to Mrs Mary Charleton. This must be one of the earliest references to a teapot.

It was not until 1680 that the first melon-shaped silver teapot was launched. There is a notable example in the Ashmolean Museum. One of its main charms is that it is only 5¼ inches high, less than half the height of the earliest known coffee-pot. The size of teapots was, of course, governed by the price of tea, and while it remained expensive, teapots and teacups remained small. The vogue for tea-drinking also influenced silversmiths to create small spoons which, at first, were as great a curiosity as forks had once been.

Forks had ceased to be the prerogative of the royal or very rich towards the end of the reign of Elizabeth, but they did not come into general use until the middle of the seventeenth century. Until as late as 1669 foreign guests touring in England complained that there were no forks on English tables, and that only the basin and ewer were supplied for a large supper party.

The earliest English fork is hall-marked 1632–3 but it was to be some time before the fork superseded the knife or spoon as an eating tool. The knife had only just replaced the dagger in the sixteenth century. The early Scottish wealthy dinner guest could be relied upon to bring his knife with him. Knives were generally made in pairs, with steel blades set in hafts of crystal, bone, ivory, ebony, silver, jasper or agate. These were often richly encrusted with jewels, and the shoulders were sometimes worked with gold and silver. A usual present from a bridegroom to his bride was a fine set of wedding knives.

That Rebecca was a good housekeeper and a superb cook is clear from her recipes. Not only did she make extensive use of all the supplies available to the housewife in her time, but, unlike most of her contemporaries, she was prepared to experiment with strange and exotic ingredients.

The Prices were sophisticated when it came to foreign foods. Sub-tropical fruits, French sweetmeats and Westphalia hams were routine gifts from Roger Price's foreign agents.

Rebecca had heard of melons, pineapples and other strange fruits, and since glasshouses were becoming a common feature of the great estates it had come to her ears that gardeners were growing vines, peaches, nectarines and even oranges and lemons under glass.

The first oranges Celia Fiennes ever saw were at Sir John Barbe's house and, again, at the Earl of Chesterfield's.

> Beyond this garden [she writes] is a row of orange and lemon trees set in ye ground, of a man's height, and pretty big, full of flowers and some large fruit almost Ripe. This has a pent house over it, which is covered up very close in the winter.

During the seventeenth century the art of gardening developed rapidly and fruits and vegetables became available and in greater variety than formerly. Many fruits are mentioned in Shakespeare's plays, including apples, pears, quinces, plums, medlars, mulberries, apricots, pomegranates, almonds, purple figs, rubied cherries, walnuts, chestnuts, hazel nuts (filberts), strawberries and gooseberries as well as blackberries, dewberries and blue bilberries. Most of the above were used in Rebecca's recipes.

Peiresc was one of the first to introduce a number of new fruits to Britain. Among these was the medlar, 'the rough cherry without stone', the rare and luxurious vines of Smyrna and Damascus, and the fig-tree called Adam's, whose fruit was deemed to be that with which the spies returned from the land of Canaan. It was from Peiresc's garden that exotic fruit and flowers were transplanted into the royal French nurseries and into the estates of Cardinal Barberini.

The apricot first known to Europe in the sixteenth century was brought from America and was in the first instance no larger than a damson. Distinguished travellers enriched English fruit and flower gardens with seeds, pips and cuttings from abroad. In the reign of Henry VIII, Thomas, Lord Cromwell, returning from a diplomatic mission, carried back home three varieties of plums.

The first oranges are thought to have been brought to England by the Carew family and they were seen to flourish at the family seat at Beddington in Surrey, and the exquisite beauty of the cherry orchards of Kent are due in measure to the enterprise of a gardener of Henry VIII's.

The currant bush was an import from the island of Zante in the same reign. To Sir Anthony Ashley of Wimborne St Giles, Dorset, we owe the cabbage, a replica of which decorates his monument. Cardinal Pole saw to it that his gardener planted figs at Lambeth. The first pineapple was grown at Dorney Court, home of the Palmer family, and around 1665 this exotic fruit was presented to Charles II by a member of the Palmer family whose gardener, Rose, had grown and nurtured this unusual gift destined for the monarch.

The first mulberry trees planted in Britain still stand at Syon. Cos lettuce was brought from the Island of Cos, and cherries from Cerasuntis, a city of Pontus. The peach or *persicum* or *mala persica* was brought from Persia where it was known as the Persian apple. The pistachio nut, or psittacia, was an import from Syria. The chestnut comes from Castegna, a town of Magnesia.[1]

Salads, extolled by Evelyn in his *Acetaria—A Discourse on Sallets*, were in great demand in Rebecca's time. Evelyn's essay covers cabbage, carrots, leeks, nettles and melons. His instructions on 'the making of a Sallet' are meticulous and detailed and would put the slapdash methods of the modern housewife to shame.

Evelyn suggests Lucca olives to 'allay the tartness of vinegar and other acids', and suggests that those who are averse to oil should use fresh butter as a substitute in the dressing. He insists that the knife with which 'the sallet herbs' are cut should be of silver and not of steel 'which all acids are apt to corrode and retain a metallic relish of'. Lastly he insists that 'the *Saladiers*', sallet dishes, be of 'porcelane or of the Holland Delftware; neither too deep nor shallow'.[2]

Though salads were popular in Rebecca's day vegetables do not seem to feature greatly in urban menus of the time. It was thought that vegetables were 'windy', and should only be eaten, well-seasoned and with oil, in salads. The English did not always boil their vegetables to pulp in water, for that shrewd observer, Monsieur Mission, writes in his memoirs that 'another time they [the English] will have a piece of boil'd Beef, and then they salt it some days before-hand, and besiege it with five or six Heapes of Cabbage, Carrots, Turnips or some other Herbs or Roots, well pepper'd and salted and swimming in butter.'[3]

Like most housewives of her time, Rebecca must have kept one or two kitchen books (or week-books) in which she recorded all the food and drink consumed in her household.

Staple foods were of course, bread and cheese.

There were various grades of bread. Manchet was white bread made of the finest quality of wheaten flour. Ravel was made of wholemeal or flour with the bran left in it. Yeoman bread was a rough brown household

[1] P. J. B. Le Grand, *L'Histoire de la Vie Privée des Français,* Paris, 1782, vol. i, p. 143. Here may be found a list of the origins of most of the fruits in British gardens.

[2] John Evelyn, *Acetaria—A Discourse on Sallets*, London, 1699.

[3] *Mission's Memoirs* translated by Mr Ozell, 1719.

loaf, generally eaten by the staff. Tems bread was rye and wheat mixed. Two Manchets were approximately equal to one loaf.

Next to the bakehouse came the dairy. Except to the wealthy, the wide range of cheeses was unknown, cheese being generally described by the district in which it was made rather than by its quality. To most people there were only soft cheese, hard cheese, green cheese and spermyse. Soft cheese was a kind of cream cheese. Hard cheese was prepared from renneted whole-milk and the cheese hardened by pressure. 'Green cheese' was a fresh soft cheese, and spermyse was a cream cheese liberally flavoured with herbs. 'Cheese of an extraordinary bigness' was made from ewes' milk in the marsh pastures of south-east Essex.

Butter was cheaper than fat and was used extensively for cooking. Clarified (melted) butter was potted for ordinary culinary use. The rest was salted and pressed into earthenware pots or barrels. Butter was usually made in quantity in the summer and 'May' butter was considered not only to be the best but also the most wholesome. Butter was also recommended for growing pains in children and to relieve constipation.

Milk was regarded as closely related to and derived from blood. 'Milke is made of bloud twice concocted . . . for, until it come to the paps or udder it is turned into milke.' Woman's milk was held to be the best, followed by that of asses and goats. Cow's milk was not held to be particularly nourishing.[1]

In poorer households most of the beasts were killed around Martinmas (11 November) because of the shortage of winter feed, and the beef was salted for use in the winter months. Custom had it that the housewife must dress the meat herself. Beef, lamb, veal, poultry and game all feature in weekly menus of the period.

Meat of all sorts, including poultry, was forbidden during the whole of Lent, every Friday and Saturday, and several other fast days appointed by the Church and added to by the state, because of the high cost of meat and to support the Navy and the building of ships, because more fish would be eaten.

Fish was always popular. Andrew Boorde speaks of the variety of fish eaten in England: 'of all nacyons and countres, England is best serued of Fysshe, not onely of al maner of see-fysshe, but also of fresh-water fysshe, and all maner of sortes of salte-fysshe'.[2]

Most of the fish was landed at Queenhythe, the chief watergate of the City of London where the fish market was situated, and it was quickly

[1] Thomas Cogan, *The Haven of Health*, 1584.
[2] Andrew Boorde, *A Compendyous Regyment, or a Dyetary of Healthe*, 1542.

salted or pickled, unless it came from the fishing grounds off the nearby
Kentish or Essex coasts. Fresh-water fish such as carp, tench or eels were
often kept in artificial 'stews' or ponds until needed for the table.

Oysters and mussels were plentiful, much in demand and fairly cheap.
Sir Hugh Platt says they were kept 'fresh' for as long as twelve days by
being plunged into brackish water.[1]

Most housewives could and did rely on the wares of the Stockfishmongers who dealt mainly in dried fish such as cod, haddock, pollack and
ling, coming for the most part from Iceland and Norway; and the Saltfishmongers also provided important supplies when fresh fish was in short
supply. The Saltfishmongers handled salted and pickled herrings, cod,
eels, whiting and mackerel which came either from the east coast or
Holland and the Baltic. In 1536 the Stockfishmongers and Saltfishmongers
united as the Fishmongers' Company.

Rebecca used great quantities of spices. This is not surprising in view
of the fact that much of the meat she cooked was tainted. Sir Hugh Platt,
who specialized in useful little hints for the housewife, had a somewhat odd
suggestion for dealing with venison. If it was 'greene', you should 'cut
out all the bones' and bury it in 'a thinne old course clothe a yard deepe
in the grounde for 12 or 20 hours' by which time, affirmed Sir Hugh, 'it
would be sweet enough to be eaten'.

Spices were all-important to the housewife of the seventeenth century.
Saffron, grown in the eastern countries, was used both as a flavouring and
for colouring dishes. Among the 'spices' sold by grocers was cane-sugar
imported from India or Arabia. Spices and salt were generally bought in
bulk. 'Spice' embraced dried fruit imported from the East. Pepper came
from India and was expensive, as were mace, cloves, currants, dates,
ginger, cinnamon, prunes and 'great raisins'. Sometimes a gift hamper
from abroad might contain dried or preserved figs, marmalade and the
much prized 'poundegarnetts' (pomegranates).

Housewives living for long months in the country had to buy in bulk
to keep their presses well stocked. They could rely on 'fresh acates' or
'emptions' (purchases) made by the 'cater' (a word which may be equated
with the modern word 'caterer') to top up their diminishing stores and
provide them with fresh delicacies. However, they must, when making
their bulk orders, keep in mind that provision must be made, not only for
the domestic staff, visiting relatives and travellers passing through, but
also for their animals.

Rebecca's housekeeping must have had its anxious and frustrating

[1] Sir Hugh Platt, *The Jewell House of Art and Nature*, 1594.

[27]

moments when carriers were late and oysters and salmon, ordered for some important occasion, arrived from London after several days' journey in hot weather, fit only to be thrown on 'ye donge heape'.

We know from the Verney and Purefoy letters that such delicacies as oysters, salmon and the like were brought to Westbury from London by the Buckingham carrier who took two days, even in fine weather. Letters ordering this or that commodity flew to and fro from Westbury to trusted London agents, often old family servants who had set up in business. Every-day purchases were sent for to Brackley which was only two miles distant.

Households in Rebecca's day were early astir. Breakfast, taken from 6 to 7 o'clock, consisted of cold meats, fish, cheese, and ale or beer. Herrings both salted and dried were a favourite breakfast dish.

Dinner was the main meal of the day and was usually eaten at noon, though later in the century there was a tendency to dine later among the *afficionados* of tea, coffee and chocolate. The introduction of these beverages had a marked effect on the habits of the leisured classes. It gave an opportunity for the sexes to meet at a social level. In time a light breakfast of coffee or chocolate and rolls 'Continental style' became fashionable. As it was taken rather late in the morning, dinner was put back to much later in the day.

The noonday repast was so substantial as to cause the good Monsieur Mission to shake his head and write, 'the English eat a great deal at Dinner; they rest a while, and to it again, till they have quite stuff'd their Paunch.'

Household servants were hired by the year. In addition to their wages they were given board and lodging and a livery allowance of clothing. John Evelyn says that his father's household consisted of 130 liveried servants. In winter the men-servants wore 'grey frieze'—a coarse woollen cloth— and in summer they wore 'grey marble'—a parti-coloured worsted which was almost as hot and prickly as their winter wear.

Maids made the ordinary clothes for the family as well as their own. The raw material, such as tow and flax for simple garments, was prepared at home. Weaving was a more complicated affair, a skilled job for which an outside worker was hired.

A serving wench did not always have an easy life. According to Nicholas Breton, a maid's lament ran thus:

I must serve the olde Woman. I must learn to spinne, to reck, to carde, to knit, to wash buckets, and by hande, brew, bake, make Mault, reap, bind sheaves, weede in the garden, milke, serve Hogges, make

[28]

clene their houses, within doores make beddes, sweepe filthy houses, rubbe dirtie ragges, beate out the old Coverlets, drawe up olde holes; then to the kitchen, turn the spitte though it was but seldome, for we had not roste meate often; then scour Pottes, wash dishes fetch in Wood, make a fire; scalde milke Pannes; wash the cherne and buter dishes; ring up a cheese clout, set everything in good order.

Household books of the period give an excellent idea of the cost of living early in the seventeenth century. Most of the following items are taken from the Household Books of Lord William Howard of Naworth Castle.[1]

In 1629, fruit trees cost 2s. each.

In 1620, oranges cost 8d. to 1s. the dozen.

In 1640, mussels cost 8d. per sack.

In 1640, salmon trout cost 4d. to 6d. each.

Between 1612 and 1640

Almonds per lb., 1s. to 1s. 10d.

Aniseed per lb., 10d.

Candles per lb., 4d. to 5d.

Wax per lb., 1s. 1d.

Capers per lb., 1s.

Cinnamon per lb., 3s. 8d. to 5s. 4d.

Cloves per lb., 8s.

Figs per lb., 3d.

Isinglass per lb., 4s.

Liquorice per lb., 6s.

Ginger per lb., 1s.

Candied ginger per lb., 4s.

Nutmeg per lb., 4s.

Pepper per lb., 1s. 7d.

Raisins from Alicante per g, 9s. 4d. to 10s.

Sugar candy per lb., 3s.

Suckett (wet) per lb., 1s. 6d.

Apples per firkin, 1s. to 3s. 6d.

During the years between the Restoration and the death of Queen Anne furniture changed more than it had in the whole century of the first Tudor dynasty and the forty-six years of the first two Stuarts. Smaller, neater and more gracious pieces of furniture replaced the enormous, clumsy side tables and court cupboards.

[1] Published for the Surtees Society.

We do not know how Rebecca's first dining-room was furnished, but we do know what her dining-room was like when she was an old woman. Few wills of the period are as detailed as that of our Rebecca who went to great lengths to describe everything in the room.

> In my Dineing Room a great easy Chair and Cushion covered with red and white figured Velvet, two Square Stools covered with the like and Six Cushions of the same Velvet Six Cane Chairs made of Cherry-tree a peir or long looking Glass in Black fframe between the Windows, a black Card table . . . covered with Crimson Velvet, one of the best painted Dutch Tables a large Japan Tea Table a Japan Corner Cupboard four red Stuff Window Curtains with Valence and Rods to them an Iron Back to the Chimney Tongues Shovel . . . a pair of Bellows, ffour Glass Sconces and a Corner Cupboard of Oak . . .

Also from her will we know that Rebecca was rich in silver and plate, much of it engraved with 'a coat of arms of three escallop shells and 3 Cornish chaffe'.[1]

During the years of exile of Charles II the silversmiths had had far less work than in the time of the monarch's father. Yet those who had done well out of the Civil War and the Commonwealth had commissioned beautiful pieces and those who had managed to remain outside the polit-ical struggle had added to their family silver and plate.

Though many of the foreign silversmiths had returned to their homes at the outbreak of the Civil War, English silversmiths had gone to great pains to keep abreast of continental developments in design by studying imported engravings and drawings.

As soon as Charles II was restored to the throne some of the Dutch and French silversmiths returned to England to give their particular *cachet* to the commissions which were pouring in. Silver bowls, porringers, tankards, chafing-dishes and spoons were needed to replace the silver and plate melted down at the time of the Civil War.

Little is known of Rebecca Brandreth's day-to-day life from the time she married Nehemiah. Yet her progress through the years can be traced through her receipt book and through family wills. Both her family and that of her husband were ardent will-writers; itemizing their possessions was obviously a favourite hobby and Rebecca herself was no exception. She, even more than the others, believed in detail and this is one of the reasons why her recipes are so unusual and so precious. That she was a

[1] In 1621, the College of Arms granted the Brandreth family their arms: the three scallop shells. The '3 Cornish chaffe' mentioned by Rebecca were Cornish choughs, the Price arms.

generous woman is obvious from the choice and variety of her recipes. She had a well-developed sense of occasion and the guests at her table, while often being guinea-pigs—a fact of which they were mercifully unaware—were always welcome.

Mrs Brandreth's later social life was extensive. Apart from her own warm, large family circle—she had four children—she had her own friends. Among the friends and acquaintances in Houghton Regis days can be numbered Lady Powis, the Countess of Desmond, Lady Danvers and Lord Grey.

It seems that of all her brothers and sisters her favourite was Anne Kerstemann. Anne was Rebecca's elder sister and when their mother died it was she, no doubt, who spoilt and cherished the little girl.

Mrs Kerstemann lived in some style in a fine brick house surrounded by gardens and orchards in Camberwell. She married twice, and both her husbands were lavish in their gifts to her. At her death she left her nieces the beautiful jewellery she seems to have collected in preference to the silver which was Rebecca's passion. Mrs Kerstemann, like all the Prices and Brandreths, was scrupulous in leaving her possessions to members of her family, and Rebecca's granddaughter, Anne Beech, a favourite of her Great-Aunt Kerstemann, inherited a 'pearle trunke and all the things that are in the said pearle trunke'. Anne appointed her younger sister, Rebecca, as sole executrix of her will and the sisters are buried next to each other under handsome black marble slabs in the chancel of Houghton Regis church.

Rebecca and Nehemiah's four children—Henry, Nehemiah, Alice and Rebecca[1]—were fortunate in their parents. Rebecca was an excellent mother. This is clear from her will in which all her possessions are carefully assessed in view of the characters and inclinations of the legatees. And Nehemiah made a point of leaving to Rebecca 'all my childbed linen and other things thereunto belonging' with the request that she should distribute them amongst her children for the grandchildren as the need arose.

Though more enlightened than the Elizabethans in the care of their children, seventeenth-century parents still believed that children were entrusted to them to be brought up in the Lord's service and to be trained as good subjects of an earthly sovereign. Most parents had read Miles Coverdale's translation of Henry Bullinger's treatise, *The Christian State*

[1] Rebecca was a favourite family name which was to recur through the generations until the history of both the Prices and the Brandreths, so detailed until the early nineteenth century, becomes shrouded in silence.

of Matrimony, written *circa* 1546 and one of the earliest books to give Protestant parents advice about the management of children and households.

Bullinger had some sound and advanced ideas. He advocated breast-feeding when mothers of rank seldom nursed their babies. He disliked 'baby-talk', insisting that even tiny infants were capable of recognizing adult English if it was clearly enunciated; and though Dr Spock's predecessor tried to get parents to cram small brains with wise saws and religious precepts, he urged that all children, no matter what their station, should be taught a trade or craft. The relationship of the Verneys with their children, which was not althogether atypical, shows a warmer and more enlightened attitude. This was also expressed by John Evelyn towards his children and grandchildren.

Rebecca would certainly have imparted to her daughters her considerable knowledge and skills in compounding the herbal remedies and nostrums whose formulae she so carefully noted in the precious companion volume to her receipt book. As we know, this book 'For Surgery and Physick' has been lost, so that we do not know how she compounded the cooling draughts and cordials, the salves, pomatums and remedies with which she kept her family and staff healthy and happy. Every household had its own particular nostrums in which everyone had faith. Rebecca was no exception. As a child she was dosed with her mother's 'Black Cherry Wine', 'rare goode for convoltion fitts, or any other fitts or vapers'. A less pleasant physick would have been Housekeeper Leech's dose 'good for worms in children' or her 'Sirop of Femetery'. No doubt both these remedies were used on the Brandreth and Price infants.

While Rebecca was fulfilling her role as wife, mother and hostess, certain developments were taking place in Nehemiah's immediate family which were to have considerable influence on the lives of Rebecca's children and grandchildren.

Nehemiah's simple-minded brother, Solomon, having died unmarried, the property at Houghton Regis passed on to the next son who was Nehemiah, Rebecca's husband. Mr Brandreth had made suitable provision for his daughter, Alice, before he died and it was in Hertfordshire, at Ware, where her estate was situated, that Alice met and married Thomas Smyth of Binderton. He was a wealthy man owning considerable estates in Sussex.[1]

Alice's husband died in 1692 leaving his widow well provided for. Alice had always longed to live near her brother, Nehemiah, and his family, and

[1] Brandreth family papers. Leases, deeds and documents concerning property in Apledram, Binderton, etc. (Lewes Record Office).

[32]

as soon as she could she returned to Houghton Regis where she bought the Rectory and the Great Tithes of Houghton Regis. This was to be the nucleus of her estate (and that of her heirs) in this part of the country. At the same time, in May 1692, Alice purchased certain other lands in Houghton Regis, 'a farmhouse which looked north over the Green and had Cook's land running down the western boundary'.

On this site she built Houghton Hall, the mansion on which no expense was spared. It was completed in 1700, by which date Alice and her second husband had taken up residence in their splended new dwelling.

This second marriage had taken place when Alice, but recently widowed, was still living at Ware. Her second choice was William Milard of London. He was subsequently knighted, making her Dame Alice Milard.

Alice, like her father, was a cautious soul, and before marrying William Milard she carefully put in trust her '4 coach horses, her nag, her saddle, coach and charriot; her diamonds, pearls and locket; her silver, furs and laces, books, looking-glasses *and* the furniture from the house at Ware, known as New House', so that no future husband could touch them.

Houghton Hall stood in 150 acres of land. In front of it was Houghton Green, much scarred with ponds and pits. Alice, who cherished the uninterrupted view across the green, came to a sensible arrangement with her brother Nehemiah, then lord of the manor, that he would prevent any trees being planted on the common which might block her view; and Nehemiah also agreed to stop pits being dug which might impede access to the house. In exchange for these civilities it was understood that Dame Alice's favourite nephew, Nehemiah II, was to be her heir and in 1713 a detailed deed of appointment disposed of her property after her death together with many of her chattels and heirlooms.

Though the house continued to appear in surveys, it is next dealt with specifically in the will of Henry Brandreth who died in 1846. Inventories made at his death give the contents of the house, room by room, and in his will he required his heir, besides taking the name of Brandreth, to live in the house at least three months each year, and he made the contents of Houghton Hall heirlooms.

The heir, Humphrey Gibbs, was willing to take the arms and name of Brandreth but he had absolutely no wish to live in the house. In 1847 Henry's trustees bought from the Duke of Bedford 'Poynter's farmstead and land' in order to extend the grounds, and in 1851 a case was put to counsel.

'The Mansion House at Houghton Regis is about 150 years old and is a very incommodious and dilapidated building. Mr. Humphrey Brandreth

[33]

the present tenant for life is desirous of pulling down the present old structure and of building a new mansion on a different site.' Humphrey Brandreth wished to know if he could do this under the terms of his uncle's will and, if so, if the £20,000 trust fund could be used to build the new house. The answer to both questions was in the negative, so he had to be content with extensive alterations. He employed Henry Clutton and the contract was signed in 1851. These alterations give the house its present appearance.

Houghton Hall still stands today among smooth lawns and cedar trees of great age and beauty. It is a fine example of William and Mary architecture with its mellow red brick and tall, well-proportioned windows. Inside, the spacious rooms retain their original panelling. Neither Dame Alice nor her sister-in-law, Rebecca, would have the slightest difficulty in finding their way about the house in which they had so often been together.

There is no record of when or how Rebecca and Nehemiah enlarged or altered their own home, the Manor House which Nehemiah had inherited from his father. We do know from the wills of both Rebecca and Nehemiah that the house in which they spent the latter years of their married life was much more sophisticated than the original house. Rebecca describes elegant panelled rooms, long windows and powder-closets as well as a number of particular closets.

> Within the light Closett in my Bed Chamber a little Oak Table with a Drawer to it and a low Cane Chair In the dark Closett in my Bed Chamber a Sweetmeat Cupboard large and high with Six Shellow boxes therein and in the said Closett is a Small Oak Table with two leaves and alsoe a Close Stool of Oak . . .

The sweetmeat cupboard must have been a great attraction to the grand-children who were no doubt addicts of Rebecca's sugar of roses, melindes, eggs-and-bacon (made of sugar) and flower pastes.

The death of Nehemiah in 1719 was a great blow to Rebecca who was deeply attached to the husband with whom she had lived in peace and amity for 'thirty five years less two days'. Though she was to survive him by twenty years he was ever present in her thoughts and prayers and at the end she planned to lie beside him.

Nehemiah had given much thought to the future of his wife should he die before her and in *his* will he made it clear to his heir, Henry Brandreth II, that Rebecca was to remain in the Manor House for as long as she remained a widow. Nehemiah, too, was specific in his instructions to those who came after him. Rebecca was to have the use of the marital bed-chamber and dressing-room, together with other rooms and selected closets. Also, Rebecca and her friends were at all times to be allowed free passage through the house. Most curious of all was his insistence that

> my said wife during the terms of her widowhood and her servants shall have the use of the kitchen, brewhouse and washhouse and all the utensills for the dressing of Victualls, brewing of drink and washing of cloths in common with my son Henry and his heirs in such reason-able manner as she think necessary.

Clearly Nehemiah was taking no chances with a daughter-in-law who might try to evict his Rebecca. Apart from storage space for wine, wood and coals, Nehemiah left his wife his plate and jewellery.

At the death of the lord of the manor the little village of Houghton Regis went into mourning. The family pew, pulpit and desk were draped in jetty black for a twelvemonth. Everyone in the village paid tribute to Nehemiah's great qualities. Then gradually he faded from the minds of all but his widow and family and life continued as before.

Though Nehemiah was dead, Rebecca was surrounded and cherished by her children. Alice, the daughter who never married, was dutiful and remained by her mother's side. The death of Henry, her elder son, was a great grief to Rebecca but she was devoted to Mary, his wife, and her grandson, Henry III, was a perpetual joy to her.

Rebecca Brandreth was not to join her 'loved ones in Heaven' until she was over eighty—a great age in the days when a woman was a middle-aged matron at twenty-five. Rebecca Brandreth's life is an interesting fragment of the history of her time. History is seldom orderly for it straddles reigns and generations and men and women live on from one era to another without realizing that they are in the midst of changes which will affect the future of their great-great-grandchildren.

Rebecca lived through six reigns. When she was a child a dark-browed Stuart was on the throne, and the chalk-white face, beaked nose, and thin red hair of the great Elizabeth would still be in the memory of a cen-tenarian; when Rebecca died, the second of the Hanoverians, George II, ruled over England.

In her life-time, much of medieval London had been swallowed up by the flames of the Great Fire and she would have seen arising from the ashes the new, spacious London and that splendid phoenix, St Paul's cathedral, built of the dazzling white stone of Portland.

Though communications were limited, town and country dwellers were assiduous letter-writers and echoes from the great world and from the court were certain to have found their way to Houghton Regis and to have been discussed at Rebecca's 'dineing table'.

Rebecca had many sources of information and she would have known of the long and tempestuous friendship between Queen Anne and the imperious Sarah Churchill. She would also have heard of the arrival of the first Hanoverian George flanked by his favourites, the one short and fat, the other thin and tall, and not one of the trio with a word of English between them!

The young men of Rebecca's family who came to London and frequented coffee shops and taverns would have told her stories of the commercial exploitation of new inventions and of new methods of doing things; of machines that helped men in their toil. All this, suitably filtered, would have been retailed to the matriarch who came to be known throughout the length and breadth of the county not only as a superlative hostess and cook, but as a fount of knowledge in household matters.

Like most of the members of her family Rebecca was conscious not only of her duties in this life but of the rites that must be performed when she left it. A long and detailed document attests to the arrangements she made to dispose of her worldly goods, and also to ensure that her mortal remains should be interred with a certain pomp and dignity.

On 13 April 1740 when the young lambs were gambolling in the pastures, when the first sweet flowers of spring embroidered the gardens of England, Rebecca Brandreth, *née* Price, aged 81 years, 1 month and 20 days, died. She died content in the knowledge that everything in her world was orderly and that ample provision had been made for all those who depended upon her. She lies in the churchyard in her beloved village and on her tomb are inscribed these words:

My afflictions have been many, my Troubles uncommon, but looking on the Hand that sent them I endeavour to bear them with that CHRISTIAN patience and resignation which becometh a Servant of Jesus Christ by whose Merits alone I hope for salvation and that Great and Gracious God Omnipotent hath of his Infinite Mercy fitted and prepared me to be received into his Heavenly Kingdom, where I may sing forth praises and Hallelujahs to him that sitteth upon ye Throne and unto the Lamb for ever and ever. Amen.

ffor all sorts of pyes both baked and fryed

USING REBECCA PRICE'S
RECEIPTS

Isabell N. Read

Department of Catering, Home Economics and Art,
College of Further Education, Chichester

Rebecca Price's collection of receipts reveal that a gentleman's wife in the seventeenth and early eighteenth century was expected to have a very wide practical knowledge of domestic matters and be an extremely capable organizer. She had to instruct the servants, and handle the housekeeping accounts and often the estate ones as well. A country house, then, was almost self-supporting, relying for most of its food on its own fields, gardens, stockyard and dairy. She would oversee the preservation of all manner of foods for the purposes of securing winter stores and making economical use of surpluses.

[37]

Every facet of running the household had to be directed by a mistress who needed far more than a theoretical knowledge of each task. For this reason, in addition to their formal education, girls then had what we would now call 'on the job training', beginning when young, helping with the simpler tasks, until in their late teens they had a sound knowledge of all aspects of housekeeping. Although there was much work to be done it was shared by many servants and so the heaviness was allayed by companionship.

The size of the household explains why the quantities given in Rebecca's receipts are so large although basically many of them are still practicable today.

A factor to be considered in using these receipts is that agricultural and horticultural developments and animal husbandry have resulted in many of the commodities being of a different size and weight. Poultry is larger, as are meat joints. Eggs in Rebecca's day would be the size of pullets' eggs—not the 2oz. standard in use now. Strains of fruit have improved resulting in larger hard and soft fruits and berries. Strong spices and flavourings are not used so extensively, as there is now no need to mask the flavour of tainted meat and fish. However, some food critics might welcome an early return of their use to give more taste to our meat and poultry, fast being made flavourless by battery production. Some of the flavourings, however, are no longer obtainable—particularly civet, ambergris and musk which are now so precious and costly that they are used exclusively in the manufacture of expensive perfume. Other ingredients such as orange flower water and tragacanth are obtainable at a chemist rather than a food shop. Hartshorn would be replaced by gelatine.

In reducing the receipts for a modern household bear in mind that all ingredients must be altered in the correct proportions, otherwise the recipe balance will be destroyed. So keep the *proportions* as close as possible to the original recipe. Flavourings would have to be adapted to suit personal tastes but retain as many of them as are obtainable, otherwise the character of the dish is changed. Obvious changes may be made in methods—it is no longer necessary to beat for three hours when a few minutes in an electric blender would achieve the same result. Labour was sufficiently cheap in those days to have a maidservant beat a mixture for several hours.

The fish recipes can all be used, but I would advise a reduction in the amount of anchovies in many of them. My Lady Howe's receipt 'To boyle a samon' differs little from our method of making a court bouillon, as does also My Lady Sheldon's advice 'To dress any fish'. Applied to salmon, the use of wine and herbs would make a delightful dish.

The section on meat receipts contains much that is impractical for present times. The salting, pickling and preservation of meat was an essential part of the domestic economy if households were to be adequately fed throughout the winter. Many of the directions are for dealing with whole animals—now a process confined to the meat trade. There is a very large section on how to 'coller' all sorts of meat and cuts of meat and this has evolved into our boiled beef and dumplings. The making of sausages has become a professional butchery process or a factory one, but some of Rebecca's receipts make up into extremely tasty savoury mixtures for rissoles or meat loaves. The 'potting' of meat is still a practical and economical process. A form of potted meat is still widely obtainable in Scottish butchers' shops and still made in many Scottish households. It is potted hough—'hough' being the name given to shin of beef. In the meat cookery, care must be taken in the use of spices for it is now no longer necessary to conceal the flavour of slightly tainted or too strong meat.

The roasting of poultry and meats was done on a spit which was rotated—the mechanism varying slightly according to the household. This method has, of course, returned to fashion in the form of gas or electric rotary spits. Small flat joints, fish and even steaks were cooked on a smaller gadget rather like a toaster—fitted with prongs on which the meat was impaled and cooked in front of the fire. Many of the recipes here can be used in the form Rebecca wrote them down—one particularly attractive one being My First Cousin Clerke's receipt 'To Boyle pullits'. Rebecca seemed to have collected a large number of recipes for scotch collops. This dish has no connection with Scottish cookery—to scotch meant to cut up or chop, and collop was a corruption of 'escalope' or small slices of meat. For any of these recipes substitute minced meat and I would add, once again, a reminder concerning the use of anchovies.

The section on sauces certainly contradicts the saying attributed to Francesco Caraccioli in the eighteenth century that England had sixty different religious sects but only one sauce. Indeed, it is a sad reflection, after reading this section, that the art of sauce-making in so many households has deteriorated to gravy and custard. Rebecca's receipts are highly seasoned and use anchovies lavishly for the reason referred to concerning meat cookery. It is interesting to note that both brown roux and beurre manie were known and used for thickening and we see the forerunner of Hollandaise and Bearnaise sauces in Mrs Whitehead's receipt for Duke of

York's sauce. The 'sawce for ducks'—Mrs Ridge's receipt—has been tested in the writer's household and found to be delicious.

The puddings 'in guts' are the forerunners of boiled puddings in cloths, and here they are cooked rather in the way haggis is still cooked in Scotland using the (well-cleansed) stomach bag of the sheep. These recipes would be quite practicable cooked in a pudding basin or mould and covered with greased paper and foil. Do note the meticulous methods of many of the recipes, e.g. the straining of the eggs to keep back the thread. In the recipes using breadcrumbs—'take a twopenny lofe grated'—base your quantites on the fact that a twopenny lofe would be the equivalent of our 2-lb. loaf and would yield $1\frac{1}{2}$ lb. breadcrumbs.

The 'pyes' did not necessarily involve the use of pastry but in many cases were similar in style to modern shepherd's pies and hotpots, where potatoes are used to cover the meat. In Rebecca's recipes they were baked in a deep dish, the cover being the lid. Use a casserole or tureen to get a similar result. However, in many of the recipes pastry, especially puff paste, is used, and a 'florendine' is referred to. This was a dish that became a florentine, the pastry being used both above and below the filling as it is now used in tarts. Also note the receipt for making puff paste on page 138. The method is basically the same as that for flaky pastry found in any modern cookbook. The emphasis on keeping the correct proportion of fat to flour is in the best cookery-class tradition.

On page 138—'my Second Cousen Clerke's' receipt for puff paste— 'taken out of a book' is the basic method for rough puff pastry even to the instruction not to work it too much, in order not to break down the lumps of butter.

In using receipts from the dessert section, experiment with small quantities at first, basing your recipe on $\frac{1}{2}$ pint of cream and using the other ingredients in proportion. For the curds and cheese recipes, the process of 'turning the cream' can be omitted by using curd or cottage cheese. For setting, Rebecca uses either hartshorn or isinglass. The latter is still obtainable, usually in health food shops as it is used by vegetarians because gelatine is of animal origin. $\frac{3}{4}$ oz. of gelatine is required to set 1 pint of thin liquid while $\frac{1}{2}$ oz. is necessary to set 1 pint of thick mixture such as fruit or vegetable purées, creams etc. Syllabubs are now enjoying a return to favour and here is a guide to the sort of quantities that would be suitable for six to eight people.

A Sillibub [*syllabub*] *My Lady Sheldon's Receipt*

¼ pt. white wine
2 tablesp. lemon juice
2 level teasp. grated lemon rind
3 oz. castor sugar
½ pt. double cream

Combine wine, lemon juice, rind and sugar in a bowl and allow to stand for 3 hours. Start whisking the mixture; whisk in cream and continue whisking until mixture stands in soft peaks. Turn out into individual glasses and leave to stand in a cold place for several hours before serving.

The section of bread receipts is of interest but it would not be practicable to adapt any to use now. The yeast in use was brewers' yeast—a perquisite of the brewer's wife who carried it to markets in earthenware jars covered with a cloth. It was in a semi-liquid state and very different from the compressed yeast in use today. In large households beer would be brewed on the premises—possibly once a month—and yeast would be obtained during that process. The measure of a peck was a variable one. Usually a wooden vessel of approximately two gallons capacity was filled with the flour, and there was no imperial bushel until 1826. The fact that a number of Rebecca's receipts include instructions for grating a penny or twopenny loaf lead one to assume that bread-making was certainly not a regular occurrence in her kitchen.

Some of the recipes in the cakes section need an arithmetical exercise in division to reduce the ingredients to a practical quantity for the present day. Nevertheless, many of them are extremely practical, especially what are obviously the forerunners of the slab fruit cakes. It must be borne in mind that baking powders were not in use until the mid-nineteenth century, therefore many of these cakes were not as light in texture as the ones we have today. Lightness was achieved by much beating to incorporate air, or the use of eggs and egg whites, or by the addition of ale yeast which was widely used in fruit cakes. If you are attempting any of the cakes and using compressed yeast, I would suggest you make a ferment with:

1 oz. yeast
½ lb. flour
1 level teasp. salt
¾ pt. milk and/or water

[41]

Leave this in a large bowl to rise (approximately 30 minutes). Then beat in the rest of the flour, butter, sugar, fruit and eggs. The ounce of yeast will raise a total of 2 lb. of flour with the other ingredients in proportion.

The cheese-making section is of interest, but it would be impractical to attempt the adaptation of any of Rebecca's instructions. The way milk is now pasteurized and processed for domestic use prevents the success of home-made cheese.

The section on preservation—jams, jellies, drying of fruit, etc.—is one from which ideas may be gleaned rather than direct adaptations made. It is in this branch of cookery that more technological advances have been made than in any other.

The pickling receipts have a curiosity value. Freezing techniques and chutney recipes make much of Rebecca's lore impractical now. The 'Conserves of Roses'—a rose-petal jam—is delicious and could be made by anyone who grows old-fashioned scented red roses.

Biskits mostly resemble in texture *langues de chat* or sponge fingers. The recipes here are not in such vast quantities, as such delicacies would be made for the use of the family and their guests and not for the servants. If you use ground almonds to replace the 'almonds cut up fine', add a few drops of almond essence as it is always necessary with the use of commercially ground almonds. The baking temperatures on most of the recipes will average 350°F and gas setting 4. For 'double refined sugar' use castor sugar—not icing, as icing sugar was called powdered sugar. The making of wafers required a special iron—it is referred to in the recipe—about the size of a small plate with a very long handle. This was to enable the wafer to be held over the glowing coal. These irons had incised designs on both sides. They were taken to America with the early settlers and in course of time became waffle irons and have returned to England in this form.

The collection of receipts for wine is fascinating. However, wine-making is a very special skill and will only be attempted by readers already familiar with the process. There are excellent modern cultures and yeasts available, but as the subject is so specialized space prevents explanations. Wine-makers will nevertheless gain many ideas from the fruits and flowers used by Rebecca.

Some of Rebecca's recipes modernized[1]

To Coller Beefe (page 97)

A piece of salted or pickled beef (flank is usual cut)
Peppercorns—1 teasp.
½ teasp. whole allspice
Thyme, sage, bay leaf, rosemary, parsley
1 onion

Cut away all gristle and fat from meat and roll up; tie with string. Place in pot and cover with water, bring to boil and pour away water. This removes excess salt. Then cover with fresh water with herbs, onion and peppercorns, bring to boil and simmer until cooked. Allow 30 minutes per lb. and 30 minutes over. Serve hot or cold. If cold, press between 2 plates or boards with a weight on top and slice thinly.
NB   If using fresh beef add 1 oz. salt to the water and omit the first boiling.

A Carett puding baked My Lady Howe's Receipt (page 121)

4 oz. breadcrumbs
4 oz. grated carrots
3 egg yolks
2 egg whites
2 oz. melted butter
2 tablesp. sherry
Grated nutmeg
¼ pt. milk
3 oz. sugar

Mix together carrots and breadcrumbs. Add yolks. Melt butter in warm milk and add with sugar and 1 tablesp. sherry and nutmeg. Beat whites stiffly and fold in. Bake ½ hr. in a moderate oven (350°F, gas 4). Add the other tablesp. sherry before serving.

[1] A guide to American measurements appears on page 46.

[43]

Plum puding boyled (page 129)

4 oz. breadcrumbs
¼ pt. milk
Grated nutmeg
2 eggs
Pinch salt
2 oz. flour (if plain, use 1 teasp. baking powder)
3 oz. prepared suet
6 oz. currants and raisins

Bring milk almost to boil, pour over breadcrumbs and leave to soak until cool. Beat in other ingredients. Turn into a greased pudding basin, cover and boil or steam for 3 hours.

An Apple puding baked My first Cousen Clerkes Receipt (page 130)

1 lb. apples
4 eggs
4 oz. breadcrumbs
4 oz. sugar
Pinch salt
Rosewater to taste
2 oz. butter
Grated nutmeg

Bake apples and use pulp; or peel, quarter and core them and stew with the butter, sugar and rosewater. Take the pureed apples, then add beaten eggs, grated bread and salt and beat well together. Put into a buttered pie-dish, sprinkle with a little melted butter and grate on the nutmeg. Bake in a moderate oven (350°F, gas 4) for ¾ hour.

An Oringe puding baked My Lady Howes Receipt (page 131)

Pastry   6 oz. flour
3 oz. butter
Pinch salt
Enough cold water to make stiff paste

[44]

Filling   Grated rind of one orange
3 oz. sugar
4 egg yolks
3 oz. butter

Cream butter and sugar, add orange rind and egg yolks. Line a dish with half the pastry,[1] put in filling and cover with other half of pastry. Bake at 400°F, gas 6, for ½ hour. Reduce heat if necessary for last 10–15 minutes.

Mince Pyes (page 141)

Mincemeat for pies: ¼ lb. ox tongue—minced or chopped
½ lb. shredded suet
1 cooking apple, grated
1 teasp. grated lemon rind
½ lb. currants
2 oz. raisins (stoned and cut)
¼ oz. spices (mix to personal taste)
Juice of ½ lemon
⅛ pt. sherry
2 oz. chopped dates
1 oz. candied peel (chopped)
4 oz. sugar
Mix all ingredients together.

To make Almond Cream   My Aunt Rye's Receipt (page 162)

1 pt. single cream (½ pt. cream, ½ pt. milk)
4 eggs
4 oz. sugar
4 oz. ground almonds
*½ teasp. almond essence
2 teasp. rosewater

Make a custard with the eggs and cream. Add other ingredients.
Pour into a dish and leave until cold.

* NB Necessary with commercially ground almonds.

[1] The original recipe suggested thin puff pastry, but Rebecca's note would suggest that short-crust was preferable.

A guide to American measurements

The main point of difference to remember is that the standard half-pint American measuring cup equals 8 fluid ounces and not 10 fluid ounces.

American	*English*
1 cup flour	4 oz.
1 cup breadcrumbs	3 oz.
1 cup sugar	7 oz.
1 cup icing sugar	5 oz.
1 cup butter or other fats	8 oz.
1 tablespoon butter or other fats	$\frac{1}{2}$ oz.
1 cup raisins or sultanas or currants	6 oz.
1 cup grated cheese	4 oz.

All sorts of Alle & strong Beer, & to fine sider or wine

A NOTE ON
THE ADAPTATION OF THE
WINE-MAKING RECEIPTS

Basil Minchin, B.Sc.

The making of wine in the eighteenth century was done in containers of a difficult size for modern use. If any of these recipes are to be attempted today, they must be made in standard gallon containers and the quantities reduced proportionately.

Modern nylon bags are better than hair sieves for straining and the small presses available to wine-makers make straining, mashing and crushing fruit an easy task.

The only yeast available in Rebecca's brewhouse would have produced a sticky deposit of dead yeast; today it would be much more convenient to use the wine yeasts sold by chemists in tablet or powder form. A red or

[47]

white wine yeast can be chosen appropriate to the recipe, and there will be only a powdery deposit of dead yeast to remove.

For the first fermentation after the addition of yeast, leave up to one third of the bottle empty and only after at least a week fill them up or transfer the wine to clean bottles if there is any scum or residue. An air lock should be used from this point until fermentation is complete.

This Booke was written by me: Rebecca: Price
in the Yare ~ [1681:]

At this end of the Booke is all maner of Cookery, and all
sorts of Creams, Custards, sillybubs, possets, jellys, and Caudles,
and all sorts of Cakes, and all maner of Wines, Alle, Beere,
and other drinks, and all sorts of pickles whatsoever:

A page from Rebecca Price's Receipt Book

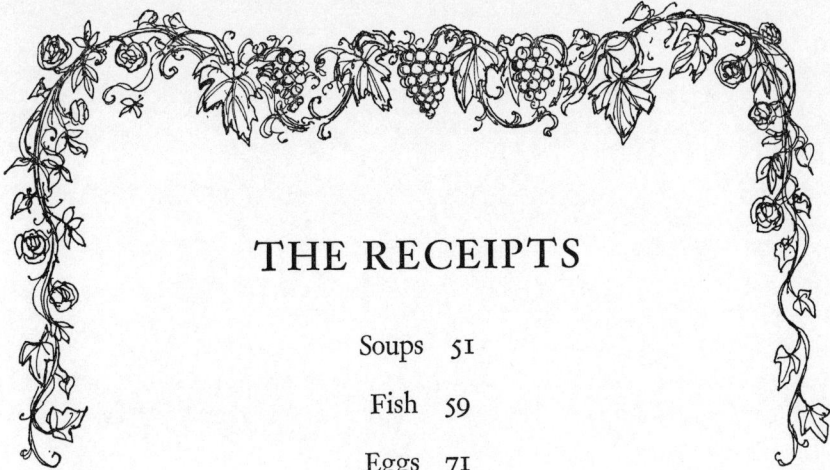

THE RECEIPTS

The reader is referred to the Glossary to the Receipts for notes on ingredients and unfamiliar terms.

All sorts of pottages, Broaths and firmity

SOUPS

SOUPS

all sorts of pottages, Broaths and firmity

A pottage: Mrs Whitehead's Receipt

Take a leg of beefe, boyle it to peeces with cloves, mace, and an oynion, and a bundle of sweet herbes, and a knuckle of veale, and beef gravie; when the meat is boyled to peeces, take out your broth and scime it, and put it into a pipkin, then put in your pigions, or palets [tongues], and frye some sweetbreads and garnish it; make tosts and laye one ye dish put in halfe the juce of a Lemon; when you are redy to serve it put in the gravie which must be but hott, you may put in a little bitt of baccon, you may in all meats pottages put in sosiges [sausages], and small birds, or what you please; when you put in whole herbes boyle them in water and butter over any meat it makes them looke very clear, and green: put in with your water about 2 quarts of good Alle.

Christmas-Broath: Leeches Receipt

Take a leg of beefe and put water with 2 quarts of Alle to it and boyle it till it is almost tender enough, then wash 3 pounde of courents and three pounde of raisons, and boyle them very well in your broathe, keepeing it stiring very well all the while it boyles after the fruite is in, and when the fruit is almost boyled put in a good quantity of grated bread to thicken it; then when your fruit and bread is very well boyled put in of cloves; mace; and nutmeg, or each alike quantity and in all an ounce, together, let it boyle a quarter of an howre after the spice is in, you may put some pruens in if you please, and also some red sanders [sandalwood], and some claret if you like it; so serve it.

A pottage of Veale: Mrs Lords Receipt

Take a large knuckle of veale, and the cragg end of a neck of mutton; or a shin of Beefe, and if you will a pullitt, or three or foure pigions, let all these boyle with so much water as will cover them well, put in 4 or 5 blades of mace, halfe a douson cloves; grosly beaten a little white pepper; put in your spice when your broath is almost halfe boyled: when the meat is enough take it up, and cover it to keepe it hott, then put into your broath salt, 3 or 4 handfulls of sorill, as much spinage, and as much of Beets-leaves, some Asparagus cutt; or green peese: if you like not the Herbes the Asparagus, and peese, will do very well off themselves alone: some will put in sliced cucumbers, when these are boyled tender take as much broath as you intend for the table in a large deep dish: set it on a chafindish [chafing dish] of coals; slice some french manchitt [bread] very thine and lay all over covering the broath: if you please you may add a little claritt 4 or 5 spoonfulls: and three or four anchoves when you put it into the dish, let it stew till it thiken to your minde: if you would have it very strong and finde this not enough, then put some gravie to it, after wch lay your veale in the broath and so serve it up: there is often times bacon boyled and sliced and layed upon the veale: also sausages layed one the sides of the dish: put in with your water 2 quarts of Alle wch will make it strong and gives it a better couller than claret does.

A chickin Broath, or veal Broath. viz

After your chickin is picked and drawn, then skin it, and with a wooden pestall or Roleing-pin beat it tell all ye flesh and bones be well broken, then put it into a pipkin with what quantity of water you think fitt, let it boyle and as soon as you have well skimed it, put into it a piece of under crust of Bred pared, and a blade of mace, keeping it gently boyleing tell all the goodness be out of ye chickin and of what strenth you would have ye broath, then strain it through a haire sive: if you please you may put in a little hartshorn at ye time you put in the crust of Bred; after the same manner you may make Broath of a small knuckle of veale, takeing the fatt off the Broath when it is cold.

A cooling Broath   Mrs Edgburys Receipt: at Montpelier

Take a chicken, and a little handfull of french barly, boyle it in an earthen pipkin two howres, then put to it a handfull of herbes, white suckery [chicory?] or endives, and burage [borage], lettis, and buglace [bugloss?], and let it boyle another halfe howre; then put in a drame of christell minerall [mineral salts];[1] then drinke of this broath every morning a poringerfull for six mornings.

To Make White Broath: my second Cousen Clerkes Receipt

Boyle a capon in fayre water and salt by it self that it may be white; then take a pinte of veale or mutton broath that is very strong, and put it in a

[1] Montpelier was a spa town where mineral salts could be obtained.

skillit with some whole mace, and a few sweet herbes, and put in also a pinte of sack, let it boyle a little; then take the yolks of eight eggs and halfe a pinte of sweet creame; beat the creame and eggs together, and mixe them with the hott broth, then take it off the fire and set it one embers, and let it not boyle after your eggs are in, for fear of turning, stir it well when you put your eggs & creame in that it may thicken; you should put in some lumps of marow into your broath before you put in your eggs, and let it boyle in the broath till it is enough; but be sure not to let it boyle after ye eggs are in; but onely keepe it heating yt it may thicken; boyle some frute by it self in some mutton broth, as raisons, courance [currants] and 2 or 3 grated dates, some pruents [prunes] to garnish ye dish; season your broath with suger, then put your capon in a dish, and poure your broath one him; and lay your pruents and grated dates one the top of your capon; and one ye dish sides; you must onely put the courents and raisons into the broath; and keepe the pruents, and grated dates, to garnish your dish withall; some will not put any fruit at all into this broath; which I beleive is much better to be left out; and onely sweeten it with suger and so serve it.

Peese-pottage: *My Lady Howe's Receipt*

Take some of your best yellow peese, boyle them and bruse them, and strayne them out; then put them in a pott and boyle them with a good great peece of butter and some sweet herbes, and an oynion stuffed wth cloves, and a little mace; shread some capers and put in, and when it boyles cutt the bottoms and tops of french manchets [bread] and tost them lay them in the dish and so serve it.

Peese-pottage: *my second Cousen Clerke's: given me by Mrs Jackson*

Take a leg of beefe and let it boyle 6 or 7 houres, then take a sive and strayne the liquor and meat through squeseing the meat; the while the leg of beefe is boyleing, set on a skillet with some peese to boyle to pap; then take them and strayne them through the sive; when so don mix it with ye liquor you strayned before and put to them a bunch of sweet herbes, and a good deale of sorrill, and some spinige; and so let it boyle about halfe an howre or more; when you dish it tost some bread and put in, if you please you may put a pullit, or a duck, in the dish for a shew, and garnish ye dish with Lemon.

[56]

Peese-pottage: Mrs Whitehead's Receipt

Take a leg of beefe, and a knuckle of veale; let it boyle till all the goodness
be out, then take it off and strayne it; boyle some peese in a bag, then
bruse them and strayne out the pulps, and strayne ye other liquor to
them, you may put in either a pullitt or a peece of baccon stuck with
cloves into the midle of the dish; boyle sosiges and balls and lay about the
dish and splits under it; some will put in a little milke with the strayned
pease to give it a couller.

Greene peese-pottage: my Aunt Rye's Receipt

Take about foure quarts of shealed peese, to about six quarts of water
boyle them well together, then take a little peny-lofe and slice it in cold
water and break it small; then put it into the porige to thicken it; then
take halfe a handfull of mints, and as many marygolds, and a little persly;
chop all small and boyle them in halfe a pounde of butter; and when your
porige is boyled mix them together and put in as much beaten pepper as
will lye one a three-pence; and salt to your likeing; if it be not thike
enough put in a spoonfull of flower and boyle it in butter and put it in;
to make them tast more of the peese put in some of the juce of the shells;
some will boyle a whole oynion in and take it out againe.

Greene pease-pottage: my Lady Sheldon's Receipt

Take a neck of veale and a henn, (or capon) put it into a skillit, with a
good deal of water, scime it cleane and put to it a bundle of these herbes,
tyme, persly, a little wintersavory, and majerom; a blade of mace, a
dousen corns of peper, while this is boyleing, boyle in another skillit halfe
a bushill of young peese before they are sheald; when they are boyled
tender take halfe of them and beat them in a stone morter very small;
then strayne them into some of the broath the flesh is boyled in; and put
yt which is strayned into the skillet of flesh, and let it boyle a good while;
then put ye other part of the peese into it, and let it boyle awhile untill it
be pretty thike; season it with salt, and halfe a spoonfull of vineger; (and
no more) and put in a good peece of butter, stir it till ye butter be melted,
then put in a dish and serve it, this pottage may be made with blanched
beans.

[57]

A pottage with cabbage: Mrs Lords Receipt

Make a good strong broath with mace, and cloves, a little of each; three or foure oynions, a bunch of sweet herbes: boyle all these with meatt in water till it be pretty strong: then strayne of and set it over the fire, then take the crust of 2 or 3 french loves well dryed and stoved over coals with some of the Broath: then melt a little butter in a sawce-pan and slice in an oynion: then have a ladlefull of cabbage cleane drayned and boyled tender, give it two or three chops with a knife and flower it, let the sliced oynion be fryed till it change couller, but not browne, then put the cabbage to it and let them frye for almost a quarter of an howre gently; and keepe them stiring; then put in a little more flower stir them together with a little gravie, and some broath: then put all into your pottage which set upon the fire and let it boyle a little puting to it a little melted butter; then put it to your stoved bread in a deepe dish or basson and serve it up: you may make the strong broath with Beefe or what other meat you please.

To Make firmety of french Barly: my Lady Sheldon's Receipt

Take the third part of a pounde of french barly; boyle it very tender in three waters, then drayne the water from it and when it is cold put it to a quart of creame, and a blade of mace, a nutmeg quartered, and a race of ginger cut into peeces; set it one the fire and let it boyle a prety while still stiring it, season it with suger to your tast, then beat the yolks of foure eggs with a little of ye creame, and mix them to the rest and let it boyle a little after the eggs are in; then have some twenty almonds blanched and beaten with some rose-water to keepe them from oyleing; then with a little of ye thynest of the firmity rub them through a strayner into your firmety; set it one the fire no more after ye almonds are in it; pick out the spice and stir in a little salt and sliced nutmeg to serve it.

That called ffermy-jelly [vermicelli], and seego, are two things that are much used in all fine pottages, you must take a little quantity of each, and boyle them in a little of your strong broth by it self untill they are tender; the seego when 'tis enough will looke clare like christall jelly, and ye fermy-jelly will be tender; boyle them both together and less than halfe an howre will boyle them enough, and just when you dish out your pottage put them both into the dish to it, and lay some of them on ye fowle, or what other meat you lay on ye midle of your dish.

[58]

to dress all sorts of fish and to stew oysters

FISH

FISH

to dress all sorts of fish and to stew oysters

To Roste A pike: My Lady Howe's Receipt

Take the pike and scalde him, then take pickled herings and cutt into long slices with which you must larde your pike all over; then take anchovies, oysters, Lemon and sweet herbes minced small; mingle them with nuttmegs cloves and mace beaten small, and a pounde of butter more or less according to ye bigness of ye fish, all which being kneaded together must be put into the belly of the pike and sewed in fast; then if you be unprovided with a hollow fish spit, put him one another spitt with a splinter of alarth [a lath] on each side tyed rounde with packthread, if you cannot conveniently roast him add to him a little whitewine and butter and so put him into the oven to bake him when he is redy to send to the table take a little vineger and butter with anchovies and oysters seasoned with salt and mixed with the ingredients that are in the fishes belly with which sawce poured one him serve him to ye table: A Barbill [barbel] dressed this way (but without either anchovies or oysters) is excelent meat.

To roste a pike: my Lady Sheldon's Receipt

Take a pike scoure off the slime, take out the intrills, larde it with the back of a pickled herring, you must have a sharpe bodkin to make the holes for a larding pinn will not go through; then take some great oysters washed in claret-wine seasoned with peper, salt, and nuttmeg, halfe frye the oysters, then stuff the belly of the pike with them; intermix with them rosemary, time, wintersavory—sweet-majerome, with a little oynion and garlick, sew this up in the belly of the pike: according to ye length of the pike prepare two sticks of ye breath of alarth [a lath], these two sticks and ye spitt must be as broade as ye pike; being tyed one the spitt tye the pike with windeing packthread about it all along; baste it with butter and claretwine and some anchovies dissolved in it; when it is rosted, rip up the belly and ye oysters will be the sawce, but the herbes that are whole must be taken out.

To boyle a pike: my Lady Sheldon's Receipt

Take your pike and either drye him with a cloath, or if he be very foule wash him cleane, then cutt him into peeces about an inch or somewhat more, then put those peeces into an earthen or puter vessell, or any thinge else so it be not brasse; let the thing you put it in be pretty deepe; that so ye less liquor may cover the fish; then take some liquor which must be three parts whitewine-vineger; and water, as much as will cover it, put to it a very large handfull of salt, then set it one the fire, and when it boyles very fairely up, put it hastily into the fish and cover it up, and so let it stand about an howre, against which time you must have redy boyleing on the fire; the water you intend to boyle the fish in, which must have in it a large fagot of sweet herbes well picked and chosen, as tyme, rosemary, peny-royall, sweetmajerom, winter savory, fenell, and mynt, either drye or greene, 4 or 5 good oynions, quartered; cloves and mace, whole ginger sliced, a Lemon or oringe pill, or both, season it to a very great height with salt, and when they are all well boyled put in the liquor the fish was steeped in, and make it boyle fast, then put in the fish but peece after peece, that the kittle leaves not boyling; when it is boyled enough take it up, for it is an injury to let it lye in the water after it hath don boyleing, send it to the table with this sawce as follows, take some three or foure anchovies (according to the proportion of sawce or the desire you have to their tast) dissolving them in some of the liquor the fish was boyled in, over a few coales, and let a clove or two of garlic lye in it whilst they dissolve, but no longer; then have good store of butter melted thike, and stir the anchovies into it, and add a good quantity of dryed horseredish-roote grated; a little nuttmeg, to all which squesse the juce of a Lemon, you must cover the bottome of your dish you serve it in with slices of manchets [bread]; garnish your dish with what you please according to your fancy, either with grated bread, Lemon, oringe, grapes or barberys,—this way is excelent for all maner of fish, so it be don without steepeing, but a proportion of viniger put into the liquor; if they have great scales take them off before you boyle them.

To boyle a carpe: my Lady Howes Receipt

Take of [off] the slime of ye Carpe with some salt, wash it cleane with water, and drye it well, put into ye dish you kill it in some vineger to keepe the bloud from cleaveing to ye dish; then take out the galle, and boyle your carpe with some vineger, and wine, and the bloud of ye carpe, some ginger sliced; a nuttmeg quartered; some mace, and salt; a little sprig of rosemary, a bundle of sweet herbes; and if you love it an oynion; let the liquor boyle before you put in ye carpe; when you are redy to put in your carpe halfe an howre will boyle it; when it is redy take it up, then put in some butter to the liquor that your carpe was boyled in; but if there be too much liquor, boyle it away after ye carpe is out to what quantity you would have it for the sawce.

To Stew Carpes: Leeches Receipt

Take two live Carpes and cutt them under the gills and in the taile and gitt out as much bloud as you can, then take a quart of claret and more if they are great carpes; after you have scaled them put them into a stewing-pann and the claret to them, and a bundle of sweet herbes, as tyme, rose-mary, and savory, then take 3 oynions and quarter them and put them in also, and a nuttmeg cutt into quarters, and ye same quantity of mace, and a little handfull of salt, mix all these together and cover it close, then set it over a gentle fire and let it stew an howre, then turn the carpes the other sides downewards and stew them an howre more; then take 3 or 4 anchovies according as you will have it tast, bone them and put them in, and also the bloud that you saved put in, and let it boyle about a quarter of an howre, after you have taken it off the fire put in a quarter of a pounde of butter; then take your carpes out of ye pan as whole as you can and put them into ye dish you desire to serve them in, and poure all the liquor upon them; takeing out the oynions, herbes and spice, you must boyle the roe of your carpes in a skillet of water by it self, and so garnish your fish with it.

To Roast an Elle [eel]: My Lady Howe's Receipt

Take an elle and rub it with salt to make the skine thine; then strip it halfe off as whole as you can; then cutt open the belly and take out all the inside; then take some sweet herbes and chop them, and two anchovies and some Lemon-pill, and nuttmeg; and a good peece of butter, mingle all this well together, and put it into the belly of ye fish and draw up ye skine again; then tye the elle to the spitt and baste it at first with alle, and salt; and when it is almost roasted then baste it with butter, the sawce must be a little wine, and the herbes that be in the belly put into the sawce and some butter.

[64]

To roast an Elle: Newton's Receipt: in peeces

Take a large ell take off the skine and gutt it, wash it cleane, and cutt it into 5 or 6 peeces, then haveing a few sweet hearbs as time, sweetmajerom, orange and Lemmon-time, persly and sage shread all pretty small mingle with them a little grated nuttmeg and beaten peper with some salt, and then strew the inside of all the peeces of Elle with it, then spitt them with 4 or 5 sage leaves betweene every peece and so roast it, flowering and basting it with butter, about an hower will roast it enough, for ye sawce take wine, anchovie, and butter, as you do for boyled fish, and so serve it in with ye sage leaves amongst it that ware rosted with it.

To Stew Elles: my Cousen Wheatlys Receipt

Take your elles and cutt them in prety big peeces after you have scined them; put them into an earthen pipkin and put to them some butter, and a little whole peper; and mace, 2 or 3 cloves, and some oynions; and a bundle of sweet herbes; then cover it close and set it in a kittle of boyleing water and so let it stew till it be enough, in the stewing you must take your pipkin up very often to turn your elles; when they are stewed enough they will be very full of liquor and gravie; when you put them into ye dish put a little vineger into them; and some sipits rounde the dish; your elles will be stewed in three howres; you must be sure to keepe the kittle of water boyleing all the while; and do not put above a quarter of a pounde of butter to two elles.

To boyle a samon: My Lady Howe's Receipt

Take as much water as will cover the bottome of a pan, and season it with salt before you set it one the fire; and when it boyles put in your samon, and let it boyle up a great passe; then take two quarts of alle, and halfe a pinte of vineger put it in, and let it boyle, and slack the fire a little by degrees; so serve it up with butter, and shrimps, and oysters.

To boyle a chine of samon: my second Cousen Clerke's

Take you salmon and boyle it in water with a little vineger, a bundle of sweet herbes, a little mace and some salt; when it is boyled take it up, and take some of the liquor and put some anchovies to it, and laye your salmon one it, and set the dish one a chafindish [chafing dish] of coales till the anchovies are melted, then poure some melted butter one it, and serve it with sipits.

To boyle and also to sowce salmon: Newtons Receipt

Take halfe a salmon and cutt of ye jole [head], then ye midle peece, and then the tayle remains for another peece, halfe a salmon will make three good peeces, wash them in fayre water, then have in redyness your kittle of water boyleing with a good quantity of water and salt in it, let it boyle a little then haveing placed your salmon on a tin fish-plate put it into ye boyleing water and keepe it boyleing till it be enough, a little more than a quarter of an hower will boyle it; if it be not very thike salmon it will quickly be enough; then if you have a minde to eate any of it hott serve it in with shrimps, and oysters and what sawce you like best: and as for that you desire to sowce lay it on a thinge to drayne until it be cold, then put it into ye pickle wch must be made as followeth: take some of the water your salmon was boyled in what quantyty you thinke will cover it, put to it as much vineger as will make it very sharpe; with some more salt a bitt of Lemon pill, a few cloves, whole mace, whole peper, a race of ginger, and some clove peper, let all boyle together a good while, then poure it into an earthen pan with all the spice remaineing in it, and when 'tis quite cold put your salmon into it, be sure let all ye salmon be coured [covered] with pickle.

A Salmon pye, my Lady Sheldons Receipt

Take a joule [head] of salmon season it with peper, salt, and ginger; cloves, and mace, and butter; so bake it tender, then draw it; and fill it with butter, and eat it when it is cold with vineger; but if you eat it hott; put in a caudle of verjuce, egge, butter, and suger.

To Roast Lobsters; my Lady Margriot Thellwell's Receipt

Take 2 Lobsters and crack the back of the shells all along, tye them to the spitt, and bast them well with butter let your basting go well into the cracks; when your lobsters become red with roasting, as they do when boyled, then they are enough, you may make what sawce you please, some will eatt them with oyle, or vineger, juce of garlick, and a little mustard, you must tye them to the spitt both together with the bellys one to another.

To Butter Lobsters: my second Cousen Clerkes Receipt

Take the fish out of the shells cut it in pretty big peeces, and put to them a little wine, butter, and vineger, season it with salt and nuttmeg, and set it over a fire and when it is thorow hott wett some sipitts in the liquor, and make sawce for your lobsters with butter and elder vineger, you may put to the lobsters if you please shrimps, or boyled oysters, garnish the dish with the best of the shells, and slices of orinnges, and Lemons; squeesse some of their juce to ye lobsters.

To stew Oysters: my Mothers Receipt

Take a quantity of great oysters when they are new out of their liquor, and wash them one by one; then take their owne liquor and strayne it and put it to the oysters, then put to them a bundle of sweet herbes and set it over a fire yt is very quick, and watch it diligently that as soon as it boyles take it off, and poure them into a coullender, and for the sawce take a little water, and butter, and squeese a Lemon or two into it, and also dissolve anchovie in it, so poure it to your oysters and serve it.

To Stew Oysters

Take a good quantity of large oysters out of their liquor, and wash them one by one in fayr water, puting them into a stewpan strean their own liquor to them, and put to them a few cloves, mace, sliced nuttmeg, and a peece of lemon pill with a bitt of horse redish, let them stew gently over a slow fire, but be sure do not let them boyle at all, when you thinke they are enough take them up and drain them and lay them in a dish with sippets and poure sawce on them made as followeth, you must for the sawce take some of ye liquor they wear stewed in and desolve therein some anchoves, and then put in some butter boyleing it over the fire tell it be thike then pour it over your oysters and so serve them with sipets fryed in butter.

[67]

To Broil Oysters in Colop [scallop] Shells

Lay a peece of Butter at ye bottom of your Colop shells; then gitt a
quantity of large oysters and cutt of the fins, then put 4 or 5 of ye oysters
in a shell with some of their liquor strained, put in also some grated bread,
a little salt, peper, and one spoonfull of whitewine, then cover them with
grated bread and set them over your stove to stew, and hold over them
your Browning Iron halfe an hour will stew them; so serve them in their
shells.

ffor the Boyleing, and frying all sorts of ffish, and how to dish it out etc

Hang your fish kettle over the fire with as much water in it as you think
will cover your fish, put into it a good handfull of salt, some time, sweetmajerom, a peece of horse redish cutt thin some Lemon pill, 3 or 4 shellots
or one oynion, some whole peper a race of ginger sliced, some cloves, mace
and a nuttmeg cutt in peeces, let all boyle together about a quarter of an
hour. Then have in redyness what sort of fish you please, either carpe,
pike, perch, tench, flounders, place, soles, or whiteings, gutt and scale
them clean, and wash them very well, then lay them one by one upon a fish
plate and put it into your kettle of boyling water poureing in at the same
time halfe a pinte of vineger, and the roes of your carpe being put into a
nett, let all boyle gently halfe an hour or less as you see that they are
boyled enough, then take the kettle off ye fire, and lift out ye plate of
ffish and set it cross ye kettle covering it with a tin cover that the fish may
drayne, then having your dish redy warme one a chafindish [chafing dish]
of coles, place therein your fish, and if any water draynes out of the fish
drye it up with a spung as it comes that no water remains in the dish,
then set the tayles of your ffish upright the heads downward of carpe,
pike, perch, flownders or the like, but if salmon that lyes flat either on
each side or in the middle of the dish, you must put your fryed fish upon
the boyled in like manner to make it lye high, and then your boyled
oysters and shrimps all over them, and here and there a few pickled
barberys. *Note.* that you must put your sawce into the dish as soon as
your boyled fish is in, before you put in ye fryed fish, or shrimps oysters
and lemon, garnish the brim of the dish with oysters, slices of Lemon, and
Barberys: ffor the frying of any fish observe to do as followeth, first gutt
and scale them, then wash them, drye them well with a cloath, then

[68]

flower them well on both sides, then having a frying pan made very clean that not ye least soile can come off put therein as much good white driping as you thinke will cover your fish, make it boyleing hott, then put in your fish and let them frye tell they are brown, then turn them and frye them brown on that side, when you think they are enough take them up and lay them on a thing with holes that the liquor may run from them, and so fry more till you have as many as you would have, still observing that as your driping wastes to put in more and to be sure to make it boyle before you put more fish in, have redy beat some yolks of eggs with a little flower amongst them, for to dip some of your largest oysters into and frye them in like manner as the fish, also you may dip smeltes [smelts] into the eggs and flower and frye them in like manner, and when you turn them put on some more with a spoon to cover them, you may if you like better, use only the yolks of eggs beaten without any flower in them.

To dress any fish: my Lady Sheldon's Receipt

Take a peece of fresh salmon; wash it cleane in a little vineger and water, and let it lye awhile in it, then put your fish into a great pipkin with a cover, put to it about six spoonefulls of water, and foure of vineger, and foure of whitewine, a good deale of salt, a bundle of sweet herbes, a little whole sorill, whole cloves, mace, and cynimon, cover it close, and set it in a kittle of seathing water, and there let it stew three howres: you may do carpes, ealls, trouts, or any other fish this way.

To souce any fish: my Aunt Rye's Receipt

Take a pike or elle, rub of [off] the scales with salt and wipe it one a cleane cloath then open it and cutt off the head and take out the back-bone and all the garbige, wipe it very cleane; then cutt a great oynion in halfe dip it in salt and rub the fish all over soundly with it; then chop some persly and majerom and 2 or 3 blades of mace and strew it all over ye inside of the fish; then bone 2 or 3 anchovies cut them in bitts and lay them all over, then role it up like brawne and tye it up with packthread; then take an equell quantity of small-beere and water and a good bundle of sweet herbes, some whol oynion and whole peper make this liquor good and salt, then put in ye roles of fish and ye bones you tooke out and boyle it untill it be enough, then souce it in this liquor; out of which you may eat it either hott or cold; when you eat it hott heat it in ye liquor at any time; and make ye sawce of 2 yolks of eggs; chopt persly; and an anchovie, and 2 or 3 spoonfulls of vineger; beat all these together and put them into a frying-pan stiring them extreamely, then beat in a peece of butter then slice ye fish and lay it in roles on ye dish and poure ye sawce all over it.

for all pancakes and Ameletts & fritters

EGGS

EGGS

frikesys of eggs and Ameletts

[73]

A fricassy of Eggs: Lady Powis's Receipt

Boyle your Eggs hard, and slice them thine, then put them into a frying-pan with some butter and when they are thorow hott poure the Butter from them, and put to them claret or whitewine wch you like best, with a little anchovies and a small quantity of sweet herbs with a little oynion, and Lemon peele shred small, let all boyle up, then have in redyness the yolks of six Eggs well beaten with a little wine and nuttmeg grated in it, put it into ye pan a little to thiken and serve it up.

To make a savory dish with Eggs a la Swiss

Take six eggs boyle them hard, take out the yolks, and cutt the whites into thine long slips, and cutt the yolks into little peeces not too small, then take some gravie not too strong and a little savory herbs chopt as time, persly, wintersavory, an oynion with 3 or 4 anchoves the bones taken out, with a little nuttmeg and peper let all boyle together a little with the gravie and then put in a pretty quantity of mellted butter with the yolks of the Eggs so stir them together and, if they be not thike enough shake in some flower and so serve them. With the herbs you may chop a little lemon pill.

An Amelet: taken out of a booke

Take tenn eggs, and more then halfe ye whites, beat them very well and put in a spoonefull or two of creame; then heat some butter in your pan and when it is hott put in your eggs, and stir them a little, then frye them till you finde it is enough; a little before you take it out of ye pan turn both the sides over that they may meet in the midle, and when you serve it laye the bottome upwards in the dish; so serve it without anythinge strewed on it; some will chopp parsly very small and mix in the eggs as they beat them, and for change it doth very well.

to coller Beefe, Brawne, pig or any fish, or any meat

MEAT

MEAT

all sorts of Boyled foule, and meats; all maner of stakes or fryed meats; for all manor of Roasted meat foule, or any other things; for all sorts of stewed Beefe foule or other meat; all sorts of Hashes of any other meat or foule; all manor of frikesys and scotch-collops; to drye Westphalier Hams, and all sorts of tongues to looke red, to salt Beefe, and porke; to coller, Beefe, Brawne, pig, or any meat whatever; all sorts of sosiges & Balls; to pott any foule, Venison, Beefe, or any other Meat whatever

a Boyle Leg of mutton with forced meat in it	79	a ffillett of veale roasted	82
a Boyled goose hott	79	a pigg Roasted	83
Boyled goose to eat cold	79	mutton roasted wth. stuffing	83
Boyled turky to eat cold	80	a shoulder of muton roasted with anchoves	83
Boyled Turkey to eat hott	80	a Haire rosted wth. ye skine	84
Boyled pulletts hott	80	a Haire roasted	84
Beefe or mutton stakes fryed	81	a Haire roasted with a puding in it	84
Beefe stakes fryed	81		
veale after 'tis roaste fryed	81	a Haire or Fawne rosted with a puding in their bellys	85
veale or mutton cuttlets Broyled	81	to Roast a Haunch of venison	85
rabetts or chickins fryed	82	a loine or rump of beefe stewed	86
a calves head roasted	82		

a rumpe of beefe stewed 4 Receips	86
to stew veale in balls	87
to stew ducks	88
to stew partriges	88
to stew pigions	88
to stew or jugg ducks	89
to stew a haire	89
an Olio, wth. a calves-head	90
a french dish	90
mutton hashed 2 receps	91
any cold meat hashed	92
to hash cold veal	92
fowles	92
rabets white	92
a frikesye of veale	93
a calves liver frikesyed	93
a white ffricasy of Lamb, Chickins or Rabbets	94
a ffricasy of chickins 3 receps	94
to stew chickins	95

a frikesy of pigions	95
to butter rabetts	96
scotch scollops 3 receipts	96
Beefe collered	97
dutch Beefe & Martlemass Beefe	97
to salt up hams	98
Westphalier-hams: 2 Receps	99
to pickle porke	100
Brest of muton collered	100
sossiges to eat coald	100
sossiges of pork 2 Recps	101
Balls for pottages	101
or Hashes 2 Recps	101
to bake a rump of Beefe	102
Beefe potted	102
porke Baked	102
potted Haire	103
or potted swans	103
vineson Baked	104

To Boyle a Leg of Mutton with forced meat

Take a leg of mutton and cutt all the meat out of the skin, leaving the skin whole, then take the meat and shred it very small with halfe a pound of Beefe suet, then put to it two handfulls of the following herbs choping them small: that is to say some sage, sweetmagerome, time, sorell, pearsley, a shalot, and a peece of Lemon pill, being all shred small mingle them with your meat, then season it with pepper, salt, and nuttmeg to your tast, then have redy beat four eggs and mingle them well in, and put it all into your skin, and lapp [wrap] it well up in a cloath, and so boyle it till it be enough, and serve it with sawce of melted butter and some anchoves desolved in it, with choped pearsley and choped capers, you may if you please chop with your meat a little fatt bacon.

To Boyle a Goose: my Mothers Receipt

powder[1] your goose 3 or 4 dayes then boyle him in water and salt one howre and three quarters; then take foure oxe pallets [tongues] boyled tender and peeled; and foure ship's [sheep's] tongues, and foure sweetbreads, when they are boyled slice them, and put them in a pipkin, and put to them a quart of strong broath made with veale, and a little gravie, with a blade or two of large mace, and one oynion, a bundle of sweet herbes, a quarter of a pounde of butter, a dousen of larkes, a pinte of fresh oysters; boyle all these together halfe an howre, so dish your goose with colleflowers [cauliflowers] underneath, and poure all these upon it and serve it hott.

To Boyle a Goose to eat cold: my Lady Sheldons

Take a fatt goose and bone it, but leave the breastbone, wipe him with a cleane cloath, and salt him foureteen dayes; and hang him up a fortnight or three weekes; being close sewed up in a cleane linnon cloath; then boyle him in runing water very tender, and serve him colde with bay leaves.

[1] Sprinkle with salt or powdered spice.

[79]

To Boyle a Turkey to eat cold: my Lady Sheldons

Take a very fatt turkey, and larde him with fatt peeces of backon being rolled in seasoning of salt, peper, nuttmeg, cloves, and mace; then take one large peece of the bacon rouled [rolled] in the seasoning, and put it into the belly of your turkey; with a sprig of bayes and rosemary, then sew it up very close in a cleane cloath and let it lye all night covered over with whitewine, then put it into a pott with the same liquor (and no more) and let it be close stoped, then hang it over a gentle fire and there let it continue simpering for six howres, then take it up and when it is cold take it out of the cloath, when you serve it stick it full of rosemary, and bayes; eat it with suger and mustard if you love it.

To Boyle a Turkey to eat Hott

Take a large fatted Turkey-cock and trust [truss] it as you do pullets for boyleing, then fill the crap of it with forced meat, when so done tye it up in a cloth and boyle it in milke and water with a handfull of oatemell in it to make it boyle the whiter, and when you thinke it is enough serve it to the table with slices of boyled, or fryed bacon in the dish, and some fryed balls, and good store of large oysters some of them being diped in yolks of eggs and fryed, and other some only boyled in their liquor, let the sawce be made with a little whitewine and oyster-liquor in wch dissolve one or two anchoves, then grate in some nuttmeg and melt in a pound of butter, and put to it a quart of large oysters being first boyled up in their own liquor, poure all into the dish to your turkey, and lay on some slices of lemon, you must let the oysters be drayned from most of their liquor before you put them to the butter or else it will make your sawce too thine.

To Boyle pullits: my first Cousen Clerkes

Take two pullets, boyle them in as little water as will cover them and a blade or two of mace with a few cloves; then boyle some rice by it self, for sawce take some whitewine and sweeten it, and put in two yolkes of eggs; and stew some dates in it; then butter your rice and laye it in the bottome of your dish, and poure your sawce upon ye rice, then lay some more rice that it may mix with your sawce; stick the pullits breast with blanched almons cutt in quarters and so serve it.

[80]

To frye Beefe or Mutton Stakes [steaks]: My Lady Howes Receipt

Take beefe and slice it thine, hack and beat it well; then put it into your fryeing-pann and frye it, then put in some water, a bundle of sweet herbes, and an oynion, some claret and 2 or 3 anchovies, (about halfe a pinte of claret is enough) put in also a little mace, and so stew it all together: instead of the claret put in Alle wch make it of a better couller.

To ffrye Beefe Stakes: Mrs Lord's Receipt

Take some Beefe cutt from the rumpe and beat it well, then put it in a fryeing-pan with a peece of butter, and a little salt, frye it till it is enough then poure out the liquer and draw your meat to the back part of your pan, and into the forepart put halfe a pinte of alle, neither stale nor too new, let it boyle keepeing the meat from it; and when it boyles and you have taken the fatt off from your liquor which you tooke out at first, put that liquor to the alle, then put your beefe to it, and shake it in it, strewing some grated nuttmeg upon it, and by that time you have given it 5 or 6 shakes, take it up into a dish and serve it in.

To frye Veale after it is rosted: Mrs Whiteheads Receipt

Take some cold rost veale and slice it very thine, beat the yolkes of 7 or 8 eggs and halfe the whites, beat them very well; then take some persly; and some other sweet herbs shread them very small, and mingle them with the eggs, with 3 or 4 spoonfulls of thike Creame, a little nutmeg, and a prety deale of salt, mix all this well together and put your meat into it, and frye it altogether like a tansy in fresh butter.

To Broyle veall or mutton cuttlets and stakes

Take your cuttlets and dip them in melted Bacon or Butter, then season them with all sorts of sweet herbs, salt and peper, and strew on them grated bread then Broyle them on your stove and serve them in with gravie sauce.

[81]

To Frye Rabets or Chickens: My Lady Howe's

Take the gravie of veale or mutton and put it in a fryeing pan, you may put a little water to it, make it hott and put in your rabets being cutt in peeces and beaten well; sprinckle them with salt, and being almost fryed put in a peece of butter, a little persly and oynions shread small; when your meat is enough stir in the yolks or 2 or 3 egges with a Lemon squeesed in, and scrape a little nutmeg one it, and so serve it.

To Roast A Calves Head with a puding in it: My Lady Howes

Take a calves head and slit it, take out the braynes wash and beat them, put to them 2 or 3 spoonfulls of creame, the yolke of an egge, a little rose water, suger, cloves, and mace; some marow shread [shredded]; with as much grated bread as will make it prety stiff, mingle all well together and put it into both sides of the head, in one side put some herbes finely shread, laye a mutton skine betweene the two sides and tye it up close, and roast it, beating [basting?] it with the yolks of eggs till it be ready to take up; then froath it up with a little butter, and grated bread, and for the sawce make it with butter, and vineger, and grated bread.

To Roast A fillit of Veale: Leeches Receipt

Take halfe a handfull of tyme and as much sweet-marjerome, and almost as much wintersavory, of straberry leaves, violet leaves, and marygold leaves, altogether halfe a handfull, and one oynion, halfe a nuttmeg grated, twenty peper corns, beat very small; two anchovies washed very cleane, two hard eggs, and one raw one, and halfe a handfull of grated bread, chop all these together very small, and then worke it very well with your hands, and put a little salt into it, then stuff your fillit of veale with it; so roast it, and baste it with butter, and flower it presently; then save the driping, and some of the seasoning you stufed it with, put the seasoning into a dish and set it in the driping-pan, that the meat may drip upon it all the while; when it is roasted blow off all the fatt off the gravie, and herbes, that stood under your meat, and put some butter and vineger to it, and so dish your meat and poure this sawce one it.

[82]

To Roast a pig: a very good way

After your pigg is scalded drye the inside with a cloth, then spitt it and put into the Belly thereof a handfull of sage, a peece of butter, and a crust of bread, then sew it up and lay it to the fire, and flower it very thike all over and as it drops off flower it again, and so roast it with a quick fire till it be almost enough and the coat thereof crisp, then with a drye cloath wipe all the flower clean off, and baste it with Butter all over, and strew a handfull of salt on it, so let it roast about a quarter of an hour, then wipe it clean off, and when it is brown and crisp send it to the table with sawce made of the gravie that runs from it in the roasting, butter being melted therein with some choped sage, and the braines of the pig.

To rost a shoulder of Mutton: Mr Cheekes way

Take above a pounde of Beefe suet and chop it small; then take a good handfull of tyme, and a little peper, and salt, then take some of the ships bloud [sheep's blood] as much as you thinke will serve, and mix it with your suet, and the rest of the things, then stuff the inside of the shoulder of muton with it; then take the kell [caul[1]] of the mutton and spread it one a dish, and laye the shoulder of muttone one it, lay the inside lowermost, then poure the rest of your stuffing that is left onc the mutton; and let it runn all over it, then scure [skewer] the kell all over it very close, and so roste it and serve it without sawce, or if you please you may make some gravie sawce for it.

To Roast A Shoulder of mutton with Anchovies

when your mutton is halfe roasted cutt crosses in many places of it to let out the gravie, then set the gravie with some claret over the fire, and slice in oynions, and when it tast a little of them take them out, then put in 4 or 5 anchovies and dissolve them in it; slice in a little nuttmeg, and a little Lemon peele minced, and some of the inside of your mutton minced small, and some capers, and oysters, heat all these together, and so dish your mutton, and serve it with this sawce: and if you will you may stuff the inside of your mutton wth oysters.

[1] Membrane of the gut. We would use aluminium foil today.

[83]

To Roast a Haire: Sr Jos. Sheldon's Receipt

Take a haire and scalde it in water, but put nothinge else in the water, be sure to scalde off all the hare very cleane, then take a pretty quantity of all maner of sweet herbes, pick them very cleane from the stalkes, which don, take a great handfull of them, and shread very small; put to them an anchovie, a nuttmeg grated, and a good peece of Lemon peele cutt very small; then knead all these together in a pounde of butter, and so put it into the body of the haire, for then the stuffing will not worke out; so roste it and when it is well roasted, melt a pounde of butter, and dessolve an anchovie in it; and so poure it into ye dish you desine to serve your haire in; then lay your haire in, and take out all the seasoning that was in the body of the hear, and mixe it in ye sawce very well, so serve it.

To Roaste a Haire: Mrs Turners Receipt

Take your haire after it is skined; and trust [truss] it short like a boyled rabet, larde it with bacon, and draw it with some young sprigs of sage, you need not draw the back of it very thike; but the belly of it, and all underneath draw as thike as you can, borth [both] with the sage, and backon, and put into the belly a good peece of fatt and leane backon; with an oynion if you love it; then sew it up and spitt it, and roast it basteing it very well with butter, and when it is roasted, for the sawce, take some butter and vineger, and grate some nuttmeg in it, and so melt it; then take a codling and codle [boil] it very tender; then peele it and scrape a little of it extreamely fine into your melted butter, put no more of it in then [than] will a little thicken the butter; then take some of the sage, and backon, that is upon the belly of the haire, and cutt it very small, and mixe it in your sawce, so serve it.

To Roast a Haire with a puding in the Belly: Newtons Receipt

Take halfe a peny lofe grated, and put to it as much or more of choped suet; grate in a little nuttmeg, and season it with salt, peper, clove peper, beaten, then put in also some sweet hearbs; as sweetmajerom, tyme, wintersavory, pottmajerom, peneroyall, persly, marygole leaves, beets, and strabery leaves a little of each, but of persly put in most; chop them small and mingle all well together with ye yolks and whites of 2 eggs; then make it up into 2 roles [rolls] and flower the outside of them a little;

and so put it into your Haire being redy skined and washed cleane; scewer ye Haire up and spitt it, and keepe it basting with creame or milke, and when it is redy to take up bast it with butter; for ye sawce you may make gravie sawce of what you like best, so serve it in with the puding in the Belly; and if you please you may larde your Haire with backon wch will make it eate moist, and look hansomely: you may also put into ye puding for the haire's belly two anchoves and some pill of Lemon cutt small.

To Roast a Hare or youn ffawne with a sweet puding in the Belly of it: my Lady Napier's way

For the puding take about three parts of a peny lofe grated and if you please you may put in some bisquit, mingle it with about halfe a pound of suet choped very fine, and grate in some nuttmeg, and put to it a little sugar, and about a quarter if a pound of curants washed, then put in two eggs; and mingle it altogether with a little milke or creame, let it not be too thike nor too thine, but off the usuall thikness you make a boyled puding off, when 'tis all stird togather put it into the body, and belly of the Hare, and then sew up the Belly of your Haire, and so roast it keeping it basted with butter, when it is roasted enough, for the sawce let it be melted butter and sugur: the same puding and sawce serves for a young fawne when roasted whole.

To Roast a Haunch, or Shoulder of venison

Spitt your venison and make some past [paste] with flower and water and role it out very thin and lay it on a sheet of whitebrown paper[1] redy buttered; and then with some melted butter let your past be buttered all over, and put the buttered side of the past all over your venison, with the paper on the outside of it, tye it hard on with packthread, and so roast it with a good fire, basting it a little with butter to keepe the paper from burning, a Haunch of venison thus roasted will require seven hours to roast it thorowly, and about an hour before you take it up cutt the packthred and take of [off] the paper and past, then bast it with butter & flower it, and so let it roast till it be enough, then serve it in with gravie sawce in the dish—some will lard the venison with bacon and roast it without past on it basting it all the time with cream; and just at the last froath it up with butter and flower.

[1] The modern equivalent is greaseproof paper.

[85]

To Stew a Sr Loin, or Rump of Beefe, called Beefe Royall

Take a s^rloin, or Rump of Beef, bone it and beat it very well, season it with salt, peper cloves mace, and Lemon peele finely shred and some sweet herbs of all sorts choped, then make a strong broath [broth] with the Bones, and lard your meat quite through with bacon, then put in a convenient quanity of butter into your stew-pan and browne it, then put in your meat to it and browne it on both sides, then put in the strong broath and one or two bay leaves, some palets [tongues] and sweet-breds, cover it very close and stew it gently till it is very tender, then take it out, and take the fatt clear off from ye liquor then put in 2 or 3 anchoves a pinte of claret, then put in your Beefe again till it be through hott, and then put in what pickles you please with fryed oysters and thiken the sawce with burnt butter and poure it one your meat and serve it.

To Stew a Rump, or any other peece of beefe: Mrs Whiteheads

Take a rump of beefe not too big, nor too fatt, rub it with a little salt, then stuff it with a little salt, beaten peper, and nuttmeg, and a little tyme and sweetmajerom, and beefe suet mixed alltogether, then put it in a pott and put to it some water, and as much Alle as water, with halfe a pinte of wine vineger, and halfe a pinte of whitewine; the liquor must be enough to cover it and no more, cover the pott close and set it over a gentle fire, the longer it is stewing the better it will be; when the beefe is stewed enough laye some sipits in your dish, then poure one your liquor that the beefe was stewed in, and laye your beefe in the midle; if you please you may put it in an earthen pott and cover it with past [paste], and bake it with house-hold-bread: remember to put in halfe Alle with your water.

To Stew a Rump of Beefe: my second Cousen Clerkes receipt: and also Mrs Lord's

perboyle a rump of beefe, (or a peece of the thine end of the brisket) an howre or less, according as it is in bigness, then put it into a deepe dish; slash the inside and let out the gravie; strew peper and salt in the slashes; then put in as much clarett wine as will cover it all over, and 3 or 4 blades of mace; cover it close and let it boyle an howre and a halfe; stiring and turning it often least it burn too; scume off the fatt, and refill it with claritt; then slice six oynions and put them to it, with a handfull of capers, or broome-buds, some persly, six hard letess [lettuces] sliced, 3 spoone-fulls of vineger, and as much verjuce, so let it stew till it be tender, then serve it with sipits in the dish; you may frye your sipitts wth butter, send it not up with too much fatt in it/if you put in Alle and water instead of claret it will be good.

To Stew a Rump of Beefe: my first Cousen Clerkes

Take a rump of beefe, bone it that it may lye flatt, put as much water to it as will cover it, let it stew all night with whole oynions, whole peper, cariets [carrots], pasnips, and turnops; put in also savory, tyme, and rosemary, tyed in a bunch, in the morning take out these herbes and roots, and put in fresh, when it is stewed very tender dissolve some an-chovies in vineger, and put them to your liquor, garnish it with your rootes, and serve it in with sipitts: put in halfe Alle with ye water.

To stew a Rumpe of Beefe: the Countess of Desmon's Receipt

in the first place season your rumpe of Beefe very well with peper and salt, put it into a pott and cover it over wth water and Alle, put to it a pinte of clarett and some lemon pill set it on the fire and let it stew for six howres, a little before 'tis redy to take up put in some broome buds, capers, gurkings, and oysters, and 2 or 3 anchoves, a little pice of lemon, let it stew tell the oysters are enough then serve it: if you put in halfe Alle with the water it will be much better.

To Stew Veal the french way: Mademoisell's Jortins Receipt

Take a fillet of veale and chop it very small with some beefe suet; then season it with some peper, persly, and tyme, cut very small, put in also eight cloves cutt into peeces, and some grated nuttmeg; mix all very well together, then put a small quantity of water to it, then take an egge and put the white in one thinge, and the yolke in another, then take the meat and roule [roll] it up in balls about the bigness of an egge, and dip the balls into the white of the egge to make it stick together; then take a quarter of a pounde of butter and put it into a dish, and set it one ye fire,

[87]

and when it is melted put in your roales [rolls]; and cover it close with another dish, so let it stew three howres and a halfe; then take a little verjuce and beat it up with the yolke of your egge, and put a little nutt-meg into it, and so heat it one the fire; but have a care it do not turnn; then laye your balls in a cleane dish and poure the sawce to them; the sawce must be well stired before you put it in, or else it will curdle do what you can.

To Stew Ducks, or Fayle [Quail?]

After they are halfe roasted put them into a stewpan with a pinte of claret, or a pinte of gravie, two oynions, a bunch of sweet herbs, and some whole pepper, and let them stew keeping the pan close covered, and when they are enough put the ducks into a dish and strain the stewed liquor on them.

To stew patridge: my scond Cousen Clerkes

when you have any colde patridges take the meat from the bones and shread it, then put to it some gravie, a little butter, and the juce of oringe: heat it together and put it into your dish with sipits under it, and poure some butter one it, being thickened with an egge.

To stew pigions: Mrs Whiteheads receipt

Take the pigions when they are picked, and drawned, and cutt them in halves, and season them with a nutmeg, peper, and salt, then put them into a pipkin with as much water as will stew them, and some gravie, when they are stewed enough put to them the quantity of a spoonfull of butter, with a little persly shread very small, and stir it together with a little verjuce, so serve them, if you please you may cutt your pigions in quarters, which will looke much better yn [than] in halves.

[88]

To jugg pidgeons, or Ducks, being a difirent way of stewing them very good

Take six pidgeons cutt off their pinnions and legs, and after you have taken out their gutts and crops very clean, fill their bodies and crops with force meat, and soe [sew] them up at each end, and dip them in water and then season them with peper and salt, and set them uprite into a high earthen pott with a broad bottom, set the crop ends downwards, put into the pott with them a bit of sallery, oynion, Lemon pill, a blade or two of mace, and a few mushroms if you have them, then tye down the pott very close with double paper and a trencher on it that no steam may get out, set it in a pot of water over the fire and so let it boyle for three whole hours, filling the pott with hott water as it wastes, and when you think the pidgeons are enough take them out and lay them in your dish, and strain the stewed liquor into a saucepan takeing of [off] most of the ffat, set it over the fire and as soon as it boyleth thiken it up with butter and a little flower, grate in some nuttmeg and pour it all over your pidgeons, garnishing the dish with Lemon and Mushroms. Note: the forced meat is made as followeth, viz. Take the livers of ye pidgeons and just give them one boyle up in fair water, then mash them all to peeces with the back of a spoon and the yolks of three eggs boyled hard, when so done put to it grated Bred, and suet choped small as may be, and some sweet herbs with Lemon pill shred small, season it with nuttmeg, mace, and salt, mixe all well together with the yolke of one or two raw eggs, and role it up redy for the stuffing your pidgeins therewith diping each bitt into melted Butter.

You may do a coupple of large ducks the same way only leaving out their livers in the forced meat, and let the ducks be layed down flatt in the pott they are stewed in.

To stew a Haire

case your Hair, cut it into peeces without washing it; put to it peper and salt, and a quart of Alle not too stale nor too new, and a quart of Water, a bundle of sweet herbs, a peece of Lemon pill, a bitt of horse redish root, 2 whole oynions, some clove-peper, and mace, but put not in the spice and herbs till it hath stewed 2 hours, and so let it stew gently close covered till it be tender; then for the sawce poure a pinte of the liquor into a sawce-pan dissolve in it 3 anchoves, then strain out the anchove bones and set it on the fire again just to boyle it up, then put to it a peece of Butter well mixed first with flower and so boyle it to be as thike as you like it, stiring it all the time, then grate in halfe a nuttmeg, and after having placed your hare in a dish poure the sawce on it, you may if you please leave out the anchoves and the sawce will be very good without them.

To make an Olio: Mrs Whiteheads Receipt

Take two calves heads and perboyle them, then pick off the meat cleane from the bones and cutt it in thine slices as big as oysters; then set it astewing in a deepe dish, with water, and salt, and an oynion or two cutt in the midle, a little peper, and some sliced ginger, and a few whole cloves, two anchovies, and some raw oysters cutt in small peeces; putt all these astewing together being close covered; and when the meat is almost stewed enough, then put in good store of large oysters, with some persly, tyme, sweet-majerom, and sorell shread it pretty small, and grapes, barberys, or gooseberys, to give it a sharpe taste, put also to it sampire [samphire], broome-buds, sliced Lemon and capers; and you may boyle or frye some balls, boyle them in whitewine by themselves, then put them into the meatt with the wine they were boyled in; stew all this together till it be enough; you may laye a boyled leg of mutton in the midle of your dish, and lay pigions or boyled chickens, or black-birds, lam-stones, and sweetbreads, and pallets [tongues], and mushroms, about the mutton; with some slices of baccon, haveing first layed one all the stewed meat, which must be mingled with butter that hath been melted with vineger, and the yolkes of two eggs, lay one slices of Lemon to garnish it, this will fill a very great dish.

A French dish with pallets and tongues: my Aunt Rye

Boyle a leg of beefe or any other bones to make strong broath; then have sweet-breads, pallets, and tongues, boyled, and peeled, and cutt in thine slices, and then take two chickens strip them and cutt them in quarters, and breake their bones, then frye all this in butter untill they are browne, then take them out and frye them in water, and put all this meat into the strong broath with a little sliced nuttmeg, and a little wine, and some whole mace, and a bundle of sweet herbes, and a whole oynion, and what other meat you please; as veale hacked to make it tender, and bigger chickins, let it all stew together in the broath, with a little salt; and when it is neere enough, put in some more wine, and an anchovie, and gravie; and at last some verjuce to give it a good tast; and a pretty deale of butter, and crumbs of bread; you may stew in it some musheroms or capers if you please, and so serve it up with some balls made as followeth: take some leane veale or mutton (but veale is best) mince it with suet as fine as for mincepyes, season it with a little spice; and salt and a few sweet herbes shread very small; beat it altogether very well, and roule [roll] them up, and frye them in butter, some will frye them againe in water to make them looke white.

To Hash a Shoulder of Mutton: Mrs Whiteheads

when the mutton is roasted cutt off the uper skine with some of the meat to it; then cutt off ye meat cleane from ye bone and mince it very small, then take as much butter as two wallnutts and put it into the fryeing-pan, let it boyle untill it looks black, then mince oynion very small and put to it, and frye them well, then season the meat with cloves, mace, peper, and salt, and add a little strong broath if you have it, the juce of an oringe, halfe a pinte of claret, and a little of ye thyne rine of oringe mincet small, then put it all into the pan and boyle it as long as you thinke fitt, about halfe an howre will do it, still stiring it and shakeing the pann, there must also be capers put in minc't very small, against this is redy gitt some bread cutt square like dice, and some peeces longer a grait deal, and frye them browne in butter, and frye some persly also; then laye the shoulder-bone into ye dish, and the fryed meat all over it, then stick the fryed bread one it, and if you please laye on fryed sweetbreads being thynely sliced, and some fryed oysters; and garnish it atop of ye meat, then strew the fryed persly over all; you may add the liquor of oysters to ye meat; and mushroms, and ye gravie which ran out of ye mutton when you cutt it, for it must not be roasted very much.

To Hash Mutton: my Mothers Receipt

Take a loyne [loin] of mutton and halfe roast it, then take a pinte of claret-wine, and almost as much water, put to it 5 whole oynions and a little bundle of sweet herbes, and one sprige of rosemary boyle them together untill almost halfe be boyled away, then set on a little claret in another thinge with foure anchovies, and dissolve them in it, then take your meat and cutt it in thyne slices, and with the gravie that runs from it put it to the liquor the oynions were boyled in, and frye it together in a pann till it be enough, then poure all the liquor from your meat and mingle it in ye wine where the anchoves were dissolved, and put to it the yolkes of six eggs well beaten, set it over [?] fire and keepe it stiring untill it be thike, but not too thike, then laye your mutton bone (being broyled) at length in a dish, and laye your fryed meat one it, and then poure the sawce one it, but remember a little before you take up your meat from the fire that you put in a little handfull of capers; and halfe a nuttmeg grated; take out ye oynions, and so serve it.

To make A Hash: Mrs Lords Receipt

Take the meat and cutt it in thine peeces, put in 2 anchoves, a bundle of sweet herbs, a little whole peper, a blade of mace, some grated nuttmeg, some salt, a little wine, 2 or 3 shalotts, then heat it as quick as you can and when it is throwly hott put in a quarter of a pound of butter and keep it stiring till it be thike: put in mushroms and what pickles you please and sipits of bread put in the dish.

To make a white Hash, or ffricassce [fricassee] of Roasted veale, chickins or Rabets

Take the leane of any roasted veal, and after it is cold cut it in little thine slices, and put some Butter into a stew-pan set it over a stove, and when the Butter is melted put in a pinch of flour, some minced cives [chives] and parsly, Lemon pill and mace also shred small, and keep it moveing over the fire a Minute or two, then put in the veal season it with salt, peper and some grated nutmeg, and give it two or three turns over the stove, moisten it with a little broth, water, or whitewine, and let it boyle a little, then thiken it up with the yolks of 3 or 4 eggs beaten up in cream with a little raw shred parsley amongst it, keepe moving it over the fire till it is thickened, then serve it with slices of Lemon: The same way you may do cold chickens, fowles, rabets, or house lamb [lamb raised on the home farm].

[92]

A Frikesy [fricassee] of Veale: as we uest to have it, by nan

Take a leg of veale and cutt some thyne slices off the fillet, then beat it a little with a roaleing-pinn; and laye it in a puter [pewter] dish, and strew one it some sweet herbes minced small, and grate some nuttmeg one it; strew one also some salt, then take some sosiges [sausages] without skins; and frye them in sweet butter; and when they are almost fryed, take some thyne slices of baccon, and frye with them; then when they are fryed take ye baccon and sosiges out, and lay them one a plate to keepe them warme by the fire; then poure out all the liquor out of the pan and wipe it cleane; then take the yolke of one or two eggs if it be a great quantity; beat them very well and put to them a pretty quantity of white-wine; or claret, haveing first an anchovie or two dissolved in it; then take as much butter as you thinke will frye the meat, put it into the fryeing-pan and when you have made it hott, put in your meat and frye it very well; when it is enough put it into the dish you desine to serve it in; then poure out the butter out of the pan but not too cleane; and take the wine and eggs yt [that] you had before mixed together and put it in the pann, and shake it one the fire for halfe a quarter of an howre, or thereabouts, if you have any gravie put in some, then poure it out of the pann upon the veale, and laye the baccon and sosiges all over your meat, and if you please squese one some Lemon and garnish your dish with slices of Lemon.

A Frikesy of Calves Liver: my Lady Sheldon's Receipt

Take and cutt the liver in little thyne bitts, then put it into a fryeing-pann with about a poringerfull of water, mixt with vineger a little more than the sharpeness of wine; put in also a whole oynion or two, and a good deale of the thyne rine of Lemon minced extreame small; put in also some salt; so let it all stew together awhile till almost halfe the liquor be consumed; then poure out all the liquor from your meat; and frye your meat with some butter and some persly browne, then put the meat out into a dish and keepe it hott before the fire, with the fatt it was fryed in, then frye some slices of baccon; and while this is adoing you must put into the black liquor (that you poured from the liver) one anchovie, and stew it in it; then put to it the yolke of an egge, and a good deale of butter, so put all together into the pann, againe, and shake them over the fire till the sawce be thike, so serve it.

To make a white ffricasy, of Lamb, Chickins, or Rabbets

Take lamb, chickins, or Rabbets, cut in peeces, wash it well from the Blood, then put it into a *broadpan* or stewpan, put in as much fair water as will cover it, and a little salt, a bunch of sweet herbs, some pepper, an onion, two anchovies, some minced mace, and let all stew till it be enough, then beat the yolks of six eggs wth a glace of whitewine, and 3 or 4 spoonfulls of cream, a little grated nutmeg, and a little green raw parsly choped, beat it all well together and put it into your stewpan with a piece of fresh Butter and shake it till it is thick, dish it on sippets, and garnish with slices of Lemon.

A ffricasy of chickins

After you have drawn and washed your chickins, halfe boyle them then take them up and cut them in pieces, put them into a frying pan and fry them in Butter, then take them out of the pan and clean it, and put in some strong broth, some whitewine, some grated nutmeg, a little pepper and salt, a bunch of sweet herbs a shalot or two, let these with two or three anchovies stew on a slow fire and boil up, then beat it up with butter and yolks of eggs till 'tis thike, and put your chickins in and toss them well together, dish it on sippets, and garnish with sliced Lemon and fryed parsley.

A ffricassy of chickins

Take off the skin of your chickins, cut off the shanks a little above the joynt, and the pinions of the wings both which you are to make no use of, then cut off the legs and break the bones and take them out, and throw the flesh into water as also the wings and the flesh of the brests, and cutt the rest of ye carcase into pieces, let all be put into water for some time, then boyle them in fair water over a stove a little while, and then put them again into cold water, and when they have lain a little while take them out and drain them; then put them in a stewpan with a little melted Bacon and fresh butter, a bunch of savoury herbs, an onion stuck with cloves, some cocks-combs, veal sweetbreads, mushroms and Trufles, seasoned with salt and pepper, toss up all this together over a stove, then put to it a little flower, and give it two or three turns more over ye stove, moisten it with halfe water halfe broath and set it over a gentle fire, Beat ye yolks of 3 or 4 eggs in cream with a little shred raw parsley, when the liquor of the fricassy is diminished as it ought to be, thicken it with your eggs and cream without takeing it off ye stove, and when it is enough lay it in a dish or plates with slices of Lemon.

A Frikesy of Chickens: my Mothers Receipt

Take a quarter of a pinte of claret, and as much water, 2 or 3 oynions and a small quantity of sweet herbes tyed in a bunch; boyle them all together, then take some claret and dissolve 2 anchovies in it, then cutt your chickins in quarters, and take 3 eggs and save out one yolke, beat them very well, and put to them a prety quantity of boyled persly shread small, then dip every peece of your chickins into it, and frye it over a gentle fire, then take the claret yt [that] the anchovies were dissolved in, and mix it with the liquor the oynions and herbes were boyled in, takeing out the oynions and herbes, then beat the yolks of 5 eggs and mingle with it, and then stir it all over a gentle fire untill it be well thickened; and when your chickens are fryed enough put them into a dish, and poure this sawce over them; garnish your dish with Lemon.

To stew chickins:

Let your chickins be quartered, then put them into a pott with as much water as will cover them, put to them a little salt, time, sweetmagerom, pearsley, a blade or two of mace, a bitt of Lemon pill, and so let it stew till they are enough, then put in some Butter and when 'tis melted thiken it up with the yolks of 3 or 4 eggs beaten well with some whitewine:

A French Frikesy of pigions: my Aunt Rye's

Take six pigions, quarter them and breake their bones, put them into a fryeing-pan with a quart of water, season your water with salt, then frye them, and shake them well in the pan; untill they are enough then shread sweet herbes, and a prety deale of persly very small, and put to them with a few cloves, and give it 2 or 3 walms [warms] in the pann then put in halfe a pounde of butter, and shake it and stir it well in the pan yt [that]

[95]

the butter may not grow thine nor burn to the bottome of the pan, then take the yolks of 3 eggs beat them very well with six spoonfuls of verjuce, and put them to ye rest; and holde it over a quick fire, shakeing and stiring it altogether very well untill it be prety thike, take care that the egg run not to flakes, so poure it all into a dish and serve it.

A Buttered Rabett: Mrs Lord's Receipt

Take your rabett and fill the belly of it full of parsly, and when it is roasted mince the flesh with the parsly, then take butter and two spoon-fulls of water, and some salt, and so boyle it allways stiring it, then take 3 spoonefulls of creame with the yolks of two eggs beaten with it, and put to it, then place the bones of your rabett in the dish, and lay some sippetts in it and so poure your meat upon them.

To make Scotch-collops: as I used to do them

Take a leg of veale and cutt it into thine slices, then hack it well with the back of a knife, and lard halfe the scollops with bacon, then flower and frye all your scollops in butter till they are a little brown, then put them into a stewpan and put to them above halfe a pinte of strong broath made with the bones of the veale, and put in also a pinte of whitewine, a whole oynion or shalot; mace, nuttmeg, whole peper, a peece of horseredish, a bitt of Lemonpill, the liquour of oysters, and some salt, let all this stew together close covered halfe an hour, then put in 2 or 3 anchoves, and some balls being first fryed in butter, so stew it till ye anchoves are dis-solved with a bundle of sweet herbs in it, then put in a good peece of butter and thiken it up with yolks of eggs very well beaten, and so serve it in with slices of bacon fryed, and some forced meat balls fryed, and also some oysters diped in eggs and fryed, lay on also slices of Lemon.

To Make Scotch-Collops: Leeches Receipt

Take a leg of veale and cutt it in very thyne slices, and beat them with the back of your knife, then take some thyne slices of baccon and oringe pille, and Lemon peele, and wintorsavory, and tyme, and potmajerom, and with all these draw your scollops, then take ye bones of your leg of veale

[96]

and put foure quarts of water to it, and a bundle of sweet herbes, 4 an-chovies, a whole oynion, and a little peper, then let it boyle till it coms to a quart, then streane it, and frye your veale in a little butter till it be browne, then poure your liquor in the pan to it, and let it frye together till the liquour be almost halfe wasted away, then take the yolks of six eggs and beat them well with the juce of a Lemon, and then poure them into your pan and holde it over the fire halfe a quarter of an howre, and so serve it with sipits.

Scotch-collops: my Aunt Rye's Receipt

Take some leane of the veal and cutt it in thyne slices, and beat them with the back of your knife, then lay them all night in claret-wine, then frye them browne in butter, and some great pickled oysters with them, then frye some slices of baccon also browne, then take it out of the pan and stew it altogether in the claret it was steeped in, with some sliced nutmeg, two anchovies, and mushroms (if you have them) and so serve it.

To Coller Beefe: my Mother's Receipt

Take a flanck of beefe and strip off the skine from of yᶜ sides; and take out the gristle bone; (the flanck will make 2 collers), take as much red wine as will cover it and so let it lye in steepe 24 howres turning it twice in that time; then take it out and lay it upon a cleane boarde and season it with mace, cloves, and peper, beaten small; and as much salt as shall be thought fitt; then take rosemary, time, savory and sweetmagerom; and Lemon peele of each as much as shall be thought fitt; shread them very small and strew it all over your beefe; then roule it up hard, and tye it hard with packthread; then put it in a long earthen pott and poure the wine it was steeped in into it; then cover it with course past and bake it.

To make Dutch Beefe: and also Martlemass or dryed Beefe: Newton's Receipt

Take a good peece of the best of the Buttock beefe cutt very thike; and mix some salt-peeter beat small with a little bay salt, and a handfull or two or more of white salt mingle them together and salt ye beefe well with it; then lay it in a thinge and strew it over with some of the salt and so let it lye for a weeke, then turne it and let it lye about a weeke longer, then take it out of ye brine and hang it up in a chimney to drye for about a fortnight or longer if you feel occation; then keepe it for your use, when you spend it tye it up in a cloath and boyle it till it be tender; but if you have conveniency 'tis better to bake it in a little pott with water; when you bake Household bread; keepe it till it be cold then with a knife shave or scrape it fine and thine into little sawcers and so serve it to table as you please.

For the martlemass or dryed Beefe, you must take a good flank of Beefe and slash the inside skine cross both ways; do not slash it deepe only just a little to break the skine that the salt may enter in the better; then salt it well with the same salts and in like maner as you do ye dutch beefe; and after it hath laine a weeke turne ye other side downe into ye brine, and let it lye so a week longer, then take it out of the brine and strew it over with bran as you do bacon and hang it up in a chimney to drye for eight or nyne days; which when you thinke it be drye enough take it downe and keepe it for your use; when you desine to spend it lay it the night before in fresh water and ye next day boyle it till it be enough and when it is cold cutt it out in thine slices like rashers of backon and eat it with vineger.

To Make a Tongue looke Red: my second Cousen Clerke's Receipt given her by Mrs Jackson

Take the third part of an ounce of salt of pruniller [sal prunella], and rub it well upon your tongue, cutting off some of ye skine that is on the sides that so it may perse [penetrate] the better into ye tongue; and when so don, mix bay salt and white salt together, and salt it well—letting it lye 2 or 3 weekes in the salt; then you may take them out of ye salt and boyle them without dryeing; and it will eat well enough and looke larger; but if you please you may hang them up and drye them: this way is very good I can assure you for I have tryed it my selfe.

To salt a Ham: a very good way

When you have cutt a hind quarter of porke into ye shape of a Ham, then take of common salt and bay salt, each a quart, and mix with them an ounce of saltpeeter beaten fine and a pound of brown suger, with these rub ye Ham all over very well, and then cover it all over 2 or 3 days, then take it out and smoke it in the manner of neats tongues etc.

To make Westphalien; my Cousen Clerke's; as she used to do them

Take a hind quarter of pig-porke, cutt it out like a Westphalierham; let it not be cutt at ye hock in ye dressing of the hogg; then make a strong brine with water and salt and peeter-salt; put your ham into it; looke after it to keepe it turned; let it lye neere a fortnight; then lay it adrayneing and tye a string about it to hang it up by; that no hole be made in it; least ye fly git into it; so hang it up asmokeing; let it be thorow drye, and keepe it for your use; when you boyle it sew it up in a cloath, and boyle hay with it; and let it be very tender boyled; then lay it one a boarde; and lay another boarde one it, and set a weight upon it untill it be thorow cold.

To drye Westphalierhams, porke, or tongues: My Lady Howe's

Take as much salt-peeter beaten to pouder as will lye on a halfe-crowne; and rub your tongue all over with it; let no part be unrubed; then lay it one a pan, and cover it all over with white salt; and let it lye a fortnight, then rub it so againe with salt-peeter, and cover it againe with white salt; and let it lye another fortnight; then boyle them in hay till they are very tender, and keepe them drye where no dampness nor wett coms to them; thus you may do bacon or porke, take porke a hinder quarter and cutt off so much of the loyne [loin] as will make it of the shape of west-phalier; salt it as ye tongues, if it be thike you must salt it three times; and let it lye six weekes; smoke them a moneth before you boyle them; in the boyleing of tongues or bacon put in some juneper-berrys, and it will make them much the reder; and to make westphalier look very black; take a roole [roll] of browne paper and rub it against a black pott's side and so rub it well on ye outside of ye hams; untill it is as black as you woulde have it; then rub it with a cleane paper untill ye black will not come off.

To pickle porke

Take your porke and cutt it into such peeces as you intend to spend at a time, and take out all the bones, then lay them in salt 2 or 3 days to drayne out the bloud, then to halfe a peck of common salt put halfe a pound of saltpeeter beaten fine, and drye them by the fire, then salt your porke, and strew a little on the bottom of your Tub, and also strew some between each piece as you lay it in, let it be put in close together and cover up your Tubb.

To coller a Brest of Mutton: Mrs Lord's Receipt

Bone your Brest of muton and put in two handsfull of forced meat, then take 3 or 4 anchoves shread small, 5 or 6 mushroms pickled, 4 or 5 oysters, sweet herbes shread very small, a shalott shred, strew all these upon the mutton, and upon these strew a little beaten cloves, mace, peper, and salt, then role it up in a coller and tye it so, then boyle it in as little water as you can possibly, before you take it up with some sipitts in the broath and lay them in the bottome of your dish: and for sawce take a little of the Broath, a little of the pickle of oysters; a little pickle of capers, or of any pickle of the like kind with cucumbers, capers, and samphire shread, give all a warme over the fire, then put in a good peece of butter, and if it is not thike enough strew in a little flower; cutt your coller into fine peeces and lay them into the dish where ye sipitts are, and poure the sawce all upon them and serve it in hott.

To Make Sosiges [Sausages] to eat colde: My Lady Howe's Receipt

Take a fresh neats tongue boyle it tender, chop it small and beat it in a morter; season it with a nutmeg, ginger, and peper, put to it some oringe pille beaten, and so beat them to a paste; then put it into a pot and boyle it in a kettle of water, a quarter of an howre, when it is cold roule [roll] them in cinemon, and ginger, then wrap them up in white paper, and tye them with packthread; and hang them up in your chimney; so you may keepe them all the yare; they are good about any baked, or stewed meat; also good to be sliced for sallet; and eaten with vineger, or to be cutt in slices and sent in for a dish to be eaten with mustard and suger.

Sosiges with skins: of porke: my Mother's Receipt

Take 2 pounde and a halfe of lean hog meat, and three pounde of hoggs fatt cut them together very small; then take an ounce of peper and an ounce of clove and mace, and 2 nutmegs beat them together and strew it one the meat; then take two good handfulls of sage and halfe a handfull of tyme, and halfe a handful of sweet majerome or potmajerom and a little rosemary and half a handfull of peniroyall chop all these herbes together very small and strew them over your meat; then strew one it a good handfull of salt; and put to it the yolks of six eggs, mix all well together and then chop it very small altogether as do meat for mynce-pyes; then take a pounder and beat it very well as you uest to beat larde; then let it lye 24 howres and cover it very close then fill them and hange them up adryeing.

Sosages with a leg of porke: Mrs Green's Receipt

Take the leane of a leg of porke and cutt it very small, take three pound of butter, one handfull of sage cutt small, salt, peper, and cloves to your tast, and yolks of 18 eggs, crums of stayle bread, mixe all well together and keepe it in an earthen pott: when you dress it make it into roles a little flat and do them over with whites of eggs well beaten and frye them in as much butter as will only moysten the pan.

Sosiges, or Balls, for any Ash [hash], or Scotchcollops, or pottages

Take either ye leane of veale or muton, and put to it some beefe suet, shread it exceeding small, then mixe with it some time, savory, and sweet-majerom, a little lemon pill, an oynion, all being shread small mixe them together, and season it with nuttmeg, and a little peper and salt, and put to it some grated bread, and the yolks and whites of eggs, as much as will mixe it to role, then role them in a little flower and frye them in butter.

Sosiges or Balls: for pottages, Ashes, or Scotchcollops

Take some leane of veale and put to it some beef suet and chop it as small as for mince pyes; then put to it some sweet herbs choped small, one hard egg, and an oynion, and an anchove, season it with peper, salt and nuttmeg; according to your tast, then beat an egg or two and mixe wth it, beat it alltogether very well, then take a little flower in your hand and make them up as you please, some biger and lesser, some long and some rounde, and either frye or boyle them; some will frye them in butter first, and afterwards in water to make them looke white, you may if you please also put in wth yr beefe suet a little bacon, and also some oysters if you like them.

To bake a rump of Beefe: my second Cousen Clerke's Receipt

Boyle a rump of fat young beefe till it is halfe enough, then stick it with cloves, and shread a handfull of sweet herbes, majerom time and parsly; take foure eggs yolks and whites, and spread them all over ye meat being mixed with the herbes, bake it in a pipkin till it be well soaked, and tender, put into it the gravie yt runs from it, the fatt being taken away, a little clarit wine haveing oynion steeped in it and 3 or 4 anchovies dissolved in it, put sipits in the bottome of your dish and sqeze in ye juce of a lemon one your meat: you may stew this in a pott if you please.

To pott Beefe: Mrs Charlton's Receipt

Take a midle peece of buttock beefe salt it well for three days; then take it and steepe it in pump water and salt for two days more; then take it out drye it and have redy an ounce of black peper finly beat and a handfull of salt, then put it into an earthen pott without any liquor; but be sure to rub in the seasoning well all over it; bake it with household bread, and let it soake well, as soon as it comes out of the oven pick out the fatt and sinews and shread it very small as quick and hott as you can, and have redy melted a pound of butter, then lay into little potts your shread meat and betweene every layer of meat poure a little butter and so continue it till all your meat be in, then poure the rest of ye butter on the top to cover it all over and if there be not enough to cover it over thike enough melt more.

To Bake porke: given me at Hackney

Take a loine of porke and cutt both the fatt and lean very small and beat it as you do for sosiges; then season it with peper, salt; cloves, mace, and nuttmeg, and thrust it very hard into a pott, and bake it with browne bread, and eat it cold cutt out in slices.

To pott up a Haire: Newton's Receipt: A Swan also may be potted up the same way

Take 2 Haires, skine and wash them, then cutt them in peeces and season it pretty well with peper, and salt, with a little nuttmeg, cloves, mace, and clove-peper beaten small, when you have so seasoned it, have in redyness about a pound of fatt bacon with some rowes of leane in it; cutt your bacon in peeces about an inch long, and half an inch thike, then put in your Haire, and bacon into a pott, putting in betweene every laying of haire, some peeces of Bacon, and let ye Haire be first and last in your pott, you may lay the Head and liver upon all ye rest to keepe it from burning, then lay upon it about three quarters of a pounde of butter, and poure in about halfe a pinte of fayre water, then tye over it a double browne paper and bake it with Household bread neare ye mouth of ye oven; then when it is baked put all your Haire into a coullender to drayne the liquor from it, and when it hath so stood a little time to drayne, take all ye flesh cleane from ye bones whilst it is hott; pull out all the skine and sinews as neare as you can, wch you will feele betweene your fingers as you take the flesh from ye bones, then breake the flesh small with your hands, and when so don take a wooden square trencher and beat it well with the edge of that as if you were choping it with a choping-knife, you must also beat ye peeces of bacon with it that was baked amongst it; beat it all together with ye trencher till it be pretty well to mash and tender but not too small, and as you so beat it put in now and then a spoonefull or two of the fatt liquor it was baked in, but be sure to take non but just ye very fatt, for if any of ye gravie be amongst it, it will sower it, you may put in by degrees in ye beating about five or six spoonefulls of it wch will make it eate moiste in ye spending; when you have don beating it, strew in amongst it some salt, with beaten peper, cloves, mace, nuttmegs, and clove-peper all mingled together, let ye spice be beaten but grosly not too small that so it may be seen in it, put in enough to season it pretty well to your tast; then worke it all well together with your hands and put it into an earthen pan laying a plate over it, and set it into ye oven it came out off just a little to warme it, you need not let it stand above halfe an hower, then put it into your pott that it is to be kept in, crush it downe close and even, and lay a borde upon it, and set a twenty pound waite upon it to press it downe, and so let it stand for 2 howers with the waite upon it, then take off ye waite and borde, and poure melted butter all over it, and to give your butter a relish scume of all the fatt as cleane as you can out of ye pott the Haire was baked in, and put it to your butter as it is amellting, you must be sure to let your butter boyle and scume it very cleane, and so poure it on your meate, but take care not to let any of ye whay (that will be in ye butter after it is melted) be poured on for that will make ye butter not looke well, put on butter enough to be pretty thike on it, and ye next day when it is cold put a peece of cleane white paper close over it, and keepe it; you may pott up a swan so and it eats very well.

To Bake Venison: my Mother's Receipt

Take your venison and bone it, and if it be a hanch slice it a little thiner; but if it be a side you need not; season it prety high with peper and salt, then put it into a earthen pott and squeze it downe harde, put good store of butter at ye bottome of your pott, and betweene your venison, and one the top of it; then cover it with course past and bake it with browne bread and when it coms out of the oven, take off the past, and fill the pott quite full with melted butter, and when it is quite cold cover it close with paper; and it will keepe good halfe a yare.

melissa

marjoram

rue

fennel

mint

tarragon

SAUCES

SAUCES

sawces of all sorts for fish and flesh: & to draw gravie the best way: to mixe spice for any seasoning

Sawce for Fish: my second Cousen Clerke's given by Mrs Jackson

Take a quantity of vineger and a good many anchovies and nutmeg; then take a bunch of herbes, time rosemary, oynion, tye this in a bunch and let it stew in the vineger and the anchovies together, then melt your butter thike, by it self, then put it together just as you poure it upon the fish.

Sawce for Fish as my Father uest [used] to have it

Take a little cloves, mace, peper and a race of ginger, with a little savory, time, and sweet majerom, and a little bitt of horse-redish roote, oynions; stew all these together in a quarter or halfe a pinte of claret according to ye bigness of your dish of fish, and when it is stewed almost enough put in 4 or 5 anchovies and so dissolve them as soon as you can crushing them with the back of your spoone; it must not be long over the fire after the anchovies are in it for if it be it will loose their sent; then strayne it all out, there should be about six spoonfulls of the wine when all the things are strayned out; then grate in halfe a nuttmeg or more and squeze in a little juce of Lemon; stir it together and when it is boyling hott put your butter into it; and melt it in it; but you must stir, and keale [keel], it apasse [apace] and have a quick fire or else the butter will turn; you must not melt your butter before you put it to this stewed liquor; for you must melt it in that: and keepe it stiring to thiken you may also put in ye yolke of an egg or two to make it thiker.

Sawce for Fish: Mrs Whiteheads Receipt

Take whitewine and boyle it with a little nutmeg and melt butter in it, and then add oysters and shrimps, your oysters must boyle up in their own liquor and the shrimps heat in the same liquor, put in one slice of oynion in the boyleing of your oysters; then scald some sipits in the oyster liquor and some of the liquor the fish is boyled in mixt together; then take the oysters and shrimps out of the liquor and put them into the butter, and so poure them over ye fish; the fish must be well dryed in a chafindish of coles and as ye water coms from them you must take it away with a cleane cloath or spunge; garnish your dish with Lemon.

Sawce for Carpes: My Lady Howe's Receipt

When you have cleansed your carps from the guts pure [pour] into their bellys some claret-wine and wash out all their bloud, save the bloud and wine and add thereto some more claret; with some whole cloves, and a race of ginger sliced, some Lemon-peele, a small bundle of sweet herbes; then take out of your carpe the melt cutt it in small bitts; and put all this astewing together a quarter of an howre before you take up your carpes; then when your carpes are redy to go in slice two spoonfulls of capers and strayne the juce from them and so put them to your carpes, not before they are redy to go in for they will make the sawce bitter; or else dissolve some anchovies and put in so much butter as will compleat your dish.

Sawce for boyled fish; Mrs Lord's Receipt

Take a pinte of clarett 3 or 4 anchoves, 3 or 4 large blades of mace, 8 cloves, 8 corns of whole peper, 3 or 4 slices of nuttmegg, 6 or 7 slices of horse redish, an oynion or shalott; boyle all these in the wine till it be halfe wasted, and wth them a sprig or two of time and as much of winter-savory and a peece of Lemon pill, when it has boyled as afore mentioned, take out all the ingredients from ye liquor, then set it one ye fire againe and when it is redy to boyle put in three quarters of a pounde of Butter, and takeing it from the fire thiken it with 3 yolks of eggs very well beaten, but have a care they do not curdle, then poure it on your fish; your fish are thus to be ordered they are not to have their scales taken off, but being opened to have their gutts pulled out, and being well washed take some water for their Boyleing, into which water put of time, winter-savory, and sage together one handfull, a peece of Lemon pill, and season it wth a little salt, and when it boyles put in your fish and as they boyle poure a pinte of wine vineger upon them to couller [colour] them, then when they are boyled enough poure your water carefully from them, and set your fish upon a chafindish of coales in a dish, drye up the water that comes from them wth a spunge or a cloath, then shift them into the dish in which you intend to serve them up: they are thus to be ordered for service, take a little horse redish-roote and scrape it very small, halfe a lemon shread small which put into the sawce before directed, and then poure all upon the fish, garnish the dish with Barberys and sippitts and slices of Lemon lay upon the fish, and about the dish.

Sawce for fryed soles: Mrs Lords Receipt

Take some clarett and anchoves boyle them together, then strayne it and put to it some grated nuttmeg, a clove or two a blade of mace, a slice of Lemon, and some white bread sliced into it: stew these together on ye fire, then beat the yolke of an egg, and take some butter and put to it, and so poure it on your fish.

Sawce for a cods Head: Mrs Lord's Receipt

The Cods-Head is to be boyled in water, and vineger, and a bundle of sweet herbes, and some salt: whilst it is boyleing take a pinte and a quarter of whitewine, put in 12 or 14 anchoves, a little whole peper, a nuttemeg grated, a pretty deal of beaten ginger, a little cloves and mace beaten; let it be seasoned very high, then put in a little Barell of pickled oysters off about a pinte pickle and all put in, grate in a good handfull of Horse redish; then give it one boyle over the fire and put in a pounde and a quarter of Butter, stir it all together till it be thike, to which you may add if you please a quart of shrimps.

Note: that anchovies, beat in ale betweene two dishes, are much better to eat, then when they are only washed.

Anchovie sawce: Mrs Whiteheads Receipt

Take six spoonfulls of claret; and two anchovies cleane washed and the bones taken out; and a little nuttmeg, and a branch of time, a little peece of oynion, a peece of horseredish roote; heat all these together till the anchovies be dissolved, then put in a peece of butter and stir it well together.

Sorill sawce for boyled Chickins: my first Cousen Clerke's

Take verjuce and make it scalding hott, or boyle it if you please then put in a peece of butter and then put in your juce of sorill but after ye juce is in you must not set it over the fire for if you do it will loose couller; so sweeten it, and haveing sipitts redy cutt lay them rounde the dish, under your chickins, so poure in your sawce; some will put in scalded goose-berys also; and juce of spinage with the sorill to make it green.

Sawce for boyled Cappons: my Lady Sheldon's Receipt

Take a little time, and sorill, cutt it pretty small, and stew it in a little strong broath or gravie, put in a little butter, and a pinte of oysters, when these have had one boyle put in a pounde of butter, with 2 or 3 spoonfulls of vineger, and 2 or 3 spoonfulls of oynion water; and 2 or 3 anchovies; and a little french bread cutt small; if you finde that your sawce be not thike enough put in a little flower; you may lay sasiges [sausages] upon your cappons, and oysters either fryed or boyled, and some thine slices of bacon fryed; poure your sawce over all.

Sawce for any black fowle: My Lady Howe's Receipt

Take some fayre water, and a little slice of oynion, a little grase [gross] pepper, a little bitt of butter, some juce of oringe; and some salt, and some gravie; and the sole [underpart] of ye birds, and wash the birds with this liquor, and then boyle it all together; and when your fowle is rosted poure this sawce one them.

Gravie sawce for fowle

Take a little water put to it a little vineger, 2 or 3 bitts of oynion a little lemon pill, a little salt, a little peper beat grosly, and the neck of your fowles cutt in 2 or 3 bitts, boyle all well together then put in as much claret as will couller it, and let it boyle for some time, then put in one or two anchoves bones and all let it boyle till they are dissolved, then strayne it and when you serve your fowles to table poure your sawce quite thorow them, if you have any gravie of meat to boyle in it when you put in the anchoves it will make it the better and give it ye better couller.

Sawce for young Roasted ducks

Take 7 or 8 spoonfulls of water put to it a peece of oynion, some peper grosely beaten, a little salt, let it boyle gently till it tast strong then straine it, and have in redyness some green tops of young oynions boyled tender by themselves and shred them small and put them in, and give it one boyle then melt in it a quarter of a pound of butter and so poure it in your dish to your ducks.

Sawce for ducks: Mrs Ridges Receipt

Take oynions boyle them in water till they are soft, then put them in a sive and bruse them to peeces, and so pulp them through the sive, with the back of a spoone; then take ye gravie of duck, and a little claret, and nutmeg sliced, and halfe an anchovie, mingle them together and when it has a little heated over the fire poure it to your duck.

Bred sawce for partriges or Turkeys

Boyle some water a whole oynion, a little salt, whole peper, and grated white bread enough to make it very thike, let all boyle together till it be as thike as you would have it, then just as you take it off ye fire stur in a little peece of Butter; you must put ye bread in at first when ye water is cold or else it will not looke white.

Sawce for a Roasted pigg

As your pig rostes save 8 or 10 spoonfulls of gravie that runs from it; put into a sawce-pan, make it just boyle then melt in halfe a pound of butter, and put in some boyled sage shred small, and also the Braines of the pigg; stir in well amongst it, and so serve it.

Sawce for a Rosted Leg of Mutton: my Cousen Wheatlys receipt

Take a good glassefull of claret and poure it into the dish you intend to lay your mutton in; and set it over a chafindish [chafing dish] of coales then cutt in two anchovies, and put in a little vineger and some gravie; so keepe it stiring till your anchovies be dissolved then take it off the chafin-dish and lay your mutton in, and so serve it.

Sawce for boyled Mutton: my Lady Sheldon's Receipt

Take a pounde of butter, and a quarter of a pinte of gravie, after you have melted your butter and gravie together put in a little french bread cutt small, and two anchovies; and a little young time striped; and a little mints, and a little sorill; let all this be cutt small; and put in ye juce of a Lemon; if you please you may put in some nutmegg and oysters; when you have mixed all together give it a warme over the fire, if it be not thike enough put in a little more bread; peele an oynion and put into your sawce, and take it out when you poure your sawce one the mutton.

Bred sawce for Roasted Venison

Boyle some clarett with a little water in it and a stick of cinomon till it tastes of ye spice, then put in of grated white bread enough to make it thike, and give it 4 or 5 boyles and take it off and sweeten it to your likeing.

the Duke of Yorke's sawce: Mrs Whiteheads Receipt

Beat 2 or 3 yolkes of eggs with water; and whitewine-vineger, slice in some shelot, or oynion, and so let it stew together with some gravie if you have it.

To draw gravie the best way: my Lady Sheldon's

Take what meat you please, either mutton, veale, or beefe; cutt it as thyne as you do to frye, pick off all the fatt, and hack it with ye back of your knife; then put it into a tynn puding-pann and cover it close with ye lidd; and set it in a kittle of water, so let it boyle 4 or 5 houres, then take it out and use it; 3 or 4 pounde of flesh will make a pinte of gravie.

To make a good gravey

Take an ounce of Butter and boyle it in your stewpan till it comes black, then strew in some flower, then put in two pound of lean Beefe cut in slices, put in a pinte of water and halfe a pinte of claret, 2 or 3 anchoves, two shallots, a little whole peper, cloves and mace, some mushroms, let all stew gently three quarters of an hour, then strain it and keepe it for your uses as you shall have occation.

To make another good gravie

Cutt a peece of lean Beefe into thine slices and fry it brown in a stewpan with an oynion, 2 or 3 slices of lean Bacon, then put to it a pinte of strong broath rubing the brown of ye pan well into it, and if you please add some claret and more strong Broath, some anchoves and a fagott of sweet herbs, let it stew well together gently then strain it and keep it for uses etc.

Another good gravie

Take a little slice or two of Bacon and put it into your stewpan, then slice some leane Beefe and frye it brown in it on both sides, then put to it some strong broath or water, some anchovies, shalots, lemon peele, peper, cloves, mace, and a crust of bread burnt black, let all stew well together then strain it for uses.

To Burn Butter: ffor the thikening of an Brown sauces, or soopes

put into a frying pan a quarter of a pound of Butter and let it boyle till it comes browne, then strew into it a good handfull of flower keeping it over the fire and stiring it all ye while with a spoone or Ladle till it be well mixed and become thike, then poure it into a pott and keepe it for your use. This burnt butter is used for the thikening of any brown sauce, or to thicken scotchscollops, and ashes [hashes], or stewed meats, and likewise very good to thiken peese soopes. It must be used as followeth, by takeing a peece of it and desolveing it in some of the hott liquor that you intend to thiken, then poure it in and boyle it together untill it be thike as you would have it.

[114]

To thiken any sauces with flower

Take some flower that is very fine and mix it well with ye back of a spoon into a peece of Butter, when so done put it into your sauce stiring it well over the fire, this will thiken instead of eggs.

To clarifie Butter

Melt your Butter in a large glased [glazed] pipkin on a gentle fire that is clear from smoke, put a little water to it, and when it is cold take away the curd and whay from the bottom, do this 3 or 4 times and put it into potts for your use and tye it down with a Blader [bladder].

To make sawce very good without either gravie or butter, viz.

put into your sawcepan some water and a little flower, stir it well together, and put to it a bit of burnt bred, a little oynion, a little lemon pill, some peper grossly beaten, let it boyle gently for a while then put in either a little catchup [ketchup] or some anchovie which when desolved then strain it and put it into your dish to either fowles or any other meat. If you have ye neck of a fowle, or any other meat you may boil it amongst the other things, and also add gravie to it if you please.

To make catchup [ketchup] to be put into any sawces

Take the largest musheroms you can gett stalks and all without washing them, only pareing them a little round the edges, so put them into a stone pott with a great quantity of salt, laying a row of musheroms and a row of salt till all in, then set them in a coole celler for ten days stiring them once a day always in the same pott keepeing it close stoped that no steam getts out, then set it in a pott of cold water but let not the pott be so full as to let any water gett into it when it boyles, let it boyle for three hours, then strain the liquor from the musheromes very clean thro a flanell bag (throwing away ye musheromes) and put ye liquor into ye same pott and let it boyle for two hours as before, then run it thro' ye flanell bag again but not squese it, then add to the liquor mace, ginger, white peper, rosemary and bay leaves of each what you thinke proper according to ye quantity of your liquor, then put it in ye pott again and boyle it halfe an hour covered as before, then let it stand till it be cold, then take out the rosemary and bay leaves and bottle up the liquor putting into each bottle an equall share of the spices that was boyled in it, corke your bottles well and seal them close that no aire getts in.

A Mixture of spices for any seasoning: My Lady Howe's

Take a quarter and halfe a quarter of a pounde of peper small beaten, halfe a quarter of a pounde of ginger; of clover; mace; and nuttmegs; of each halfe an ounce, beat these spices very fine, and mingle them together, and put to them two pounde of white salt, then put it in an earthen pott cover it close, and keepe it for your use.

for all sorts of pudings both Boyled, baked & fryed

PUDDINGS – SAVOURY

PUDDINGS — SAVOURY

all sorts of pudings and Hogs pudings

To make Black pudings in guts: My Lady Sheldon's Receipt

Take the bloud of 2 porkers strayne it and put into it a good quantity of salt stir it till it be almost cold; then put into it a quarter of a peck of oatemell yt which is caled cuttlings; so let it stand 2 or 3 days sometimes stiring and tasting it; if you finde the bloud to grow sower you must not let it stand so long; then take sage; parsley; wintersavory; sweet marjorome; peneroyall; of each a like quantity; and a very little time and fenell, the body onely of a Leeke; greene onions if they are to be had, if not take one whole oynion; shread all these as small as may be and let them be at least a poringer full when they are shred. Take a groat's worth of mace and a nutmeg, beat them together with two spoonefuls of sugar; then take a pinte of Creame and as much milke as you thinke will make ye pudings thyne enough; boyle it and put it into the puding-stuff; put in 2 or 3 spoonfulls of rosewater; and all ye things before mentiond; then have eight pound of Beefe suet redy shred and beat with a roleing-pin; put to it ye rest of the things and so fill them; beevers guts are beter to fill ym in then any others; be sure you do not fill them too full.

To make Liver pudings in gutts: either of calfes-liver or Lams Liver

Take 2 pound of grated white bread and sift it, and put to it 2 pound of suett finely choped and also sifted; then have redy a pound and a halfe of curants washed and picked cleane; halfe a pound of suger; one ounce of cinomon, halfe an ounce of cloves, halfe an ounce of mace, two nuttmegs; all beat small and mingle them together with a little calves-liver or lambs-liver choped small; then put in five eggs with a little rosewater and creame enough to mix it of a fitt thikeness; then fill it into gutts; you must boyle the liver first and then chop it and sift it; or else you may grate it fine on a bread-grater. You may fill them in Hoggs gutts or in Sheepe-gutts which you please.

Greene dumplings: Mrs Lords Receipt

Slice a pounde of the crume [crumb] of browne bread, then haveing your pott boyleing with beefe scume of ye fatt and put it to ye bread in which let it soake an houre, then beate it with a spoone very small, then put in

5 eggs whites and all and a little ginger and sweet herbs shred small, whereof two parts must be penneroyall stir it all together and strew in flower with three quarters of a pound of suet cutt very small; then haveing a litle flower rubed one ye palmes of ye hands role them rounde and put them into ye pott when it boyles very fast three quarters of an howre boyles them.

A Cabidge puding: My Lady Desmons' Receipt

Take a leg of veale cutt it in peeces and shread it with the best part of a very good cabidge, then being shread season it with beaten cloves, mace, nuttmeg, sinomon and a little peper, then take the green out-leaves of the cabidge and role it up fast and put it into a cloath and boyle it, but when you take it out of the pott take it out of the leaves and serve it with melted butter over it.

A Carett [carrot] puding baked: My Lady Howe's receipt

Take a twopeny lofe grated; and the same quantity of raw caret grated very small; mix them together; and put to it the yolks of eight eggs, and the white of 3 beat them well and put them in, then stir in a quarter of a pounde of butter being melted, and a little sack; and grated nutmeg; put in milke enough to make it of a good thickness, about a pinte I believe will be enough; sweeten it prety sweet to yr tast; mingle all well to-gether; and bake it in a dish, halfe an houre will do it; when you draw it, poure a little melted butter with sack in it; one ye top of it.

to stew apples & to bake apples & pares

PUDDINGS – SWEET

PUDDINGS — SWEET

for all sorts of pudings both Boyled, baked, & fryed

An Almonde puding boyled Mrs Whiteheads' Receipt

Take a pinte of Creame and boyle it with Sliced nutmeg and mace; take of almonds blanched and beaten very small, foure ounces; stir them with ye creame and add the yolks of the eggs and four whites well beaten; and four ounces of suger; and a little oringe-flower water: wet your bag and flower it. Halfe an hour will boyle it; for sawce take buter and Sack and suger; where almons are used oringe flower water is much better than rose-water.

An Almond puding baked Mrs. Whiteheads' Receipt

Take a pounde of Almons blanch and beat them; then put to them 3 quarters of a pound of suger beaten small; and 3 quarters of a pounde of melted butter and 18 yolks of eggs; with six whites; the crumbe of 2 french roles soaked in creame as much as it will take in; mingle this all together and bake it in a dish; with past [paste] or without it as you like it best.

To make a Rice puding whch may be boyled, baked, or put into gutts as you please

Rube halfe a pound of rice well in a cloath, then boyle it in a quart of new milke till it be tender, keeping it stired, then take it off and put it into a pan covering it close and let it stand all night, then put to it a pinte of cream, the yolk of eight eggs well beaten with 2 spoonfulls of Sack as much oringe-flower water, a nuttmeg grated, and suger to your tast, about half a pound I believe may do, stir all well together and mixe in it a pound of suet shred very small, and also some marow cutt ye bigness of ye dice, you may either boyle it in a cloath, or Bake it in a dish, or put it into gutts as you please; and if you like plums in it you may put in a pound of curants well washed and dryed; and if you add a little muske or ambergreece [ambergris] 't 'will eat the richer.

A Rice flower puding to be baked, or boyled

Take a quart of milk and when it boyles put into it six ounces of the flower of rice and let it boyle till it be thike as hasty puding and a spoon will stand in it stiring it all the while that it do not burn too, then put it out into a pan and put to it halfe a pound of fresh butter, some mace shred pretty small, two spoonefulls of oringe flower water and as much suger as will sweeten it to your likeing; stir it well together and when it is cold put in the yolks of six eggs with three of their whites well beaten; put in like-wise cittron and candied oring and Lemmon pill sliced thine, then put it into a dish well-buttered and bake it in an oven no hotter than for tarts—three quarters of an hour will bake it; this puding eats as well cold as hott. If you please you may boyle this puding but then you must leave out the butter, and be sure to wett your puding cloath in hott water and then flower it well; halfe an houre will boyle it; for the sawce take melted butter with suger and a little sack in it if you please.

A French Barly Puding—my first Cousen Clerkes receipt

Take halfe a pinte of french barly; water it and boyle it very tender; then take blanched almons beaten very fine with rose water strayne them with creame into ye barley, put in some grated bread 4 yolks and two whites of eggs; season it with mace, nutmeg and suger; so bake it.

An Oatemell puding baked: Mrs Brownes receipt

Take a little above a quart of creame, and a pinte of great oatemell: bruse it a little in a morter; then put it into ye creame and put to it a blade of mace; and let it boyle softly untill it hath drunke up all ye creame; then let it stand till it be cold, then put in the yolks of 8 eggs and ye whites of 2 well beaten; with six spoonefulls of rose water; season it with cinimon and nutmeg and suger to your tast and a very little salt; then melt a good peece of butter and put in also some suet minced very small, or marow if you please also a little grated bread; mix all well together and butter a dish and put it in; and so bake it.

A Oatemell puding to boyle: My Aunt Ryes Receipt

Take a pinte of oatemell, lay it asteepe in new milke all night, then in the morning set it over the fire to boyle a little; then put in your suett, and courents [currants], and spice and suger and eggs, and then boyle it in a bagg.

[127]

A sego [sago] puding Baked

Take a quart of milke boyle it and thicken it with foure spoonfulls of flower a litle over the fire, then coole it and put to it a quarter of a pounde of sego, grate in a nuttmeg and put to it the yolks of 6: eggs and one white beaten well, and halfe a pounde of curants redy plumped, and a quarter of a pounde of suger, and if you please put in some sliced citron, when tis all mingled together put it into a dish well buttered, an hour bakes it.

A puding with suet: My Lady Sheldon's Receipt. Boyled

Take halfe a pounde of Beefe suet shred small; halfe a pinte of raw creame; 8 spoonefulls of rose water; beat six yolks of eggs and 1 white; a little nutmegg and suger to your tast; and 2 peny loaves grated; mingle it together and tye it up round in a cloath; put it into boyleing water and let it boyle 3 houres. This puding is also good with curants in it.

To make little plum pudings: My Lady How's Receipt

Beat 2 eggs well with some suger and rosewater; put it a few courance [currants]; some grated nutmeg, 2 handfulls of Beefe suet shred small; a little salt and grated bread enough to make it stiff to wrap in balls; it being in some balls worke them up and downe in flower that the outside may be hardened; let ye water boyle before you put them in serve them with buter and suger and a little rose water and vinegar; you must boyle them halfe an houre but not very fast.

Pudings in guts with plums in them: as Leech uest [used] to make them

Take 3 pound of grated bread and sift it; then take 3 pound and a quarter of beefe suet, chop it and sift it; then take halfe an ounce of cinemon, and halfe an ounce of nutmegs, a race of ginger and halfe an ounce of cloves and halfe an ounce of mace; beat all these very well together, and put to it ye bread and suet; then take 12 egg yolks and whites, beat very well and put them in, then take three quarters of a pound of suger and put in also; and take two quarts of good creame boyle it and coole it a little and then poure in it; then put in 2 pound of courance [currants] and 16 spoonfulls of Rosewater; mix all these well together; and fill them in hogs guts; boyle them in milke and water. Let it boyle before you put them in; halfe an houre will boyle them. Some will shred a little Lemon peele very small and mix in with ye rest of ye things.

A plum puding Baked: my Aunt ffrancklines Receipt

Take a peny lofe (but of London bread take a little more) cutt of the crust, and slice the crume [crumb] very thine, then boyle a quart of milke and put it boyleing hott to the bread, and grate some nuttmeg to it, so let it stand all night, and the next morning put foure eggs into it, and beat them very well in the bread, and milke, and as you beat it strew in a little flower, till you have made it of a fitt thickness, it must not be too thine for then all the plums will sink to the bottome, neither must you make it too thike for then it will not be so light, you must keep it with continuall beating for a great while, for that will make it light, then put in about a quarter of a pounde of suet cutt very small, stir it in well, then wash almost halfe a pounde of courence [currants], and as many raisons, and shake them very well in a cloath till they are drye, and stir them well in the puding, with a little salt, and so bake it in a puter dish, well buttered.

A plum puding Boyled

Take a peny lofe and pare off ye crust, then slice the crume very thine, and poure to it boyling hott a pinte of good milke, or creame, cover it up close and let it stand awhile to soake, then break ye bred small, and grate in halfe a nuttmeg, break in 4 eggs whites and all, and beat it all together, puting in by degrees 2 good handfulls of fine flower, then put in a full quarter of a pounde of suet choped small, and 3 quarters of a pound of curants and raysons together, stir all well together with a little salt, and boyle it either in a cloath, or in wooden dishes well buttered and boyle it 3 howers.

A Shakeing puding: Mrs Greens' Receipt. Boyled

Take a quart of creame and boyle it with cinomon and ginger and sliced nuttmeg, then put in some almons blanched and beaten fine with ye rosewater; mix with it 12 eggs leaveing out 6 of the whites beat them well and put in a full spoonfull of flower; beat it all well together with a spoone then boyle it in a flowered cloath being first buttered; halfe an hour boyle it.

A quakeing puding boyled: Leeches Receipt

Take a quart of Creame and 2 peniworth of bread grated; put it to ye creame; if ye see ye creame will be too thike of bread, do not put it all in because the eggs will thiken it; when you have stired it together set it over the fire and let it boyle almost halfe an houre stiring it all the while; then put it in a dish and coole it and beat 14 eggs very well, leaveing out 2 or 3 of ye whites and mix them with ye bread and creame; grate in above halfe a nutmeg and sweet it to your tast; then flower your puding-bag very well and put it in; tye it very hard so that the water may not git in; be sure ye water boyles all ye while; two houres will boyle it, then blanch about 2 handfulls of Almons and when ye puding is enough stick ye Almons all over it; and for sawce melt buter and suger with 2 or 3 spoonefulls of Rosewater; so serve it.

Aple [apple] pudings in broath boyled: Mrs Whiteheads' Receipt

Take flower, and new milke, and an egg; and make it into a soft past; then take large aples pare them and take out ye cores; and put in suger and a little butter in ye midle where ye core was; close and wrape ym up in ye past; keepe your pudings to boyle in but just water enough to cover them; when they are boyled enough take ye liquor they were boyled in and put to it some whitewine; butter, and suger; and a little salt; and some creame; serve the pudings up in this liquor.

An Apple puding baked: my first Cousen Clerkes Receipt

Take 12 pipins and scald them tender: then take ye pap of them and 12 eggs well beaten; and some grated bread, nutmeg, sugar, salt and rose water to your tast; and a good peece of butter; beat them all well together; and bake it in a dish.

[130]

An Oringe [orange] puding baked: My Lady Howes Receipt— also Mrs Lords

Take the pareings of 2 large oringes cutt it in little bitts; and pounde it very well in a morter; then put to it 3 quarters of a pounde of sugar and a pounde of fresh butter; and the yolks of 12 eggs well beaten, then beat it well together till it be throughly mixed; then put it into a dish be- tweene two leaves of past; which must be made of butter rubed into ye flower and weted with cold water, set it into a quick oven for half an houre; a pounde of flower will make ye past and halfe a pounde of butter.

Some will grate the rines of 2 large oringes instead off cutting them: and some says that puff past is not so good to put between it, as other past made as good as can be; an oven as hott as for tarts will bake it.

An Oringe puding baked: My Aunt Ryes Receipt

Take 2 large Sivill oringes, cut them in ye midle and squeese out all the juce into a silver poringer; pick out ye seeds and pith or skin yt growes in ye midle of ye oringe; then boyle some of ye out rinde of ye oringe in 3 or 4 waters; yt it may not be bitter; then beat ye meat and inner rine of ye oringe with as much of ye peele yt you boyled as will give it a good tast, and beat them together into a fine past, and put into it a quarter of a pounde of fine sugar; and halfe a pounde of butter beat them in; then put in six yolks of eggs and 4 whites, and 4 spoonfulls of thicke creame; mix all well together; put in also halfe a graine of muske finely rubed in with sugar, yn [then] put it into a dish with a thine puff past in ye bottome and cover it with ye same; put it into your oven let it be no hotter then for manchets, halfe an houre will bake it, this puding is very good hott in ye first course; and cold in ye second; put not in ye eggs till it is redy to go into ye oven.

An Aprecock [apricot] puding baked: My Cousen Wheatly's receipt

Boyle a quart of creame with a blade of mace; then take it from the fire and put to it a peny lofe grated; nutmeg, sugar, rose water to your tast; a good handfull of marow minced; and the yolks of six eggs with ye whites of 3 beaten very well, mix all this well together, then laye six aprecocks preserved in halves and quarters into ye dish and so poure ye creame with all ye rest of ye things one them; and then bake it; halfe an houre will do it.

a fine Lemon puding Baked

Take the parings of 2 large Lemons, boyle them in water till they are tender, then beat them in a morter very fine, then put in a pound of suger and a pound of fresh butter beating them well together, then have redy a pound of almonds Blanched and beat very fine with a little oringe flower water to keep them from oyleing, put them in and beat them together till well mixed, then put in ye juice of ye 2 Lemons and the yolks of 12 eggs well beaten and beat all together till well mixed, then put it into a dish between two leaves of fine past, and put it into an oven no hotter than for manchets [bread], three quarters of an hour will bake it.

A greene puding with cittern [citron] in it: Boyled

Take the crume [crumb] of a penny lofe and slice it very thine put to it boyleing hott a pinte of new milke, and breake the bread as small as you can possible in the milke, then put in halfe a pound or more of pound-cittern being cutt in thine slices as you can posibley cutt it the crosse way of the cittern; then have redy a good quantity of the juce of spinage; or, for want of that take violet leaves, strabery leaves, beats [beets], of which make as much juce as you thinke will couller it green enough; when you have made it as greene as you would have it, put in foure or six eggs whites and all being beat well with some rose water and grated nuttmeg; mingle all together and sweeten it to your tast with suger; you may either boyle it in a bagg or in wooden dishis with a cloath tyed over them, but if in dishis, you must be sure to butter them well to make them turne out; an houre will boyle it, for the sawce melt butter and suger: if you would have it very rich, instead of ye milke take creame, and you may put in also more eggs; ye must not fayle to breake ye bread with ye back of your spoone extreame small.

A Sack puding baked: My Lady How's receipt

Take about 20 almons blanch and beat them; then take 2 eggs well beaten and a poringer full of creame, stir them together; then have redy a marow-bone boyled, melt it and put it to ye rest of ye things; mingle it all well together and let it boyle in a skillit over ye fire a little while; then put it into a dish and set it in a oven to harden a little; before you take it out of the oven to send it up you must strew a little sack upon it; you may put in suger and dates or rosewater if you please.

A biskit puding baked: My Lady Sheldon's Receipt

Take 4 naple biskits; and 2 peny loves slice them thine; and put them to a quart of milke boyleing off ye fire; and when it is cold put to it 4 eggs and a little rose water; and some salt; and nutmeg, stir all well together and butter a dish; and put it therein and bake it; so serve it.

To Make a white pott with plums in it: Leeche's Receipt

Take a quart of new milke; but creame will do better, put to it as much grated bread as you thinke will thicken it, a peny lofe will do, then boyle it for halfe an houre keepeing it stiring all ye while; then put it out into a dish and coole it, and put to it ye yolks of 12 eggs beat very well, with six spoonefulls of rosewater; and a nutmeg grated; then wash halfe a pounde of courance [currants] and plump them; and mingle them with ye rest, sweeten it to your tast; then butter a dish and put it therein and when you are redy to put it into ye oven cutt some thine slices of butter; and put here and there a slice one ye top of it; your oven must not be too hott an houre will bake it; serve it in with scraped suger one it.

A Devonshire Whitepott: My Second Cousen Clerkes

Take a peny white lofe, pare it and slice it thine, drye it in a slow oven; or by the fire; take a quart of creame boyle in it a little cinimon and a good handfull of raisons; when it has boyled a little while put it to the bread and let it stand till it be colde, then beat 5 yolks and 3 whites of eggs very well put them to ye bread sweeten it well; and stir it together;

then put it into a dish and put to it peeces of marow; or butter into many places of it, bake it in a gentle oven.

Pudings to frye; my Lady Sheldons Receipt

Take a pinte of milke and 3 eggs, a little rosewater and nutmeg grated; a little salt, a quarter of a pounde of courance [currants]; a peny lofe grated, a little suet 2 or 3 spoonfulls of flower; and as much sugar as will sweeten it; and make them into cakes and frye them in butter.

Puding Cakes fryed: Lady Howe's Receipt

Take the yolks of 4 eggs and 3 whites, halfe a nutmeg, beat the eggs very well with two spoonefulls of rosewater, and as much sack, with a little flower, and grated bread, and beefe suet shred very fine, stur them alltogether with creame, so drop them into ye pan being very hott, and the fire quick, you may put courance to them if you please.

A Hasty puding that Butters itself: Mrs Westons Receipt

Take a quart of Creame and set it one the fire, then take a penny white lofe and grate it in, put in also as many courence as you think fitt, boyle this altogether till it be thike, and a little before you take it up, take the yolkes of foure eggs well beaten with a little suger, and rosewater, and some nuttmeg, and a little salt, and so let it boyle till you thinke it is buttered enough, then serve it in.

To make a puff: my first Cousen Clerkes Receipt

Take about a quart of new milke, and put a little runit [rennet] to it, it may make a tender curd, then drayne out all ye whaye very gently, and put in the yolks of 4 eggs, and 2 whites, and as much grated bread as will make it as thike as batter, put in a little flower to bind it, and also nutmeg, suger, and rosewater, when it is baked poure over it some melted butter wth suger and rose-water, it must have but a coole oven.

Batalia Pie
Chicken Pie
Umble Pie
Meat Florentine
Florentine of Tongue
for all sorts of puff past and other past

PASTRY AND PIES

PASTRY AND PIES

for all sorts of puff past and other past, for pastys, pyes, and tarts; ffor all sorts of pyes both baked and fryed

An exelent puff past [pastry] for a vineson [venison] pasty, or pigeon pye, or any other pye—by wch I make mine by

To every two pounds of fine flower [flour] take the yolks of 3: eggs and one white; and a pound and quarter of butter, beat your eggs well in cold water, then break into little bitts halfe a pound of your butter into the flower and make it up with your eggs and water into a limber past, knead and handle it as little as maybe, then take the other three quarters of a pound of butter and devide it into three parts, and role [roll] out your past and stick in little bitts one part of your butter all over it and strew flower prety thike upon it, then turn it up together and role it out again, and stick on another part of your butter strowing on some more flower as you did before, and so do it in the like manner the third time, handling it as little as you can, and if you role it out one way every time it will be the better: note: that the flower you are to strew on the butter must be taken out of your two pound of flower before you make it into a past: Remember just before you put your pasty into the oven that you wash it all over with 2 spoonfulls of melted butter and the yolks of 3: eggs well beaten and mixed in it, wch will make it looke of a fine shineing yellow when it comes out of the oven:

it is much ye best way to make your pasty whilst your oven is aheating both for ye crust, and venison wch is apt to taint if covered with past all night, five hours generally bakes it very well, covering it all the time with paper, with a hole in the midle of ye paper to let out ye steam of ye pasty.

Puff past; taken out of a book: my Second Cousen Clerkes

Take a little above a peck of flower; then breake into it little bitts of butter the quantity of 3 pounde; then put in one egge; and as much cold creame as will worke it into a stiff past; do not worke it too much for yt will melt ye butter; and it should not be melted; but be in lumps in the past; or else it will be spoyled; so soon as you can posible, rowle (roll) it abroade, and make it into what fashon you please; this will be extreame good, if you observe to do it carefully.

Puff past: Mary Tooth's Receipt

Take to a pounde of flower, a pounde of butter; then laye by halfe the flower, and wet ye other halfe with cold water, but be sure to make it as

stiff as you can posible; for ye stifer it is the better it will be; molde it
very well; then rowle it out and lay some of your butter one it being cutt
in thine slices; then double it up and rowle it so yt non of ye butter coms
out by the sides; then put some more butter one it, and rowle it as before;
and so do till all your butter be in; as you do it you must use some of ye
flower you layed by in rowleing it out; and when all your butter is in;
beat it with a rowleing-pinn untill you have used all ye rest of the flower;
then use it according as you please, the oven must be prety quick to puff
it up; but not so hott as to scorch it.

Puff past: Leeches Receipt: as she used to do it

Take to a pounde of flower three quarters of a pounde of butter, breake it
into small bitts into ye flower; and put in 4 eggs whites and all; then take
a little cold water and mix it prety tender; so moulde it up; you must not
roule it, nor beat it; but the bitts of butter must be seen in the past: you
may mixe it wth milke instead of water, and for any past milke is better
then water to mixe it withall.

To make a rare hollow puff past for tarts or cheesecakes: given me by Mrs. Allome

Take a pounde and a quarter of flower put in a little suger, then take two
eggs leave out one white, mix this quantity of flower with your eggs and
some water to a limber past; then take halfe a pound and two ounces of
butter, devide it into three parts, and role out your past three times, each
time sticking in one part of your butter in small bitts upon your past, and
strow flower upon it pretty thike, and turn it up together, do this three
times and handle it as little as you can; if you always role it out one way
it will be much the better: you must remember to beat the eggs well.

To make a puff-past that is not very hollow: Mrs. Allom's Receipt

Take a pound and a quarter of flower, and halfe a pound of butter, breake
the butter in the flower, then beat two eggs leave out one white, put some
water to your eggs, and mixe it up to a past, this is good for tarts; and
will not be too hollow, remember to put a little suger into your flower.

[139]

To Make puff past: my mothers Receipt

Take a pounde of flower, and a pounde of butter; and six whites of eggs, put them all together, and worke it betweene your hands till it coms like grated bread; then put in 2 or 3 spoonefulls of cold water; and mix it with your hands a little only to worke the water into it; then take the rouleing-pinn and spread it out and turn it up againe seven times; and be sure you do not turn it upside-downe.

French past; my first Cousen Clerke's Receipt

Take a little butter; one egge; cold water, and flower; then roule it prety thine; have redy some melted butter, and with a brush or feather wett it all over, then foulde it up and rowle it out againe; then cover your pyes with it.

A Fyne past to frye; my first Cousen Clerkes Receipt

Take the yolks of 2 eggs, and one white; and as much butter as a wallnutt; a quarter of a pinte of sack and water mingled together; worke them with flower to a fine past; then roule it and frye it with butter.

To make past Royall

Take a pound and halfe of flower, a pound of butter, one Egg and a quarter of a pound of fine suger sifted, and so worke it all into a past for use.

Oyster pye: my Lady Howe's Receipt

Take great oysters as many as will fill a pretty hansome pye perboyle them in their own liquor, season them with a little peper, nutmeg whole mace, shred some time, persly, sorill, sweet-marjerome, with a great deale of buter: and if you love it sweet strew some suger one it, lay one ye top slices of Lemon, and when it comes out of ye oven put in a caudle of whitewine and eggs, it must not be over baked, neither must you put a caudle in except you make it a sweete pye.

A Lobster pye: my Lady Sheldons Receipt

Take 4 lobsters boyle them, and take them out of their shells, cutt the ferm [firm] flesh in slices about an inch square, and take all the other out cleane; then take oysters boyle them, and beard them; and put them to ye lobsters; and season it with mace salt, nutmeg, to your tast; make your crust good and proportinable to your meat; put butter into your pye and close it; when you put it into your oven put a little oyster liquor into it; and let it bake almost an howre; when you take it out; cutt up ye lidd, and put out ye fatt; and put in a layer of thike butter; five or six anchovies dissolved; the juce of an oringe; 2 or 3 yolks of raw eggs; and a little sack; and a lemon parted; and cutt grosely; make your leere [juice] a little sharpe and put it into your lobster pye; shake all together and so serve it.

Mince-pyes: Leeches Receipt

Take some neats tongues and parboyle them, but do not boyle them too much, to three pounde of tongue, take three pounde and a halfe of ye best beeves [beef] suet, chop ye meat and suet very fine, then take of nuttmeg, cloves, and mace, of each a like quantity and altogether let it be an ounce, take also a little peper, beat all very fine and strew it on your meat, with a little spoonefull of salt, and ten spoone-fulls of Rosewater, and six pipins pared and choped very small, then take three pounde of courance [currants] washed and put them in, then put in also a pounde of raisons being stoned and cutt very small, then take a handfull of dates cut them small and put them in, then take some Lemon peele and cut it exceeding small and put in also, then take a pinte of verjuce with a pounde of suger, and poure it over all, mix all very well together and let it stand all night, ye next day fill your pyes, you may put in what sweetmeats you please: and with the other things put in a good glace [glass] of sack, and the juce of 4 Lemons.

Mince pyes to be made as followeth, viz

Take a pounde of tongue after 'tis parboyled, two pound of suet, chop them very small, three pipins choped small, and one Lemon pill shred small, two pound of courance a few raisons shred, one ounce of spice, the juce of one Lemon, halfe a pinte of sack, some dates shred, a quarter of a pound of canded cittron Lemon and oring pill, and suger to your likeing, mingle all well together for use.

A pigion pye with Balls in it: Burgiss Receipt

Take a douson of pigions redy picked and quarter them, then take two nuttmegs, a little mace, and as much beaten peper as you can take up betweene your foure fingers and thume; take also some wintersavory, time, and sweet majerome finely shread, mingle all the seasoning together with a little salt, and so season your pigions with it, then lay at the bottome of your pye some thine slices of baccon, and strew on your baccon some sweet herbs redy shread, then lay in your pigions and some balls made of what meat you like best, and here and there little slices of baccon; then put in what quantity of butter you thinke will serve, put in also some gravie, and so bake it; the balls must be seasoned and made just as those you put into scotchcollops.

A Turky pye: Mrs Lord's Receipt

Take your turky and parboyle him, then breake the breast bone, and cutt of the neck which with the other giblets lay under your turky in the pye to make him lye ye more to vieu, season him, with an ounce and halfe of peper, one nuttmeg grated, and a good handfull of salt, and let your turky be stuck with cloves, laye him into a pye made with a good a past as you can, if you please you may put in also two rabetts parboyled and quartered some of wch lay under him and some of each side, but just before you put the turky into ye pye poure in a pounde of melted butter, and after he is in lay in small bitts a pound and half of butter all over him, then close up your pye, and when you bake it you may couller [colour] ye out side with yolks of eggs beaten, and as soon as you draw it put in two pound of melted butter, and so you may keepe it to eat cold; some will put the turky into the pye without parboyleing it at all.

A Chicken pye; my Second Cousen Clerkes Receipt

Take small Chickens trusted; and dryed, season them with peper salt cloves, and mace; then fill their bellys with puding-stuff made with veale perboyled and shread small and well seasoned with ye former spices, and mixed with beefe suet finely shread; courance, sack; and suger, some raw yolks of eggs; and sweet herbes shred small; so laye in you chickens being filled; and put one them potatos, marow; dates; skerets [skirret];[1] or chesnuts which you must rowle [roll] in raw yolks of eggs; lay one ye top of all, slices of lemon, a little sack and some butter; so bake it and before you serve it put in a caudle of sack butter and suger.

A Chicken or Lame [Lamb] pye: given me at Hackney

Take three prety big chickens, and cutt them in peeces, and season them with one good spoonefull of nutmeg; peper, and salt; being all mixed together; then put them in the pye, and put to them ye marow of 3 bones dyped in yolks of eggs; and also put in six ounces of preserved littis-stalks [lettuce-stalks]; and a quarter of a pounde of raisons and as many courance; and 12 quartered dates; six blades of mace; and halfe a lemon sliced; and halfe a pounde of butter; so bake it; an howre and a halfe will do it; when you draw it, put in a caudle of verjuce; whitewine, butter; and suger; in ye summer you may put in a few greene goosberys into your pye; the same ingredients serves to season a lam-pye; onely leaveing out the marow.

A Rabet [Rabbit] pye: my Lady Sheldons Receipt

Take Rabets strip and wash them; then cut them crosse in peeces; then take parsly, time, winter-savory majerom, shred all small and put them all about the meat, with peper, and salt; strew the yolks of 3 eggs upon it; put butter one the top and bottome of your pye.

A veale pye: Leeches Receipt

Take a quarter of an ounce of peper; and of Cloves mace and nutmeg halfe an ounce all together; then put to it a little salt; and after you have cutt your loyne [loin] of veale in peeces fitt for a pye, rub it all over with the spice; then lay some butter at ye bottom of your pye and so put your meat in; and put to it three quarters of a pounde of courance and 3 quarters of a pounde of raisons; strew your fruit all between your meat yt it may mix together; lay some sprigs of barberys upon ye top of the pye; then lay some butter upon it, and if you please put in some greene

[1] Sweet white fleshy tuberous vegetable with a delicate flavour and fragrance, very popular in medieval times; still grown in Scotland and known as crummocks.

goosberys, instead of barberys; so bake it, and when you draw it put in
a caudle of verjuce, suger, and a little butter; so serve it.

A Florindine of veale: Mrs Whiteheads Receipt

Take a fatt kidney of veal and parboyle it; when it is cold shred it small,
and put to it, nutmeg, suger, cinimon; cloves, mace, and a little salt; the
yolks of hard eggs chopt small; a few courance, 3 or 4 dates finely chopt;
crums of bread; 2 spoonefulls of rosewater, the juce of 2 oringes; 3 or
4 raw yolks of eggs; the marow of 2 or 3 bones; mingle all these together;
make puff past and put it in the bottome of a dish, which must be buttered;
cover it with past and bake it 3 quarters of an howre will bake it.

Pastys to frye of a kidney of veale: Leeches Receipt

after your veale is rosted cutt out ye kidney; with all the fatt that belongs
to it; when it is cold shred it very small as for mince-pyes; then season
it with about halfe a nutmeg grated, and a handfull of suger; and a little
salt; then plump two handfulls of courance, and when they are cold mix
them to ye rest of the things; then make them up in puff past and frye
them; to frye them put into your pan 2 pounde of tryed [rendered or
clarified] suet and make it as hott as you do for fish; then put them in, and
and turn ym once or twise; this quantity will make about 5 or 6 pastys.

A Calves-foot pye; or an humble-pye; My Lady Howes Receipt

Boyle the feet very tender, and peele them, and shred them very small;
season them with rosewater, suger, and nutmeg, a little Cinimon;
courance, and suet; according to ye quantity of feet; so put them in your
past; in like maner you may season the humbles of deere; you may shred
in the yolks of hard eggs; with some quartered dates and large mace.

A Tongue-pye: My Lady Howe's Receipt

Boyle a tongue very tender, and cutt it in thine slices ye bigness of your
thume; lay it in whitewine all night to steepe, then season it with nutmeg

[144]

cinimon, and suger; with a little salt, put in some raisons; marow, canded oringe or lemon peele; or letis-stalks [lettuce-stalks]; dates quartered; with what other sweetmeats you will; put in butter, and bake it; when you draw it liquor it with verjuce and suger.

A pig-pye: Mrs Whiteheads Receipt

Take your pig when it is scalded and opened; and cutt it into peeces not too bigg; season it with nutmeg, salt, and suger; then the pye being made and butter at the bottome, put in the pig, and upon it strew courance and raisons; large mace, sliced dates; preserved or pickled barberys; citron pill; and good store of butter one the top; then lid it, and set it in the oven; and when it is baked poure into it halfe a pinte of whitewine with the yolks of 3 eggs; and as much suger as will sweeten it, so serve it.

A French-pye: my second Cousen Clerks Receipt

Take sweetbreads of veale; lam stones, sheeps tongues, and tooters being first boyled tender and sliced thine like two-peny ribon; cocks combes boyled; pudings of veale seasoned with nutmeg, peper, and salt, beefe suet, and sweet herbes, and raw yolks of eggs, rowled like little sosiges [sausages] and some make roune ones; when you have made these sosiges boyle ye tongues and sweetbreads a little; slice ye sweetbreads in the midle, you may put in larkes, younge chickens, and pigions, a great many great oysters, marow as whole as you can take it out of the bones role it in the yolks of eggs to keepe it from melting; take also two chessnuts boyled and peeled; in ye season of the yeare take hartichoke [artichoke] bottoms boyled tender and quartered; season all this with nutmeg, peper, and a little slice of ginger and halfe a very little oynion, put in good store of butter, you may leave out nutmeg if you please, and put in large mace, you should larde the tongues, you may make ye pye of what form you please, when you put it into ye oven if it be a large pye put in a quarter of a pinte of whitewine, if it be but a little one then 3 or 4 spoonefulls will serve; that which is caled pudings of veale in ye begining of this receipt; is only sosiges made with some leane veale.

A Lumber pye: given me at hackney

Take a peece of rosted veale and mince it very small, then grate a peny lofe and put to it, then put in halfe a pounde of courance and a good spoone-full of sweet herbes, minced small, then take curd of a pinte of milke turned with eggs, then take two makeromes [macaroons] and 2 Lemons minced very fine, and one nutmeg grated and the same quantity of cinimon beaten finely, and six spoonfulls of rosewater, worke all these things well together like paste, then make it up in balls as big as eggs with a peece of marow in ye midle of each, then put them in a pye with a Lemon sliced, and halfe a pounde of butter, and six blades of mace and 12 quartered dates, then cover it and bake it, an howre and halfe will do it, when you draw it put in a caudle of verjuce, suger, and the yolks of eggs and butter.

A Lumber pye: my Lady Sheldons Receipt

Take a pounde of beefe suet finely minced, grated bread, sweet-majerome, savory, and a little penyroyall, shred all small, cinimon and nutmeg, beaten, halfe a pounde of courance and some suger, stir it all together, and make it into balls, and lay them close together in your pye, then take some sweetmeats as oringe, Lemon citron, slice them and barberys put some in, and some one the top of ye pye, with lumps of marow, so close it and bake it, and when you send it in beat rosewater suger vineger to-gether and poure it in and so serve it.

A Betaily-pye: my first Cousen Clerkes Receipt

Take foure tame pigions to bake; three ox pallets well boyled; peele them and cut them into little peeces; take also six lamstones; six sweetbreads of veale cut into halves; and parboyled; and 20 cock stones boyled and blanched; 4 hartichokes bottoms boyled tender; a pinte of oysters per-boyled; the marow of 3 bones; season it with nutmeg and salt; put these into fine past of what fashon you please; put in halfe a pounde of butter and a little water; and so lid it; let it stand in ye oven an howre and a halfe, when you draw it you may if you please liquor it with gravie; and ye juce of lemon; so serve it in.

[146]

A Hartichoake-pye: my Lady Sheldon's Receipt

Boyle your hartichokes [artichokes] very tender in ye beefe-pot; then laye ye bottoms in soake in whitewine; a little vineger and suger all night; the next day make a pye of good crust and lay butter at ye bottome; then laye in the bottoms; with marow, sliced dates, and sliced oringe, and citrons, and have eggs cutt into quarters, so lid it, and bake it when it is bakes put in a caudle of butter, and ye yolke, of an egge or two, with 2 or 3 spoonefulls of ye liquor the hartichokes were soaked in; and a little suger.

A Hartichoke-pye: given me at Hackney

Take the bottome of six hartichokes boyled; cut every bottome in 4 parts and season them with halfe an ounce of beaten cinimon, and a quarter of a pounde of suger mixed together; then laye them in ye pye with ye marow of 3 bones; dype the marow in the yolks of eggs being seasoned with the same cinimon and suger, put in also 12 quartered dates, and six ounces of canded Ringo-roote [Eringo]; and six blades of mace; one sliced lemon; and halfe a pounde of butter, so lid it and bake it, an howre and a halfe will do it; when you draw it put in a caudle of verjuce, and whitewine, and buter and suger, with the yolke of an egge; the same ingredients serves for a scarit [skirret][1] pye, or potato-pye.

A potato-pye; or any root-pye; My Lady Howes Receipt

Boyle your potatows almost tender peele them and lay them in past; put in the yolks of hard eggs, dates and marow; season it with a little cinimon beaten, and suger; and large mace; lay slices of butter at ye bottome of your pye and one ye top also; when it is baked put in a caudle of whitewine butter and suger; then set it in ye oven againe for a little while; so you may make any kinde of root-pye.

Egge pye: my Lady Sheldons Receipt

Take 12 eggs boyled hard, mince them very small with a pounde of beefe suet, then put into it a pounde of courance, halfe a pounde of suger, a

[1] See note 1, page 143.

quarter of a pinte of verjuce, a little sack oringe and Lemon peele canded, citterns and dates, salt and spice to your tast, mingle all very well together, and put it into past and bake it as you do mince pyes, you may also bake it in a dish wth puff past, or leave out the sweetmeats and dates if you do not like them.

Egge Tart: my Second Cousen Clerkes Receipt

Take six yolks of eggs, a little creame, beat them well; then melt a little butter, rose water, and suger, and a little muske stir in it; mix them well together; and put it into puff-past; bake it in a dish or patty-pann.

To make an Apple-pye to eat Hott

Take 3: pintes of water set it on the fire with some quine sliced very thine, and take as much scutcherneele [cochineal] beaten very small to pouder as will lye upon a shilling, tye it up in a bitt of muslin and put it to your water and quince, boyle them together till the quince be a little tender, then put in near halfe a peck of apples pared and quartered and let them boyle till a little tender keepeing them stired, but do not boyle them too tender, then poure it out into a puter [pewter] dish, and if there be any liquor left straine it out, and take out the scutcherneele also, mash the apples and quince pretty small, then cover your dish over with puff-past, and bake ye pye an hour or not quite so much, then serve it to the table buttered, and sweetened with good fine pouder suger; this way makes the apples looke of a charming red, you may if you please make it without quince in it.

An Apple Tart with Oringe: my Lady Sheldon's Receipt

Take either paremaines [pearmains] or John-aples, pare and quarter them, put a raisonable quantity of faire water to them; boyle them a while then put good store of suger, and a good deal of preserved oringe minced to them; let it boyle a good while till it is a very clear marmelet; with a little muske or amber-greece tyed up in a tifiny [tiffany]: before you take it up put into it ye juce of a lemon and the juce of a good many oringes; and a little rose or oringe flower water; when it is cold put it into fine thine past [paste] and cover it; ye tart must be rounde, you must not laye the stuff too neere ye edge for fear it fly open; wet ye edge with rose water close it and cutt it rounde with a rowell; as far as it is closed pick it with a knife, bake it upon flowred [floured] paper, and be sure you burn it not; eat it cold.

Aprecock, Apple, or Goosbery Tart with Creame: my Lady Sheldon

Take Codlings in summer, John Apples in winter, pare and quarter them; then rayse arounde tart and lay in ye aples in, one by one very thike; put one them a good deale of suger; then close it up, and bake it; then take it out of ye oven and cutt up ye cover; and laye it by till ye tart be don; poure into your tart about halfe a pinte or more (according as your tart is in bigniss) of custard-stuff just such as you make for custards; then set it in ye oven againe, and let it harden then draw it, and lay the cover upon it; and serve it cold; greene goosberys makes a good tart this way; and so doth likewise ripe aprecoks [apricots].

Plum, Raspe, or Grape Tarts—my Lady Sheldons Receipt

Take a quart of plums wipe them very cleane and slit them; then take halfe a pinte of creame put it into a skillit with ye plums; and let it boyle till the plums are all broke; and it be pretty thike stiring it all the while; whilst it is pretty hott strayne it, then put to it three eggs well beaten, a little ginger, rosewater; and suger to your tast; boyle it againe till it be thike still stiring it; then put it into a dish and when it is cold rayse a tart and put it into; cutt a cover, ice it and bake it; To Rasberys or grapes you must have 5 eggs; and if in the winter take a pinte of Creame and boyle it; then dissolve in it halfe a pounde of concerves of any of these fruits and put to it six eggs so doing as before.

A peach pye: my Lady Sheldons Receipt

Take your peaches and put them into scalding water, and when you may take of ye skins take them up; and then make your crust of good almond milke seething hott; make your pye 3 square put in the peaches; and season it with Cinimon; to 12 peaches put halfe a pounde of suger; and a good quantity of whitewine; so bake it an howre and serve it to ye table cold.

[149]

Almond Tart: My Lady Howes Receipt

Take halfe a pounde of suger, and halfe a pounde of almons, blanched and beaten small with rose water; a pinte of creame, ye Crum of a peny-lofe [bread] soaked in the Creame and small broken; mingle them together with the yolks of six eggs; and so bake them in a little fine past [paste].

for all sorts of possetts

DESSERTS

DESSERTS

───◦◦◉◦◦───

for all sorts of Creames, fooles, Sillybubs, posetts, Caudles and jellys, look for hear as followeth; to stew apples, and to bake apples; all maner of cheese-cakes: custards, and Almon Butter; for all sorts of Tansys and flantants; for all pancakes and fritters

To make Barly Creame. my Lady How's Receipt

Wash french Barly and boyle it, shifting the water till it does not dis-couller the water; then take your Barly out; and steepe it in new milke; let it boyle in the milk, till the milke be boyled from it againe. Then put in a good quantity of cream; some almons blanched and beaten small with a blade of *mace*; then let it boyle almost halfe hour, keeping it stiring that it burn not too; sweeten it with suger to your likeing; put in also a little Rose or oringe-flower water; if you please, you may strayne in ye almons with some of the cream.

To make Barly Creame my Lady How's Receipt

Take a nutmeg quartered and boyle it in a quart of creme; then put in a little Rose or oringe-flower water; and two spoonefulls of barly flower, sifted; boyle it a little in your creame, then put in the yolks of three eggs well beaten with some ambergreece [ambergris]. Then sweeten it. Let it not boyle after the eggs are in.

Rice Creame. My first Cousin Clerkes receipt: and also my Lady How

Take two spoonefulls of fine rice-flower [rice flour]; and three or four spoonefulls of fine suger. Mingle the flower and suger together; put it into a quart of good cream, and the yolk of an egg well beaten; and two or three spoonefulls of Rose or Oringe-flower-water. Mingle them all together; then stirr them on a quick fire; and when it begins to be thike enough, put it into your dish, stiring it till it be almost cold, that it may not creame on the top. It is best to make it overnight to eat the next day.

To make Lemon Cream: My first cousen Clerkes receipt

Set a quart of cream on the fire, stir it gently till it be bloud [blood] warme. Sweeten the juice and meat of three Lemons very sweet, and put to it a spoonefull of oringe-flower-water; you must make the Lemon juice so sweet that it may not turn the creame. then put it into the cream upon the fire, and when you thinke it is thike enough put it into your dish and eat it cold.

[155]

To make Lemon Cream. My First Cousin Clerkes receipt

Take four great Lemons, chip them very thine and shred the chipings and put to them the juce of the foure lemons; and so let them steepe 3 or 4 houres, or more; then take the whites of six eggs or more, and the yolks of three of them; beat them well together and put them to the juice and pills; with a porringer and halfe of faire water, and a quarter of a poringer of Rose or oringe-flower water; stir them well together, then strayne it thorow a cotten strayner, sweeten it with double refined suger; ading a little embergreece [ambergris] or muske. Then put it upon a chafen dish [chafing dish] of coals, stiring it continually till it be scalding hott, but not to boyle; so keep it over the coles till it be as thike as the best cream, then put it into your Dish and eat it cold. It will keepe 2 or 3 days. If you would have the jelly not yellow, then put in no yolks of eggs at all.

To make Lemon Cream. my second cousen Clerkes receipt

Take a quart of sweet creame boyled. Poure it into a vessall [vessel] to coole, keepeing it stiring gently till it be lukewarme then put in a good handfull of the best suger; and the juice of six lemons strayned, keeping it well stired till it be cold, ading more suger if need requires.

To make Lemon Cream. Mrs. Yorkes receipt

Take halfe a pinte of juice of lemons; and half a pinte of water. Then take 10 or 12 very small bits of lemon pill cutt very fine that the white be not left on just to give it a fine taste and no more; then boyle all this together a little while just to give it a tast; then sweeten it with fine suger being first strayned; then beat the yolks of 3 eggs and cool a spooneful of the liquer and put into them to thine them; then put it to the rest and set it on the fire and let it just thicken and just boyle. So serve it in, cold.

To make Lemon Cream: My Lady Sheldons receipt

Boyle a quart of cream with a blade of mace: when it is a little boyled quench it with the juice of lemons and coole it a little. Then, cast it into a cloath [cloth] and hang it to whay [whey]; when it is whayed have some almons finely beaten with rose or oringe-flower water and suger; then beat the curd and almons together; then lay into a dish first a row of cream and then off [of] curd, and so fill the dish; but let the cream be first and last.

To make Lemon Cream. My Lady How's Receipt

Take a quart of cream and boyle it; then put to it a spoonfull of grated lemon pill very fine and small; the yolks of six eggs well beaten, and let it boyle a little, always stiring it; then, take it off and stir it till it be almost cold, then squeeze in the juice of 2 lemons and sweeten it; stir it till it is cold that it may not skin on ye top.

A Lemon Caudle: My Lady Hows' Receipt

Take a poringerfull of water and the yoks of two eggs well beaten; then take a Lemon, cut of ye peele very thine, and mince it very small and put it into your water and eggs; and squeeze in ye juce of your Lemon. Then set it over ye fire and keepe it stiring yt it may not curdle; take it off and sweeten it.

A Lemon Caudle: My Second Cousen Clerke's Receipt

Take a pinte of springe water; and a pinte of Renish-wine [Rhenish wine]; or whitewine and 4 or 5 eggs; ye juce of 3 or 4 lemons; beat these well together and sweeten them to your tast; then slice in as much whitebread as you thinke will make it pretty thike; then set it over ye fire, and let it boyle leasurly at ye first for fear of curdling; afterwards as fast as you will till it be enough; some will make it with only water; but some wine is better.

To make Oringe Cream. My second Cousin Clerkes receipt

Take the juce of 5 oringes; and the yolks of three eggs, beat them very well; and put them to the juce, and when they are stired in well together put to them halfe a pound of fine suger or more. When the suger is dissolved strayne it through a lawne or tifiny [tiffany]; then set it over the fire till it be so thike you think it will jelly. You must not let it boyle; only keep it scalding hott. When it is enough poure it out and let it stand till it be cold.

To make a Cream of Oringes or Lemons or Gooseberys or White Courans Mrs. Frances Typings Receipt

Take the juce of a Lemon and make it very thike with suger. Then take a pinte of cream and set it on the fire and make it lukewarm for, if you make it hotter, it will turn; and if you put not suger enough into the juice 'twill turn nevertheless; take the cream off the fire and put in the juice with the suger and keep it a stiring for a good while; then beat it with your spoone till it riseth with a froath [froth[and be thike; then, put in some oringe-flower water of Ambergreece [ambergris] if you please; thus you may do with the juice of orinces, courants [currants] or Goosberys.

Quince Cream—very fine

Take a large quince and scald it prety tender, then pare it and mash all the clear part thereof and pulp it through a hair sive; then way [weigh] it and put to it like weight of double refined lofe suger beaten and sifted, and also the whites of two eggs well beaten. Then beat it all together with a wooden spoon untill it be as white as snow, then put it into little sawcers.

Quince Cream: My Aunt Rye's Receipt

Take a good pinte of cream; boyle it and thiken it with the yolks of six eggs; or the flower [flour] of rice; then, take it off the fire; and stir in it two ounces of marmalade; sweeten it to your taste. You may put in two or three spoonfulls of oring-flower water [orange flower water] if you please; and you may lay in ye bottom of the dish, slices of preserved quince; so, put it in your dish and when it is cold, you may stick it with citron.

Codling Creame. *My First cousen Clerke's receipt*

Take the codlings being very soft boyled in whitewine; slice them and rub them through a thin strayner with the back of a spoone; then, take a pinte of good cream, boyle it and thicken it with the yolks of three eggs. Whilst it is hot, put in the peels, having suger enough in it to sweeten it all; keepe it with continuall stirring till it is cold; if you please, put in some rose or oringe-flower water.

To make Eringoe Creame. *The Countiss of Desmon's Receipt*

Take a quarter of a pound of eringoe roots and a quart of the thikest cream; give them one boyle together, then take out your roots and beat them in a morter till they are very fine past [paste] then mingle it very well in your creame and boyle it till it be as thike as a custard when 'tis cold.

Goosbery Creame. *My First Cousen Clerke's Receipt*

Take a pinte of goosberys whilst they are green; put them into a skillet [dish] with a pinte and a halfe of water; so, gently scald them till they are tender then break them well with the water; and rub them through a thine strayner and boyle a quart of cream and thicken it with the yolks of six eggs; then put in your gooseberys, being sweetened with suger; let it stand over a gentle fire, keep it continuall stiring till you thinke it thike enough. Poure it out and eat it cold.

Gooseberys Cream: *My Second Cousen Clerke's receipt*

Take gooseberys before they are ripe and scald them in a jugg till they are soft; then worke them through a strayner and season them to your tast with suger, then take cream boyled and thickened with an egg or two, and when it is cold mix them together; thus you may make cream of Rasberys; but strayne them raw into ye cream.

Goosbery, Raspbery, Mulbery; or Courant [Currant] Cream. *Second cousen Clerke's Receipt*

Boyle your cream with mace; and thicken it with beaten Almonds and let it boyle a little; then sweeten it to your tast, and when it is cold, strayne your fruit into it.

Gooseberry Cream, without cream in it

Take a quart of the greenest gooseberrys, top and taile them and put them into as much water as will just cover them. Boyle them all to mash, then run it thro' a sive with a spoon, and to a pinte of the pulpe you must have three eggs well beaten, and whilst the pulpe is hott put into it halfe an ounce of Butter. Sweeten it to your tast and put in the eggs and stir it over a gentle fire till it grow thick, then set it by and when 'tis almost cold put into it one spoonfull of the juce of spinage, and a spoonfull of orange-flower water. Stir it well together, put it into little glaces [glasses] and serve it cold to table. *Note.* The juce of spinage is to make it look green, but it being apt to give a little tast, care must be taken not to put in too much thereof.

Goosbery foole: My Lady How's Receipt

Take two quarts of goosberrys before they are full growne; scald them very tender and bruise them very small; the water being first drayned from them. Drye it a little on a chafin dish [chafing dish] of coles [coals]. Then put in the yolks of 3 eggs; and sone [some] creame and the white of one egge; then let them boyle till they be enough. Sweeten it to your tast.

To cook Gooseberys. My Lady How's Receipt

Put two quarts of gooseberys with 2 or 3 spoonfulls of Rose or oring-flower-water and a good quantity of suger in a skillit; boyle them to mash, stiring them all the while; being all broken, take halfe of them out; and stir to it the yolks of 2 or 3 eggs; a little sweet butter or creame instead of eggs and butter; you may eat it either hott or cold.

Apple Cream. My Second Cousen Clerke's Receipt

Take pipins quartered and cored; set them to stew with a little rose water and faire water tell they are tender; then boyle a pinte and a half of cream, and when it is boyled put in the whites of three eggs well beaten with rose or oringflowers water and suger. Then lay the apples in a dish with sippits about it; poure the cream on and eat it cold; or you may strayne the Apples and Cream into a Coffin of past [paste] and bake it as a custard.

[160]

Cherry Cream: My Second Cousen Clerke's Receipt

Scald the cherrys with suger and a little water till they are soft; then, when they are cold; lay them into the bottome of the basin and boyle some cream and thicken it with yolks of eggs; and when it is almost cold; poure it over your cherrys: mix with your cream some rose or oringflower water; sweeten it to your tast.

Courant Creame: My Lady How's Receipt

Take a pinte of thike cream; put to it three spoonsfulls of the juce of red courants [currants]; or Raspes [raspberries]; Sweeten it to your tast, then whypt [whip] it with a whiske, and, as the froarth [froth] riseth take it off and lay it in your dish; if you please you may put in the white of an egg; before you begin to whypt it, to make the froarth rise the better.

Rasbery Creame. Mrs. Whiteheads' receipt

Boyle ye Raspes [raspberries] with suger to take away ye rawness; strayne them into thike creame and season it with suger to your likeing.

To make Grape Creame: The Lady Desmon's Receipt

Take grapes and pill them and stone them, then take halfe a pinte of very strong pipin water and take the weight of suger to the weight of water, boyle it together, then scume [skim] it, then put in your grapes and boyle them till the grapes be sweetened and the sirup thike, then let it stand till it be almost cold then put to it as much creame as you thinke fitt and boyle it, and if you please you may put in a little ambergreece [amber-gris] and so eat it.

Almond Cream: My First Cousin Clerkes Receipt

Take a good handfull of blanched Almonds: beat them very well with rose-water; then take a pinte of good cream; boyle it; take it off the fire, and put in your Almonds; with a blade or two of mace; sweeten it, put in some rosewater, set it on the fire; let it boyle till it be thike enough; stir it often. Eat it cold.

To make Almond Cream. My Aunt Rye's receipt

Boyle a pinte of cream with a blade of mace, thiken it with eggs well beaten, either yolks or whites, sweeten it, put in halfe a pound of blanched almons beat well with rosewater; then stir them well in the cream; let it not boyle after the almons are in. Dish it out and eat it cold.

Almond Cream. My Lady Sheldons Receipt

Boyle some cream and have some almonds finely beaten; and boyle them in the cream with a blade of mace and suger to your taste; strayne it and stir it till it is almost cold. Eat it.

Almon foole My Lady Hows Receipt

Boyle a quart of Creame with a nutmeg quartered and sweeten it with fine suger; let it boyle half an hour or more; take it off and stir it till it be almost cold; beat ye yolks of eggs very well; blanch a quarter of a pound on Almons in could water; beat them very small with a little cold water; strayne them with some of the boyled creame and beat them several times and strayne them againe; and so do till the strength of them be quite out; so mingle ye eggs and creame together and let it stand over a slow fire till it be prety thik, then dish it.

Almond flumery

Make a very strong jelly of Calves Ffeet, and take an ounce of almonds and beat very fine with a little Sack; then put them into your jelly-bag, and squeeze it through until your jelly is as white as you would have it, then season it with juce of lemon and 2 spoonfulls of Sack; sweeten it to your likeing with fine suger, and grate into it a little lemon peele; and when it is cold, cutt it into slices and so serve it.

To make Snow Cream: My Lady Sheldons receipt

Take 3 pintes of cream, the whites of 7 or 8 eggs; some oringeflower water and as much suger as will sweeten it; mix them together and strayne it;

then take a stick as big as a child's arme, cleave one end of it across and widen it with your finger. Beat the cream with this stick or a bundle of reeds tyed together; and roule it between your hands standing upright in the cream; then as the snow riseth, with a spoone put it into a collender that the thin may run from it; when you have soficiently done having enough of the snow; take the cream that is left and boyle it in a skillet; put thereto whole cloves, a stick of cinemon [cinnamon], a little ginger brused: boyle it till it is thike; then strayne it; when it is cold put it into a dish and lay the snow upon it.

To make Snow

Take a pinte of thike cream and put therein 4 pieces of lofe suger a little *iseing-glace* [isinglass], and a little lemon peele. Let it stand half an hour, then, whipp it with a whiske and skim off ye bubbles as they rise, into a dish or glass and so it will stand 3 or 4 hours.

To make Snow Cream: My Lady How's Receipt

Take a quart of cream and steep a little mace in it, and having seasoned it a little with some lofe suger and a little rose or oringe flower water; beat 4 or 5 egg whites till they run like water with a little milk in them to keep them from froathing; then put them in the cream; and let them just boyle up; then, as fast as you can, poure it into your dish; and when it is cold lay some thike snow one it made with whites of eggs; spread it all over, and scrape if you will, some suger over it.

To make Whypt Sillibubs. My Lady How's Receipt

Take a pinte of cream and a pinte of whitewine and a glasse of sacke [sack] and a little oringe-flower water; The white of three eggs, a peece of Lemon pill [peel]; sweeten it to your tast, then mingle some milke and whitewine in the bottome of your glaces [glasses] about a quarter full; then, with a twige of whiske whypt [whip] your cream, and as the froath riseth scum [skim] it off; and lay it in your glasses upon ye milk and whitewine. Beat the whites of the eggs and suger together a little first before you mix in the other things [ingredients].

To make a Whypt Sillibub My Lady Sheldons' Receipt

Take 2 quarts of thike creame and put to it one quart of whitewine the juce of 2 lemons, with suger to your tast: stir it well together in a large tray; then whyp it with a whisk, and, as ye froath riseth, take it off with a spoon, and put it into ye Sillibib-pot; to continue whiping till it is all froath, and put it into ye pot; then let it stand 12 or 16 houres before you eat it.

To make a sillibub My Lady Hows' Receipt

Take a quart of creame and a pinte of milk and boyle them. Then put into your sillibub pot a pinte of whitewine and a glass of Sack with ye juce of one lemon. Sweeten it then poure in your creame stiring all the while. Then let it stand four houres; or you may make it in ye morning and eat it at night; you must let your creame be as cold as milke from ye cowe before ye mix it with ye wine.

A sillibub. My Lady Sheldons' Receipt

Take a quarter of a pinte of whitewine, steepe in it all night a little nut-meg and cinimon [cinnamon] and a little inner peele of a Lemon; next morning put in a skiming dish of creame; so milke it up with milke from ye cowe; and eat it at night.

A Whypt Cream. My Second Cousin Clerke's receipt

Take 7 or 8 spoonfulls of thike cream, halfe as much Sack and a little suger and so whypt it three houres and lay it in your glaces [glasses].

A Fine Cream; churned. My Lady How's receipt

Take thike cream, season it with oring-flower water and suger and a little mace; put it into a glasse churn and churn it till the butter be redy to come; but not to let it come to any butter; put it into a dish and serve it.

To make the Blanch Cream: my First Cousen Clerke's Receipt

Take a pinte of the thickest cream you can gitt; season it very well with Rose or oringe-flower water; boyle it; then, take the whites of ten eggs, take the treads [threads] out and beat them with a little cold cream; When your cream is upon the fire and boyling up, then put in your eggs, stiring it till it comes to a thike curd; then take it up and passe it through a haire strayner, then beat it with a spoone till it be cold.

Long Biskit Cream. My Aunt Rye's Receipt

Take a role of Bisket [sponge fingers] and break it in thine peeces; then take a pinte of cream and boyle in it a blade of mace, thicken it with the yoks of eight eggs well beaten; put in 3 spoonfulls of Sack and 2 of Rose or oring-flower water; sweeten it to your likeing, when you take it from the fire, poure it on the Bisket, and let it stand tell it be cold without stiring.

To make a Piremide with Cream. My Second Cousen Clerke's

Take a quart of water; and six ounces of heartshorn [hartshorn], put it into a bottle with some gumdragon; and gum-Aribeck [gum arabic]; of each as much as a nutt; corke ye bottle close, and boyle in in a pott three houres; then take as much cream as there is jelly: beat halfe a pound of Almons with some Rose or Oring-flower water; beat them very small, then strayne ye cream and Almons till you thinke all is gotten out of ye Almons, then put ye jelly when it is cold into a bason; and the cream to it; sweeten to your likeing; ading a graine or two of muske or ambergreece. Set it on ye fire, stiring it continually and scuming it till it be scalding hott; but let it not boyle, then poure it into an old fashon drinking glase [glass]; standing so till it be cold; and when you would use it hold the glase in a warm hande, and loosen it with a knife and place it upright in a dish; and serve it either in cream or without; the pot you boyle your jelly in must be bigger by a pinte than you use it for or else it will breake; you had better boyle your jelly in a pott; then in a bottle.

Clouted Cream: My Lady Sheldon's Receipt

Take foure quarts of new milk hott from the Cowe; set it over a coale fire in a pan of earth; when it is ready to boyle put in a quart of cream: then take coals from the bottome; and so let it stand twelve houres; then slice it out and strew suger betweene it.

Clouted Cream: My First Cousen Clerke's Receipt

Take two gallons of new milk; and make it scalding hott; then put it into 4 or 5 pans, and let it stand till it cream all over. Then take a plate with holes and lay it over a dish; take your cream as whole as you can and lay it round upon the plate; between every one of the creams strew lofe suger; And Rose Water; then, heat your milke againe; and againe; till it be as thike as you would have your dish.

Spanish Cream. My Lady Sheldon's Receipt

Scald your mornings milk and set it in a pan as for clouted cream; when it hath stood as long as that cream rest to do scume [skim] it off; and put it into a bason; and beat it till it begins to be thike; you may make it thiker or thiner, as you please; not too thike is best; sweeten it with Sirrop of Aprecocks [apricots], or suger; and so serve it.

Spanish Creame: Mrs Duncombs Receipt

Take two quarts of creame and boyle it with mace and cinomon, and keepe it with stiring on the fire as it boyles for a quarter of an hower, and then poure it into two milke-pans and stir it once rounde; and let it stande from the morning till the next day at Diner; then take the creame that is on the top off it, and put it into another pan, and season it according to your tast with orange-flower water and suger, and so whip it with a whiske till it be thike, then putt it on a silver salver in spoonefulls, and it will keepe in single spoonefulls without runing together; so serve it to table; some will put in a spoonefull of Sack with ye orange flower water, but that will be apt to make it turn to butter.

A French Cream. My Lady Sheldon's Receipt

Set your cream and milke as for clouted cream; then take out the clouts and put them into a bason; season it with suger and Rose or Oringeflower-water wherein muske hath been steeped; beat it all together with a spoone; and when it is thike put it in a dish; You must keep one bolde [piece] of the clouted cream whole to lay on the top; poure raw cream rounde about and so serve it.

To make a trifle. My Lady Sheldon's Receipt

Take Cream with a blade of mace and put it in a skillit, put to it suger and Rose or Oringflower-water to your tast; make it bloud warme; then strayne it and put a little runett [rennet] to it; cover it and serve it cold.

To make a trifle. My Second Cousen Clerkes' and Mrs Harisons'

Take Stroakings [milk] and boyle it with mace, or what spice you might like. Sweeten it with fine suger, and put in some Rose or Oringflower water. When it is almost cold put in a little Sack and a little rennet not too much, and so, let it stand till it sets; before you put in your runet, put it in ye thinge you will serve it in either dish or bason; if you will you may cutt it out into great spoonfulls and put it into cream: it will eat richly; take out the spice before the runet goes in.

To make a whitewine possit. My Lady Sheldons Receipt

Take a quart of whitewine and a pound of Suger, boyle it and scime [skim] it; then take 2 quarts of thike creame and boyle it in an other skillit; when they are both boyleing put them together into a bason, cover it close with a dish, wraping a blankit about it; so let it stand neere ye fire three houres; by that time it will come like a possit; so serve it.

A Possit without Milke or Creame: My Lady Sheldons Receipt

Take a pinte and halfe of Sack and halfe a pinte of ale; and three quarters of a pound of suger; set it on the fire and when it boyles, scime it; then take it off ye fire and let it stand till it be cold; then set it on a coald fire and take thirty eggs, (whites and yolks) well beaten; let them run through a cleane cloth into ye skillit, continually stiring it untill it is thike; then poure it into a bason and serve it.

To Make a possit without milke; My Lady Sheldons Receipt

Take halfe a pound of Almons, blanch them and beat them very small with, now and then a spoonfull of fayre water. When they are very small rub them through a strayner with a pinte of Sack and 2 spoonfulls of Rose or oringe flower water; sweeten it with suger, put into it a little nutmeg; set it the fire. When it is hott, put into it ye yolks of 4 eggs and one white well beaten; let it stand on ye fire and give it one stir; and let it boyle a little yt the curd may be hard enough; then take it off ye fire and strew suger on ye side of ye bason and serve it.

A sack posset: My Lady How's Receipt

Take the whites of six eggs and beat them with a whiske till it is like snow; now and then strewing in some suger with ambergreece, then take halfe a pinte of Sack, and as much alle; sweeten it and let it be bloud warme; take a quart of creame boyling hott, sweeten it and poure it to your eggs and liquor; give it a stur, and cover it very close. This will make it thine in the bottome, curd in ye middle and snow on ye top, and if it be too cold before you eat it it will be tuff.

To make a posit like a custard: Mrs Bornford's receipt

Take 3 pintes of Creame and one pinte of Sack; 18 eggs. Mix your eggs, Sack and Suger together. Sweeten to your likeing and slice in a little nut-meg. Heat your Sack and eggs together scalding hott keepeing it stiring all the while; let your creame just boyle and so poure it on ye Sack being boyleing hott; hold up your creame on high and set your bason with ye Sack on the grounde; and as soon as ye creame is in set it on a few coles [coals] of a very soft fire for a quarter of an houre, or rather more, being covered, you must not stir it all lest you breake ye curd.

To make a possit. Lady Sheldon's Receipt

Take halfe a pinte of sack and as much ale; as much suger as you thinke
will sweeten it; set it on ye fire in a bason, when it is warme poure into
it a quart of cream boyleing from the fire; and have redy six whites of eggs
beaten with a whiske to a perfict snow; with a little rose or oring-flower
water and suger; and, at ye instant you poure in ye creame strike in the
eggs with the whiske; stir it once about in takeing it off ye fire; and so
serve it; if it be too cold before you eat it; it will be tuff; if it be right made
it will be snow on ye top, thike in the midle, and clear liquor at ye bottome; you may just put in a little ambergreece if you please.

The Popes Possit: My Lady Sheldons Receipt

Take a pound of Sweet Almons blanch and beat them in a stone morter
till it be as fine that it will spread between your fingers like butter; in the
beating put a spoonfull of fayre water or as you see occation to keep them
from oyleing; then put them into a cleane skillit with a quart of fayre
water, and stir it continually till it boyles and grows thike; then, have
ready upon a chafin dish of coles in a bason half a pinte of Sack or some-
what more; and a little ale, and halfe a pound of suger (or according to
your tast) when this liquor is scalding hott, poure ye almons into it
boyling off ye fire; stir it together and serve it.

Fresh Cheese and Creame. My Lady Howe's Receipt

Take as much cream as you will, and put in so much runet [rennet] as will
make it turn like cheese but very tender; when it is come, hang it up in a
cloath that the whay may run from it; beat the curd in a morter with
Rose or oringeflower-water and suger; then put it into a coullender that
the moisture may run from it; then laye it in a dish and put creame and
suger to it.

To make French curds: My Second Cousen Clerkes and
Mrs. Jacksons

Take a quart of cream and a pinte of new milk, and five egg yolks and
whites beaten very well; put them all together and sweeten it with fine

[169]

suger according to your tast: set it over the fire and let it scald, tell you see ye Creame turn; and, when it is come to a tender Curd take it off the fire, and whay it through some tin moulds in what shapes you fancy, and when they are well setled and could turn them out into a dish and serve it up with creame and suger.

Jelly of Heartshorne. *My Mothers Receipt*

Take two quarts of water and put into a pipkin well glazed; put to it a quarter of a pound of Harts-horne [hartshorn], and one race of ginger, and a nutmeg, sliced, and a little mace. Let these boyle very leasurely till it comes to a pinte; then strayne it and put in ye juce of two Lemons and sweeten it according to your tast with fine lofe suger: and when your suger is melted let it run through your Strayner againe into a silver or earthen thinge; you must keepe it in a coole place and when you serve it lay some Lemon peele at ye bottome of your dish; and ye jelly upon it in careless lumps.

Hearts-Horne Jelly. *Mrs Whiteheads Receipt*

Take a bottle and put into it six ounces of Harts-horne [hartshorn]; a quart and a half a pinte of spring water; stop it [stopper it] and tye it up cloase then let it boyle in a pott of water full 5 houres; then strayne it and put into it ye juce of 3 good Lemons and half a pound of refined suger (and if you like it, a stick of cinimon), let it run through the jelly bag againe.

A rare Harts-Horne Jelly: *given me by Burgise*

Take a Harts-horne halfe a pound and put to it one gallone of spring water, let it boyle modirately fast till there be not above three pintes left; then strayne it throw a sive and let it settle; then peare away all the *clearest*, and put to it the juce of foure Lemons, and a peece of Lemon pill [peel]; also a little mace, a little cinimon and a nuttmeg quartered; and as much lofe suger as will sweeten it to your likeing; then sett it over some clear coals in a silver bason or a silver skillett; and when it is redy to boyle, put in the whites of 8 eggs well beaten, and let it boyle a pretty while not scumeing [skimming] it. Then take it off, and run it altogether 2 or 3 times thorow a thike jelly Bagg; then put it into cheny cups [cheney cups] or glaces as you please; if you would have it extreordnery clear you must have the whitest and largest Harts-horne you can gitt.

If you would have your jelly of Harts-horne off severall coulers you must, when you have gott it redy to the sweetening, instead of the lofe suger put in sirrup of clovegilliflower enough to sweeten it and couller it to your likeing; which will make it a fine red: and for blue, sweeten another part of it with sirrup of violets, which will give it a fine couller; and for yellow you may dye it with saffarn [saffron] as yellow as you would have it; when you have finished your jelly take Lemon pills [peels] cutt in halves; take out all the meat very cleane, and whilst your jelly is hott poure it into the pills till you have filled the halves; and so let them stand till they are cold; then cutt them into quarters, the jelly and pills together, and laye them on a silver server, and the severall coullers mingled one among the others will look very finely in ye lemon pills; but when you have not pills enow [enough], you may put your jelly into glaces and the severall coullers will looke well throuw them also.

Note That in the above said jelly of Hearts-Horne, the whites of eggs must be put in at the same time with the suger, spice and lemon juce, while the jelly is cold, before you set it on the fire for boyleing; also it must be kept keeleing and stiring all the while 'tis on the fire till you take it off to run it thro' the jelly Bagg.

To make Leech. *My Lady Hows Receipt*

Take 2 ounces of iseing-glass [isinglass] sliced into water and let it lye an houre before you use it; take halfe a pound of Almons beaten with Rose or Oringe flower water; boyle the iseing glase in a quart of milke till it be disolved with nutmeg sliced; a stick of Cinimon and a little mace; then stir in your almons and let it boyle awhile; then strayne it and sweeten it with lofe suger to your taste, then strayne it again, and let it be cold. Then cutt it out in slices and serve it.

To make Chocolate Creame: *Newtons Receipt*

Take a pinte of sweet creame just boyle it up then take it off ye fire and put to it 2 ounces of chocolate, stir it well with ye chocolate stick till ye chocolate be all disolved and mill it a little with the stick, then set it over the fire and let it just boyle up, take it off ye fire and stir it about with the chocolate stick for some time, but not mill it for fear of its turning to butter, then put in it the yolks of 2 or 3 eggs beaten in 2 or 3 spoonefulls of raw creame stir them well in and set it over ye fire again just to give it one little boyle, then take it off and put in as much fine suger as will sweeten it to your tast then keele it out of one pott into another ten or 12 times one after another, holding it high as you do it that it may froath as you do it, when so don poure it leasurely into your cheny bason holding it as high from ye bason as you can that so it may lye with a great froath all over it, let it stand till it get cold before your eat it and just before you send it to table, whip up a little raw creame with some chocolate in it and ye white of an egg; you may also put a little suger to it, and as you whip it take of ye fraoth to lay upon your creame just as you send it to table.

To Make Black-Caps

Take John apples and cutt them in the midle, core them, but do not pare them; then laye them single in a puter [pewter] dish, and take some candied oringe pill cutt very small and strew it amongst them; and also a little rose or oringe-flower-water, strew in some suger; and then set it into the oven and bake it with white bread, serve ym in hott.

To Stew Apples

Take about 12 paremains [pearmains], pare, core, and cutt them in halves, then laye them in a puter dish, and take foure quinces boyled very tender; pare them and slice them thine; and mix them with ye apples; then put in a little rose-water and ale, and a little suger; then stew them upon a chafindish of coles [coals], till they are tender; then put to them a slice of fresh butter.

To Stew apples: Mrs Brownes Receipt

Take pipins and pare them and cutt them in halves, and put them in cold water; then take to a pounde of suger; a pinte of whitewine; and a pinte of water; make it a sirop and scume it well; then put in the apples and let them boyle very fast; and when they are halfe boyled put in ye juce of a

[172]

lemon; and a little of ye peele; but you must not let the peel lye long in it; when ye sirrop begineth to be thike put in a little ambergreece; and shake it all together; so take them up, and let them stand untill they are cold; then laye the jelly in lumps upon them and so serve them in.

To Make Cheese-cakes: Leeches Receipt

Take 2 gallons and a halfe of new milke and make it into a very tender curd; then take almost a quart of creame, and 1 pounde of courance [currants] washed cleane, mix them with ye curd, and creame, grate in a nutmeg, and put in a pounde of butter cut in little bitts; then put in the yolks of 5 or 6 eggs—and six spoonfulls of Rose-water; sweeten it according to your tast; put them into puff past:—it is much better to beat the curd and butter together in a stone morter.

To Make Cheese-cakes: my Aunt Rye's Receipt

Take ye Curd of Creame before it is too hard come; and drayne it very leasurely; then hang it up; have some almons redy beaten with a little sack; boyle them awhile in some good Creame, beat ye curd in a morter— with some butter; then put in some grated bread yt [that] has been dryed; and put in cloves, mace, and suger to your tast; and some courance [currants] yt hath been heated over the fire; mix all together with some yolks of eggs; for ye Crust take some butter not salted, and beat it very well, and rub it in drye flower as hath a little suger in it; put in also some rosewater and eggs, and so beat it well together.

To make Cheese Cakes off Egg Curd

Take three pintes of new milke and when it boyles up, put in 12 eggs whites and yolkes being well beaten, stir the milke and eggs together upon the fire till it come to a curd, and when it is so take it off ye fire and let ye whay run from it thro a cullender, and when it is well drayned from all the whay, beat it by a little at a time in a marble morter with halfe a pound or more of butter, then grate in halfe a nuttmeg, and put to it halfe a pinte of cream, the yolks of 5 eggs well beaten, with 5 spoonfulls of rosewater, put in as much suger as will sweeten it to your tast, and halfe a pound of curants stiring it well together: put in also with the rosewater two spoonfulls of oringe flower water.

Orange Cheese-cakes, with a past for them

Take halfe a pound of blanched almonds beat them very fine wth oringe flower water to keep them from oyleing, take halfe a pound of fine suger beat and sifted, then melt a pound of Butter and let it be almost cold before you use it, beat the yolks of twelve eggs and the whites of four very well; take two canded oringe pills, or raw oringe pieles with the bitterness boyl'd out, beat ye peeles in a morter as fine as possible, then mix altogether; The past [paste] for your cheesecakes make as followeth— take a pound of the finest flower and three ounces of the finest suger; then worke with your hands half a pound of butter till it cometh to a froath, and then put into it by degrees the flower and suger, and worke it together with the yolks of three eggs and the whites of two, if it be too limber [supple] a past put in more flower and suger till it be fitt to role out: If you please to Ice your cheese-cakes gitt in redyness some fine suger beat up with the white of an egg as thike as you can, and as soon as they come out of ye oven Ice them all over, and then set them in ye oven again to harden: this same past will serve to lay over fine puddins.

To Make Custards: my Aunt Franckline's Receipt

Take a quart of creame and a nutmeg quartered, and some whole cinimon, boyl ye creame with the spice a pretty while; then take 12 eggs and leave out 8 of the whites, beat your eggs very well; and when ye creame is prety coole put your eggs in, and stir it together very well and then strayne it, and fill your dishes, bake them in an oven not too hott; you must sweeten it to your tast wn. ye eggs go in.

To Make Lemon Custard: my second Cousen Clerke's Receipt

Take the juce of a large Lemon or 2 little ones; and twice or thrise as much water as juce; sweeten it with suger to your likeing; take ye yolke of one egge, and the white of two, mix it together and boyle it up as you do a foole.

To make Orange Butter, pistacia Butter, and Almond butter

Take the yolks of five hard Eggs, a pound of Butter, a little fine suger, and a spoonfull of oringe flower water, then worke it all through a sive;

you may make Almond, and pistacia [pistachio] Butter the same way having first blanched and beaten them small.

To make an Almond Custard: the Lady Desmon's Receipt

Take a quart of creame, boyle it wth whole mace and a nuttmeg cutt in quarters, then have redy a quarter of a pound of Almonds blanched and beaten very fine wth a little creame to keepe them from oyleing; and when your creame is boyled and cold againe strayne them and put in also the yolks of 8 eggs and suger to your tast, so fill your dishes and bake them; or if you please you may put it all into a puter [pewter] dish and set it over a pott of boyleing water covering your dish close wth another and as the steame riseth on ye top of the dish take it often off and dry it; and if you like it you may if you please strew in by digrees two handfulls of curans having some at ye bottom of your dish first; and the rest strew in as it hardens, so let it stand on ye boyleing water, till it be enough baked which it will be over the water (if it be kept boyleing) as well as if it ware in an oven.

To make Almond Butter: the Lady Desmond's Receipt

Take a quart of creame and a quarter of a pound of Almonds blanched, beat them fine with a little of the creame to keep them from oyleing, then strayne them into the creame and let it boyle, then put in the yolks of ten eggs well beaten and let it boyle till it curdles, then put it into a cloath and let the whay run from it, then take it out of the cloath and season it with rose, or oringe flower water, and suger to your tast, bruise it with a spoone that it may looke smooth.

To make Almond Butter

Blanch a pound of jordin almonds in cold water, and as you do them throw them into fair water, then beat them very fine with some rose or orange flower water to keep them from oiling, then take a pound of fresh Butter out of the churn before 'tis salted, but it must be well washed, mix it with your almonds with near a pound of double refined lofe suger beaten and sifted, and when it is very well mixed set it to coole, and when you are

[175]

going to use it put it into a colander and pass it through with the back of a spoon into the dish you serve it in, you must hold your hand high and let it be heaped up.

A Tansy: my second Cousen Clerkes Receipt

Take tenn eggs, leave out halfe ye whites, beat them very well, green it with spinage, or wheat juce; put in a little juce of tansy to give it a tast; and put in above halfe a pinte of good Creame; halfe a nutmeg grated; suger to your tast, 2 or 3 spoonfulls of grated bread, and as much flower; frye it and serve it up with ye juce of an oringe, suger, and butter if you please; some will bake a tansy.

A Tansy: Mrs Lords Receipt

Take 26 eggs leaveing out 8 of the whites, beat them extreamly well, put to them a grated nuttmeg, a pound of lofe suger finely beaten, a pinte and halfe of thike creame, and a great poringerfull of the juce of spinage wth a little tansy stamped with it, mix all these together with two spoonfulls of rose water then strayne it, grate not your nuttmeg in till after you have strayned it, then put it into a skillet and set it over a gentle fire stiring it only one way when it begins to thiken put into it a peece of butter as big as two wallnutts, then keepe it stiring till it be thike enough to lye together, then put it into a dish that is very well buttered and patt it downe smooth in the dish with a spoon, then cover it close and set it over some gentle coales and so let it stand till you thinke it be hard enough, then turne it out upon a pye-plate and serve it wth slices of Lemons on it, this way of doing a tansy in a dish is much better than fryeing of them; you may do any tansy so if you please, this quantity will make a very large tansy, except it be for a great company halfe this quantity is enough for a good hansome tansy.

A White Tansy: my second Cousen Clerkes Receipt

Take 16 eggs with but 2 or 3 of ye whites; beat them very well and put to them halfe a pinte of Creame; 2 spoonfulls of rose-water, and some grated nuttmeg; suger to your tast; then frye it with butter; but do not stir it in ye pan as you do a green tansy; you must remember to put in 2 little handfulls of grated bread into your Creame and eggs.

[176]

An Apple Tansy: my Aunt Rye's Receipt

Take about 12 apples or more, pare, core, and slice them thine; and with a little rosewater set them astewing, put in also a little sack; let them stand till they are very tender, then strayne them through a pulping-sive, that no strings be left in them; then beat ten egge whites and all very well; mix them together and put in some grated bread, and halfe a pound of suger; a pinte of creame; and some juce of spinage, or wheat; to make it greene; mix all well together and frye it with butter; this will bake as well for a puding.

An Apple Tansy: Mrs Whitehead's Receipt

Pare your apples and slice them very thine, and frye them in sweet butter till they are very soft; then take the yolks of 5 eggs, and 2 whites, beat them well and put in a little nutmeg; spread the apple abroade in ye pan, and poure the eggs over them; when it is a little hardened turn it one a plate, and frye it a little more.

A Flantant: my first Cousen Clerke

Take 3 soft apples pare them, and slice them in cakes very thine; beat 3 or 4 eggs very well and put to them; then put in ye pan and frye it like a pan-cake, and so serve it with some suger one it; some loves sawce with it, which if you make let it be a pretty deal of vineger, or verjuce, and grated nutmeg, and good store of suger, being warmed together poure it one.

Curd puffs to ffrye

Take of curd a quart and let it drayne through a sive from the whay, then beat it in a morter with a halfe a pound of butter, then mix with it six yolks of Eggs and two whites, grate in the peele of one Lemon, some nutt-meg, mace and cinamon beat fine, some rose water, a little suger, and a little flower, mixe all well together, then role them in flower about ye bigness of wallnutts and frye them: your sauce must be melted butter with a little sack, oringe flower water and suger, so serve them.

[177]

To Make pan-cakes: Mrs Whiteheads Receipt

Take a pinte of creame and the yolks of ten eggs; and ye white of two; foure spoonfulls of sack; and 2 of rose water, a little nutmeg grated; beat all these together with a little flower very thine; the pan must first be rubbed with a little butter, and after dryed with a cleane cloath; before you put in your stuff; make your pan very hott otherwise they will heave [rise] too light; and not bake so well; you may frye ym with butter, or without.

Rice pancakes: My Lady Howe's Receipt

Take some rice and boyle it prety tender, and a pinte of creame, the yolks of foure eggs; (well beaten) two or three spoonfulls of yeast, some flower, a little sack, cinimon, and suger; put these together, and set it by the fire a little; then frye them as other pancakes; and scrape suger over them.

Oatemell pancakes: my second Cousen Clerke's, given by Mrs Jackson

Take a pinte of new milke and let it boyle, then take half a pinte of half grates [groats] pick them cleane, and put them in an earthen pan; and when ye milke boyles poure it one ye oatemell; and cover it very close and let it stand an houre; then take nyne eggs and leave out the whites of three; (beat them very well) then take halfe a pinte of creame and put to ye eggs, beat them well together, and put them to foure spoonfulls of whitewine; and one spoonfull of suger; one nuttmeg, 2 small races of ginger; mix all together and beat them well together; then put in a good handfull of flower; and beat it all together, frye your pancakes with butter, and turn them with your pye-plate; if you please you may squeeze some oringe over them; and scrape suger on them; season them with salt to your tast.

To make ffritters

Beat six eggs whites and all with a spoonfull of yest, and 2 or 3 spoonfulls of sack, then grate in a race of ginger and some nuttmeg, put to it a pinte of milke, then put in as much fine flower as will make it a thin batter, and sweeten it to your tast, and when you are redy to frye them, mix in it a good quantity of choped apples, or if you like it better dip in only some rowne [round] slices of Apples into the batter, frye them in tryed Beef suet.

for ffrench=bread, wiggs and bunns

BREAD

BREAD

for french-bread, wiggs and bunns

Trencher-Bread: my Lady Jones Receipt

Take to 3 pounde of flower, six eggs, and six spoonfulls of very good east [yeast]; mix them together; then take halfe a pounde of butter and put it into some milke; and set it over the fire; and let it stand till it be melted; then set it acooleing till it is as cold as water for other bread; then put it into your flower and mix it together; and make them up; your oven must not be too hott; halfe an howre will bake them; you must put a little salt into the flower.

French Bread: my Second Cousen Clerkes Receipt

Take a peck of flower, and breake in eight eggs; and put in a quart of east [yeast]; and a little butter as big as an egge; make it up with warm water and milke very tender; lay it by the fire to heave up [rise]; let your oven be redy; make it up into little loves and put them into a quick oven.

To make French-Bread the best way, my Lord Gray's Receipt:

Take halfe a peck of fine flower, a quart of new milke bloud warme, and a pinte of new Ale-yest, mingle it with the milke puting in two yolks and one white of egg well beaten; then strayne it into the flower, and beat it up very light together, and let it lye in the Boule till it rises, then make it up and put it into little wooden dishis hott, and let your dishis be hott also, cover them with a cloath and let them stand and rise in the dishis, then turn them out of the dishis into a quick oven, let them be pretty hard baked, then chip them with a knife, then put them into the oven againe for a little time, then take them out and Raspe them; but if you have no Raspe then you may rub them all over with a grater, you must take a peece of one days leven to put in the next day, and that will make them rise and be the lighter; this is the truest way for french-Bread.

To make ffrench Roles: Mrs ffrenches Receipt

Take a quarter of a peck of fine fflower a quarter of a pinte of good ale yest, three ounces of fresh butter, halfe a pinte of milke, make it into a soft doe and let it lye a quarter of an hour to rise in a hott Wollin cloath, and when you mold them up lay them on a warme board flowred, covering them with a warm cloath, and after a little time put them into a very hott oven, a quarter of an hour will bake them, then chip them and set them edge way against a wall to agive [soften], then put them into the oven again the bottome; upwards till they are crispe, and then raspe them: if you keepe some a day or two, you may rap them up in paper and set them in ye oven to make them eat new.

To make Wiggs: Beeches Receipt

Take halfe a peck of flower by measure, put to it a pound of sugar, and as many careway-seeds as you thinke will be soficient, then put in six eggs leaving out two of the whites, and a pinte and halfe of good elle-yest [ale yeast], and having a pound and halfe of butter redy melted in warme milke make it all up into a past, put in milke enough to make it a pretty limber [supple] past, then role it all up together and lay it warm before the fire for halfe an hour to rise, then make them up in little thine wigs as you like them best, lay them upon flowered paper, halfe an houer will bake them.

To Make Wigs: my Cousen Clerks Receipt

Take one pounde of butter, a poringerfull of good ale-east, and halfe a pounde of suger, 2 ounces of cariway comforts; halfe a nutmeg grated, one egge, 8 spoonfulls of rosewater, melt your butter in a skillit and put your rosewater into it when it is melted; then take two quarts of fine flower; the first thinge you put into your flower let it be your east strayned; and mingle it well together; then put in your other things; then worke it well together; but let it not be too stiff; you may heat your oven as hott as for french bread.

To Make Bunns: my Second Cousen Clerke's Receipt

Take 3 pounde of flower, 4 or 5 spoonfulls of ale east [yeast], make this into a stiff past with warme milke or creame; lay it before the fire till ye oven be hott; then worke in a pounde of fresh butter, when the butter is well wrought in put in one pounde of careway seeds; make them up with as much speed as may be and lay them one flowered papers and put them into a reasonable hott oven and bake them.

for all sorts of Plume cakes & seed cakes

CAKES

CAKES

━━◦◯◦━━

for all sorts of plume cakes and seed cakes: and how to make
iceing for them: short cakes

A Cake not very rich: my Mother's Receipt

Take tenn pounde of flower, and six pounde of courents, wash and drye them, then take one pounde of raisons stone them and cutt them small, then take almost an ounce of mace; 3 nuttmegs, a few cloves, a little cinemon, and halfe a pounde of suger, then take foure pounde of butter and rub three of it in your flower, then put in your spice, and suger, being beaten small, and melt the other pounde of butter in three pintes of good creame warmed, then put in your fruit into the flower, and affter you have mixed them well together with a little salt, then make in your flower 3 holes, and in the first hole put in a good quart of alle east [ale yeast], and in the second hole put in your creame, and butter, and in the third hole put in halfe a pinte of sack, and a quarter of a pinte of rose water, then mixe every hole severally by itself, and when so don mix it altogether, and let it stand halfe an howre to rise, then make it up and put it into a hott oven and let it stand two howres, butter your paper well that you lay under it, my mother used to make two cakes with this quantity.

A Receipt for a very good Cake, my first Cousen Clerkes

Take foure pounde of flower, put into it halfe a pounde of suger, one nuttmeg grated, six cloves, and as much cinemon as will lye upon a shilling, and a little salt, put in the yolks of tenn eggs beat very well with a little flower, mingle with the eggs a pinte of good ale east beat them well together, boyle a pinte of good creame put in a pounde of butter, when the creame is indefirent colde put into it a quarter of a pinte of rose water, then make a hole in the flower and put in all the things together, and cover it with flower, and then laye a dish and a cloath over the pan or bolde [bowl] that you make it in, to keepe it warme, not stiring it for a quarter of an howre; then stir it very quick together, and put in foure pounde of courents well dryed, and one pounde of raisons stoned and shread, mix in the fruit very quick; worke it as little as 'tis possible for fear of makeing it sad; butter your paper you laye it one, and you must butter a border of paper to compass it, giveing it liberty enough, then have a quick oven, bake it an howre, and when it is baked ice it and put it in the oven againe for a quarter of an howre with the stone [lid] downe, that the suger may looke the whiter; you may if you please soake in your rose-water some muske and ambergreece [ambergris], and when you put

your fruit into your cake put in if you please some sweetmeats, cutt in
little bitts; the sweetmeats that you may put in are lemon pills, ringer
[eringo] roots, and citton [citron]: this is the cake my second cousen
Clerke used to make: you may put in a pound of sweetmeats and two
grains of muske, and four grains of ambergreece beat fine with a little
suger to a pouder, and mixe it in flower, wch is better than soaking it in
rosewater.

A Good Cake: my first Cousen Clerkes Receipt

Take seven pounde of flower, three pounde of butter, one quart of creame
if very good or else 3 pintes, a quarter of a pinte of sack, as much rose-
water, 16 yolks of eggs, one pounde of suger, two graines of Muske, one
graine of ambergreece steeped in rose-water, tenn pounde of courents
washed and dryed the day before, one quart of good ale east [yeast]; then
boyle your creame and put the butter into it, then make a trough on one
side of the flower and let the yeast and eggs being well beaten together
lye on the other side of the flower, when the Creame is bloud warme put
the sack and rosewater into it, mingle some of the flower with it first,
while the oven is heating, in the meantime set your courents before the
fire to drye, and when your past [paste] is risen worke in your fruit, and
spice, which must be halfe an ounce of nuttmegs, halfe an ounce of mace;
and a quarter of an ounce of cloves, then put it into a paper hoope,[1] and
bake it, it will require three howres bakeing.

A Good Cake: my second Cousen Clerkes Receipt

Take one peck of flower, foure pounde of butter well rubed into the flower;
two ounces of cinemon, two ounces of nutmegs; halfe an ounce of cloves
and mace, three pounde of lofe suger, two pounde of raisons stoned and
shread, two pounde of almons blanched and finely beaten, eight pounde
of courents, two graines of muske, one pinte of sack, one quart of ale
yeast, halfe a pinte of rose water, 18 eggs halfe the whites taken out; and
one quart of Creame warmed; mixe all these well together and bake it.

[1] A hoop of greaseproof paper to line the cake tin.

A Cake: my Lady Sheldon's Receipt

Take seven pounde of flower; 3 pounde and a halfe of butter, rub it in the flower till it becomes a pouder [powder], then take three pounde and a halfe of courents; one pounde and a quarter of suger, halfe an ounce of mace, a quart of good ale yeast, or a little less; halfe a pinte of rosewater, a pinte of creame, with a little sack, mingle all the drye things together; and all the wett together, and before you put all together be sure to have your oven redy.

A Rich Cake: Mrs Ridges Receipt

Take 8 pounde of flower, and 3 pounde of courans [currants] well washed and dryed; when you go to make your cake put your courens in a dish and set them upon the fire with almost a pinte of sack to plump them; let them stand upon the fire about two howres stiring them continually, then put your flower in a traye and make a hole in the midle; take two quarts of yeast, well beaten halfe an howre, and two quarts of creame boyled well and stired till it be colde; then take the yolks of twenty eggs and 4 whites, well beaten with six spoonfulls of flower, then mingle the yeast with them, and beat them well together, then set the creame one the fire again, and when it is scalding hott melt in it gently two pounde of butter; then put in it almost halfe a pinte of rosewater, then take off the top of it with a porenger and mingle it with the yeast, as much as you thinke will wett the cake, which will be the most part of it; then putt into the flower three quarters of a pounde of lofe suger searced; almost halfe an ounce of mace, three nuttmegs, and a little salt; then put in the yeast as it is mingled into the flower; mingle it up lightly with your hand, or a spoon for it may not be kneaded; you may beat a pounde and a halfe of almons and mingle them well with halfe a pinte of ye boyled creame and then straine it out, and poure it in with the rest of the things, put into the creame 2 graines of muske, and as much of ambergreece, then bake it in a hoope of paper, or tinn, let it be put in a very hott oven, that has been cooled and heated againe.

A very good, and a Rich Cake, often made by me

Take eight pound of fine flower and put to it a pound of good pouder suger, a little salt, 3 nuttmegs grated, and of cloves, mace, and cinomon of each a quarter of an ounce beaten small, put in also foure grains of Muske and eight grains of Ambergreece beaten very fine with a little lofe suger, mingle all well together in your flower, then have in redyness two pounds of sweet Almonds beat very fine puting in the beating of them a little milke to keep them from oyleing, beat also twenty eggs with foure of the whites, beat them with a little flower very well, and then put to them almost three pintes of good Ale yest beating them well together a considerable time, then strain it thro' a hair sive, and boyle a quart of good cream and put into it two pound of good butter, and when it is indiferent cold put into it a quarter of a pinte of oring flower water, a quarter of a pinte of damaske rose water and halfe a pinte of sack, then stir into it all your beaten Almonds and make a great hole in your flower poureing into it your eggs, and yest, and then poure to it ye creame, covering it all over with flower and lay a dish and a cloath over the pan or bold [bowl] that you make it in, keeping it warm by the fire not stiring it for halfe an hour, then take it from the fire and stir it very quick together puting in nine pounds of currants well washed and dryed, and two pounds of raisons of the sun stoned and shred with a knife, and one pound of dates cutt into bitts, and one pound of canded oringe pill, and one pound of canded lemon pill, and two pound of canded cittern [citron] all cutt into bitts but not too little; be sure to mix in the fruit and sweetmeats very quick and worke it as little as tis possible for fear of makeing it sad, butter a double paper to lay it on and put it into a tin hoope well buttered, bake it in a quick oven and when it is well risin cover it with a paper, and let it stand two hours and a halfe, and when it is baked take it out of ye oven and ice it, and put it in the oven again for a quarter of an hour with the lid down that the suger may looke the whiter: this will make a very large cake, and it will take up foure pound of lofe suger to ice it.

If you would have an extraordinary great cake you may add one third part of every thing, that is to say 12 pound of flower and so every thinge proportionable to it, and if you make it so bigg it will require 3 howers bakeing; and 6 pound of suger to ice it: If you please you may make this cake with but 4 pound of flower and so every thinge proportionable to that quantity wch will make a good midling sise cake.

A cake of 6lb. of flower wch. is usually what I send away

6:pound of flower
6:pound of curants
1:pound and halfe of raisons
3:quar. of a pound of suger
1:quar of a ounce of cloves and mace together
1:quar of an ounce of cinamon
2:nuttmegs
2:grains of muske
4:grains of ambergreece
1:pound and a halfe of sweetmeats
1:pound and a halfe of butter
1:pinte and a halfe of cream
1:pinte and a halfe of yest
1:quarter of a pint of Rosewater
1:quarter of a pinte of orringe flower water
1:quarter of a pinte or more of sack
15:yolk of eggs and a little salt
2:pound off lofe suger will ice it well

about two hours bakes it: the tin hoop must be at ye full bigness: about 12s:6d this cake cometh to.

Little plum cakes: Leeches Receipt

Take a pounde of butter, a pounde of flower, and halfe a pounde of courents, and six eggs leaveing out 2 of the whites, and six spoonfulls of rose-water, and a little mace; mix all together, and bake them in little tinn pans; be sure you do not make your oven too hott, make them about the bigness of broad biskitts [biscuits]: you must prick them.

Little plum Cakes: Mrs M. Weston's Receipt

Take a pounde of suger, six yolks of eggs, and the whites of two, a little mace, beat them up together for about an howre; then take a pounde of butter and set against the fire untill it be melted; then put in a pounde of flower; and a pounde of Courents; sett the Courents against the fire to plump them, so mingle them up together and bake them in panns.

[194]

Little plum cakes: Mrs Whyfells Receipt

Take halfe a pound of the finest flower, halfe a pound of fine suger, halfe a pounde of Butter, the yolks of four Eggs and a quarter of a pound of curents plumped; mixe your flower and suger together an put in ye eggs being well beaten working it with your hand, and by degrees put in your butter a little bitt at a time keeping it beating with your hand till all be in for halfe an howre together then put in the courents mingleing them well in, then put it into small pans buttered and bake them in an oven not too hott—if you will Ice them, as soon as they are baked take them out of the oven and mix some fine lofe suger being sifted with a little water and spred it over the cakes, and set them in the oven again with the Lid down for to harden them.

A seed cake

take 4 pound of flower and 3 quarters of suger, of cinnamon, mace, nutmegs cloves and ginger of each a little the whole to make half an ounce, and 2 ounces of careway seeds, mix all into the flower, then take almost a pinte of milk 3 quarters of a pound of butter wch. melt in the milk, take a pinte of new yest and put into it a quar. of a pinte of rosewater and a wine glass of brandy the yolk of 3 eggs well beaten, then mix it in the flower and last of all put in ye hott milk and butter, set it by ye fire to rise, then stir it all together a quarter of an hour before you set it into ye oven, about an hour bakes it.

Jane Swanells ordenary seed cake

Take a pottle [small pot] of flower and put to it a quarter of a pound of suger an ounce of careway seeds and halfe an ounce of coleander [coriander] seeds a little brused [bruised], and a race or two of ginger beat fine and a little salt, then take halfe a pinte of Ale and warm it and put it to halfe a pinte of good yest and poure to it halfe a pinte of cream warmed and mixe it all together in your flower very well then butter your hoope or pan that you desine to bake it in and let it stand therein to rise before ye fire half an hour or longer and bake it in a quick oven an hour.

A Seed Cake: my Aunt Rye

Take foure quarts of dryed flower, rub into it a pounde and a halfe of butter, and a quarter of a pounde of suger, some ginger, cloves, mace; and nuttmeg, cinemon, and a little salt; put into the flower halfe a pinte of sack, and the yolks of 8 eggs beaten well with some boyled creame, put in also a quart of good ale yeast; mix all these together with creame yt hath been boyled and is pretty cold againe; put no more in then [than] will wett it, that it may not stick to your hands; then put a pounde of careway seeds, and so make it up, an howre will bake it, and to know when it is baked enough, it is by thrusting a knife into it, and if the knife coms clear out, then it enough, but if any thinge sticks to ye knife, then it is not enough.

A rich seed cake

Take six pound of flower grate in it two nuttmegs, and halfe a quarter of an ounce of beaten mace, and two peneworth of saffern [saffron] poudered, one pound of suger, and one little handfull of coriander seed: then boyle a quart of creame and melt in it one pound of butter, beat the yolks of 12 eggs with a little sack and rose water and a little sirop of sittorn [citron], and one pinte of good yeast, mingle all together in your flower and let it stand halfe an howre by the fire to rise, then mixe in it one pound of caraway-comffitts and halfe a pound of cittern cutt in bitts, and halfe a pound of canded oringe and lemon pill cutt into little bitts, then bake it in a hoope wth a double paper under it well buttered, and let ye hoope be also buttered, an howre or a little more will bake it.

To make a seed cake very good as followeth

Take two pound of butter and beat it with your hand in a puter [pewter] dish for an hour over a very few coles [coals] just to keepe it a little warm, puting in now and then a spoonfull of cream to the quantity of halfe a pinte in all, then have in redyness 18 eggs leaveing out foure of the whites, well beaten with one spoonfull of good yest, strain them and put to them a pound of good pouder suger sifted, then put them in by degrees a little at a time into your butter continueing beating it all the while over ye coles for another hour; after which stir in with your hand two pound of ye finest flower by degrees being redy dryed and sifted; then set it before a fire covered for halfe an hour to rise, and as soon as the oven is redy stir in a pound of ruff sugered careway comforts and then put it into a tinn hoope well buttered with a buttered pye plate under it, bake it in a quick oven and let it stand an hour or better.

To Make a seed cake

Take three pound and a halfe of fflower well dryed, two pound of butter wch melt in a pinte of cream bloud warm, take twelve eggs leaving out eight of the whites beat them very well, and put to them halfe a pinte of ale yest beating them well together, and then strain them, take a pound of fine pouder suger beat it and sife [sift] it and mingle it well in your flower with a nuttmeg grated, then divide your flower with a rige [ridge] in the middle, puting in ye yest and eggs on one side, and the butter and cream in on the other side, mixeing it well together and beat it with your hand a quarter of an hour, and set it before the fire to rise for about a quarter of an hour more, then take it from the fire and strow [strew] in a pound and halfe of ruff sugered careway-comfortts, and if you please you may likewise put in halfe a pound, or a pound of citron cutt in little slices mixe all well together and put it into a Hoope well buttered, and set it into a quick oven but not to burn it, one hour and a halfe will bake it.

To make a seed cake

Take two pound of flower, one pound of Butter, one pound of suger, halfe a pinte of cream, half a pinte of yest, six eggs leaving out three whites, one ounce and a half of careway seeds, a quarter of a pinte of rose water, a quarter of an ounce of spice, let it be mixed together as you do other cakes, an hour will bake it.

Seed Cakes: My Lady Howe's Receipt, also Mrs Green's

Take foure pounde of fine flower, one pounde of fresh butter rub it well into the flower, mingle it with as much cold creame as will make it in a light past [paste], if it be colde weather warme your creame a little, mix with it halfe a pinte of alle yeast and 4 spoonfulls of oringe flower water, then lay it by the fire ariseing, till the oven heats, then strew in halfe a pounde of carewey comfetts, and a pounde of suger, do not knead it, but graspe it in your hands; bake them in an oven prety quick; but not to scorch them, you may make 10 or 12 cakes of this quantity, about halfe an howre, or less will bake them: you may make it all into one cake if you please but yn twill require more bakeing.

To make a seed cake, or dyet [diet] Bred, without any butter

Take a pound of flower, and a pound of Eggs waying [weighing] shells and all, and a pound of suger, and as many careway seeds as you please, drye your flower over some coles, then mixe the suger and flower with the seeds together, then beat your eggs very well and put them in and beat it up with your hand for halfe an hour together, and bake it in a tinn pan buttered, three quarters of an hour will bake it.

Portingall Cakes: Mrs Brownes Receipt

Take a pounde of butter, and a pounde of fine sifted suger, put them to-gether in an earthen pan, and stir them extreordenerily with a wooden slice. Then take a quarter of a pounde of Almons being blanched, and well beaten with a little rose-water; and put them in, then take 3 eggs being well beaten, and put them in also, then stir it together very well, then put in by digrees a pounde of flower, and when that is in; last off all put in a pounde of Courents, and so make it up in little rounde cakes like balls, and lay them upon papers flowered and bake them, and when they are baked ice them, but let your Iceing be thike, you must not forgett to prick them, when you put them in the oven.

Short Cakes: Mrs Whiteheads Receipt

Take a pounde of butter, a pounde and quarter of suger, a nuttmeg or mace, as much flower as will make it into a past; a little ambergreece, the yolks of 2 eggs, mingle these well together, and make them into rounde cakes as you please.

[198]

To Make Iceing for A Cake; my Lady Sheldon

Take a pounde of lofe suger beaten, and sifted; then put to it as much gum-dragon [tragacanth] that hath been steeped in rose water, or oring-flower-water, as the quantity of a nuttmeg; mix with your gum the white of an egg, and 5 or six spoonfulls of rose, or oringe-flower-water, so straine it altogether into your suger, and put it into a morter and beat it extreamely for an howre or more if you see occation, for the longer you beat it the whiter it will be, and if you will you may add a little muske, or ambergreece [ambergris]; when your cake is baked poure it one the top and spread it all over it, and also the sides, you may spread it with a knife, then set it in the oven againe and let it stand a little till it harden, but not couller: be sure don't put to much water to make it than three spoonfulls of ye waters is soficient.

To pott up Butter to keep sweet and good

BUTTER AND CHEESE

BUTTER AND CHEESE

for butter and severall sorts of cheese

To pott up Butter to keep sweet and good

Let your Butter be churmed very coole, and then worke the Buttermilke extreordnery well out of it without any water, for it must not be wasted [washed] with any water at all, neither the least drop of water to touch it; when ye Buttermilke is very well out of it, then salt it, but not to be very salt, then strew a little salt in the bottom of your pott and lay in the Butter in pretty thike layers strewing a little salt betweene the layers and at last on the top.

A Slip-Coate[1] Cheese: Mrs Duke's receipt

Take a gallon of new milke and put to it a quart of warme water, to make it of the ordenery heat that you put other cheese together; add to it as much runett [rennet] as is convenient to make a tender curd, then when it is come throw it gently into a cloath, in a cheese-fatt [vat or mould], and have a care that you breake not the curd; then set a cheese-fatt over it and if that be not heavie enough, put one 3 or 4 pounde weight; you must turne it every halfe howre, for six howres, and then take it out and strew a little salt one it; and so let it lye upon a boarde till the next morning; then wipe the salt off with a wett cloath, and laye it betweene a drye cloath till the next daye; then laye it upon rushes for 8 or 9 dayes; turning it twice a daye, and then you may eat it. If you please you may tye up a little beaten mace in a cloath, and wett it in the milke, and squese it in the milke, to give it a pleasant tast, squese it in before you put the runnett in.

Slip Coate Cheese: Mrs Lord's Receipt

Take a gallon of new milke and halfe a pinte of creame, and halfe a pinte of cold water so run them together, put in a spoonfull or a little more of quick renet [rennet], and when it is thorowly come drayne the whay [whey] through a strayner, so press the curd with a weight of 2 pound 6 or 8 howres, then take it out and lay it in a wett cloath and change it

[1] *Editor's note*: Slipcote is judged to be one of the oldest and best of English cream cheeses, originating in Rutland. It was traditionally ripened in cabbage leaves. Its name comes from the fact that it has a loose skin which slips off when the cheese is ripe.

twice a day and in 6 or 8 days it will be redy. Make your rennet thus, take
the curd out of the bag and put a pinte of new milke into the bag with
six cloves brused and a little salt, so tye it up and it will be fitt for use in
two days.

Slip Coate Cheese: Mrs Duncombe's Receipt

Take a gallon of milke and 2 quarts of creame, warme the milke a very
little and put the cold creame to it, put a very little runett to it, and cover
it close with a cloath and a cheesefatt [cheese vat], and when it is come
breake it a very little with ye scimingdish, but not with your hands, then
fill ye cheese-fatt, but handle it not with your hands, and then press it
with a three or foure pound waite from morning till night, then take it
out of ye fatt, and lay it on a fresh fatt, and so continue turning it twice a
day from one fatt to another till it comes to a white coate wch in very
hott weather will be in 3 or 4 days, then lay it very thike on nettles, and
cover it with nettles very thike, and if the weather be cold cover it with a
blankett, and in about a week's time it will be redy, to know when it will
be redy the skine will be apt to slip off in the turning and it will have
a black molde on it: But if you would have it with magotts, just wash
the outside with a little sack when you take it out of the fatt the first
time.

A Thike Cheese: my Aunt Rye

Take the milke of 15 cowes; let it stand all night in boles or pans in the
morneing stir the milke and the creame together, then set it over the fire
and make it scaldeing hott, then take if off and strayne it and keepe it
stiring that it may not creame, then take as much mornings milke and
put to this scalded milke, it must be put together some-what hotter
then [than] it comes from the cowe, but not much hotter, when the cheese
is come it must be well broken, which you may well do with a charme-
stafe [stave], then let it stand awhile, before you take out the whaye; and
when you take the curd to put it into the fatt [vat] you must break it
very well, squesing out the whay very well before it be put into the press,
turn it offten into drye cloaths, let the cheese stand two dayes and a night
in the press, after you have taken it out set it one a smooth plaine boarde,
and rub it pretty thike with salt, top, botttome, and sides, so turn it twice

a day for 3 dayes, salting it as before; untill it be very harde leting the brine runn from it; when it is harde let it stand where you please to drye; turning it once a day: this cheese is to be made in maye or the begining of june.

To make the water Cheese: my Lady Howes Receipt

Take about seven or eight gallons of new milke at night put runett to it as you do for ordnery cheese, when it is come *sinke* the curd, but break it as little as is possible, drayne out the whey and worke it into a fatt [vat] that will hold all the curd, set it in the press about 2 hours, then take it out and lay it in water all night, the next morning make another cheese after the same maner and of the same bigness, and let it stand in the press about two howrs, then take it out, and the other out of the water, break them together as small as is possible, and strew so much salt among the curd as you thinke will season it, then worke it into a hoop, and let it stand in the press two or three days; then take it out, and pin a napkin round it in the dryeing for a weeke or longer.

The last water cheese I made I had six cowes, and ordered ye milke as followeth:
I made the first cheese on fryday night with thursday nights and fryday mornings milke, then on saturday morning I made the other cheese with fryday nights and saturday mornings milke so that in the 2 cheeses there was 4 meales milke, and ye milke of 24 cowes in the whole cheese which made it very thike and hansome.

To make egg cheese: Mrs Bunker's Receipt

Take 2 gallons of new milk and a gallon of creame, first boyle the cream and coole it till it be as cold as new milk, then strayne it to your milke, then take 15 yolks of eggs well beaten and strayne them into your milk and creame stiring it well together, then put in your runett as for other cheese, and when come put it into the fatt [vat] as you do other cheese, let the cheese be about two fingers thikeness after it is dryed. When it is turned it must be on two boards not touching it with the hands for fear of breaking. The moneth of may is the best time to make it in.

[206]

For to make sage cheese

Take all the night and next morning's new milke of six cowes devideing the milke equally into two things, and into one of them strayne in as much juce of sage and spinage as you think will give it a tast strong enough, and green enough, about a pinte and halfe of juce I beleive may do, put in the juce when you put in your runett and so set it to be a tender curd, and likewise the other milke in the other thing set at the same time to be a tender curd also, then whay both your green and white curd severally and put them into two severall cheesefatts [cheese vats] just of an equall sise strewing salt into the curd as you put it in, then sett both your cheese in the press for about a quarter of an hour or longer till you thinke it be enough, then take them both out and turn them out of ye fatts, and with a pack thread slitt each cheese just through, wch when so done there will be two white cheese, and two green cheese, then take one of the white cheese and lay it into a great deep fatt (big enough to hold it all) and lay a green cheese on that, then lay on another white, and then the green on the top; when you have so lay'd in all your 4 cheese put it again into the press and let it stand about a quarter of an hour, then take it out of the press again, and with a packthred cutt it into narow slipes quite downe the cheese, and then cutt it the cross way again that so the peeces may be about an inch square or biger, when so done, take great care to place every peece right into your fatt that is to say a green and a white that so it may lye checkered, and be sure to put it all into the same fatt again, and set it into the press for 2 or 3 days till it be well pressed, but you must turn it the day after you put it in ye press.

Butter cheese

Take the night and next morning's milk of six cowes, sett it to be a tender curd, and when the whay is well drayned out of it break into the curd 2 pound of fresh butter, be sure to break the curd and butter extraordinarily small, and well together, then put it into your fatt strewing some salt amongst the curd as you do other cheese.

ffor all tarts: and to keepe fruiet for them.

PRESERVES

PRESERVES

marmelett of all sorts of fruit: and jams; all sorts of jellys of any fruite whatever; to preserve whole orenges and lemons, whole quinces, and all manor of wett sweetmeats whatsoever: and to green codlings or any other fruit; to keepe fruiet for tarts; for all sorts of sirups and conservs

[211]

PRESERVES

Marmelett [jam] of Cherys: my Lady Sheldon's Receipt

Take three pounde of cherys pul'd from the stalks, and stoned, then take halfe a pounde of lofe suger beaten, strew some of it in the bottome of your preserveing-pan, and then lay in some cherys, and then more suger, so do till it be all in, then set it one the fire, and when the suger is well melted, let it boyle, as fast as it can; stiring it till it be thike enough then put it into glaces [glasses], scrape suger upon it, and set it in a stove awhile.

To Make Marmelett [jam] of Cherys: my Aunt Ryes Receipt

Take your cherys and stone them, then way [weigh] them, and breake them very well with the back of a spoone, put them into a clean skillet, and boyle them untill good part of the liquor be consumed, then to every pounde of cherys put in six ounces of suger, so boyle it up to the height of a marmelett [until it reaches setting point]; it will keepe if you boyle it not too high, for it will stifen in the keeping, put it up in glaces, or potts: when it is almost boyled enough if you put in a little juce of white or red curants it will be the clarer.

Marmelett [jam] of Aprecoks: My Lady Howe's Receipt

Take a pounde of aprecoks before they be too ripe; whilst they be very paile, pare them, and stone them, and cutt them in foure peeces, or smaler, as you please; then put in a pounde and a quarter of fine suger beaten fine, then strayne in a quarter of a pinte of the juce of white courents [currants]; or pipin [pippin] water, set it over the fire, and when the suger is melted, boyle it very fast, and keepe it stiring and scimed till it be cleere and jelly.

Marmelett [jam] of Aprecocks: Mrs Beriges Receipt

Take your aprecoks and codle [boil] them, till they be soft, then peele them, and squesse all to mash with a spoone, then pulp them through a haire sive then to a pounde of that pulp take a pounde of lofe suger, then boyle it up halfe an howre will do it.

[213]

Greene Marmelett [jam] of white plums: Mrs Beriges Receipt

gerther your plums whilst they are greene, and scald, and greene, them just as you do those you preserve, and then stone them, and take their weight in fine suger, and a spoonfull in a pounde over; then boyle them together till it be thike enough, and put it up.

Marmelett [jam] of white pare-plum: My Lady Howe's Receipt

Take a pounde of white pare plums, skine them, and cutt them from the stones; into a pounde and quarter of fine suger into a silver basson, then drayne out a quarter of a pinte of the juce of white pare plums as you do for jelly; and put to it, then set it one a slow fire till the suger be melted, then boyle it very fast and stir and scume [skim] it well, till it be a jelly, then put it up.

To make jam of damsons: Mrs Whiteheads Receipt

Take foure pounde of damsons stone them; and put them into an earthen pitcher into a kittle of water, till they are boyled all to mash; then put in a good pounde of suger to each pound of mash and so boyle it well; then put it up in glaces; some will let the stones be in it.

Marmelett [jam] of quinces white: my Aunt Rye's

Take quinces newly gathered of the trees, let them not stand so long as to be yellow, for green ones are best to make it white, codle them in a great thinge of water as soft as can be without breaking, let them not be so long adoing for fear of looseing couller [colour], the while you are prepareing your quinces in this maner, make in another skillett some pipin water, quarter your pipins as fast as you can, without pareing or coreing them; boyle them quick untill the water is slipery, then put as much of that water as will thine [thin] it when it is pulst [pulped] fitting, about halfe a pinte to a pounde of quince will be enough, then take the weight of all in double refined suger, and boyle it uncovered as fast as you can, untill it be cleere, minde not the thickness of it, for if it be cleere it will stifen with keepeing.

[214]

Marmelett [jam] of quinces Red: my Mothers Receipt

Take your quinces and pare, and core them, but still as you pare them put them into fayre water, or else they will looke black, then to every pounde of quince, take a pounde of suger, and a wine quart of water then set them over the fire and keepe them boyleing, with some of the seeds out of the cores tyed up in a cloath, when your quinces are boyled tender breake them with a spoone, then set them one the fire againe, keepeing it stired, that it do not burn, when you thinke it is enough put it up into your glaces; you must be sure to keepe it close covered all the while it boyles before you breake the quinces for to make it the reder.

Marmelett [jam] of pipins: my Aunt Rye's Receipt

Take pipins or John apples, pare them, and cutt them in little slices, to a pounde of aples, take a pounde or better of fine suger beaten, as you cutt the aples put them into the suger, to a pounde of apples put at least a pinte of water; let them boyle, and when it is halfe boyled put in the peele of halfe a Lemon; or oringe, which hath been boyled in severall waters to take out the bitterness; mince it very fine, then put it in, and boyle it till it be enough, then put in juce of Lemon, according to the quantity you make, and let it stand to heat over the fire a little, but not boyle, for then it will rope [become thick and stringy].

Marmelett [jam] of popling-pare: my Aunt Ryes Receipt

Take your pares [pears] before they are too mellow, pare them, and core them, and put them into drye suger as you do them, that they may not loose their couller, to a pounde of pares, put neere two pounde of suger, set them one a soft fire, till the suger be well melted, you must not put the least water to them, boyle them apasse [a pace], and scume [skim] them, keepe them with continuall sturning [stirring], put in some slices of green sittarn [citron], when it is halfe boyled, a little more than halfe an howre will boyle it up to a marmelett, if it be too high boyled it will rope, put in a little ambergreece [ambergris], to give it a tast, wett it in a little rose-water and so put it in, you may lay some of this in little cakes, they will candy quickly and eat very finely.

Marmelett [jam] of Orin:: My Lady Howe's Receipt

Take a pounde of oringe-peele, lay them in water a day and a night, shift
the water 3 or 4 times; boyle them very tender; and drayne them drye,
then beat them very fine in a morter, then put to it two pounde of double
refined suger, boyled to suger againe; put to it a pinte of the juce of John
apples as you make for jelly; and the juce of 3 or 4 oringes, then boyle it
very fast, and keepe it stirring till it be a jelly, then put it up.

Marmelett [jam] of Oringes: My Lady Howe's Receipt

Take the fayrest oringes and scoure them well with salt, then wash them
in fayre water; and then pare, or grate, the outward rine [rind] off them,
then cutt them in the midle, and take the pulpe cleane out off them, boyle
the peeles in fayre water, shifting the water some-times, let them boyle
till they are very tender, and the bitterness gonn, then dry them well
in a cloath, and cutt them in little peeces, and to every pounde of oringes,
allowe three pounde of fine lofe suger; put halfe your suger in at first, then
take pipins or John apples pare and cutt them into water, and boyle them
to a strong jelly then put one pinte of this liquor to the oringe, and suger,
and boyle it together; and in the boyleing add the remainder of your suger
by digrees; then take the pulpe, and the juce of the oringes, which will
come out as you pull out the strings, and kernells, pulling them out with
a knife very cleane; put in the juce of two Lemons to it in a pott, and sett
it one the fire, when your jelly is almost boyled which you may see by the
cleereness of the oringes, then put in all the juce and the meat into the
jelly and let it boyle a little, sciming it clean as it boyleth.

Marmelett [jam] of Oringes: my Mothers Receipt

Take the best sivill [Seville] oringes you can gitt, take the rine off and
cutt off some of the white which is within from it, then slice your rine
very thine; and let it boyle in a skillt of water, till it makes the water
bitter, then have in rediness another skillet of water boyling hott and
shift your peeles into it, and let them boyle till they are very tender, then
take them out of the water and squese them hard in a cloath that no
water remaine in them, then cutt them as small as you can, then take the
pulpe of the oringes and with a knife breake it very small, and take out

[216]

all the seeds and white strings, then mixe your rine, and pulp, together and take to every 4 oringes a pounde of double refined suger, beat it very fine and drye it well over coles [coals], then put your oringes into it, and sett them over a slow fire, and so keepe it with continuall stiring till you thinke it be enough, do not let it boyle at all; for if it doth it will be spoyled, it will not be so stiff as other marmelett, to be cutt, but must be taken out wth spoons.

Marmelett [jam] of Rasberys: my Mothers Receipt

To every pound of rasberys [raspberries] take a pound of lofe-suger, or good pouder suger, boyle your Rasberys all to mash, and then put the suger to them, set it over a gentle fire till all the suger be melted; then make it boyle pretty fast keepeing it stiring, and cleane scimed, till you thinke it be thike enough, then take it off and put it into glaces: it will keepe a yare or longer.

Jelly of pipins: My Lady Howe's Receipt

Take two quarts of water, and twenty pipins, and two John aples, pare, core, and quarter them, and put them into the water, and let it boyle till halfe be consumed, then take to every pounde of juce (that is to say a pinte) take a pounde of fine lofe suger, drye your suger well, and warme the juce, and mixe them together, and have redy one Lemon pill [peel] boyled and cutt, and the juce of two Lemons, put in a bag, muske, and ambergreece, mixe alltogether, and set it one the fire; but do not let it boyle when it is enough put it in glaces, and let them stand in a drye place, for the juce of Lemon will make it apt to give.

Pipin jelly with Cittorn: Mrs Whitehead's Receipt

Take cittorns [citrons], or oringes, which you like, choose them with hardest rines, for they are the best for this use, cutt them into halves and quarters, then take out the meat, and put it into a clean glasse, with the juce of the oringes; cover it and set it by, lay your oringes to water in a silver dish all night, the next day take out the quarters of the oringes, and slice them slanting as thine as paper; be sure that your knife be cleane and

[217]

offten wiped, or else it will disscouller your oringes, when they are all sliced put them into a skillet of boyleing water; and let them boyle till they are prety tender, then drayne them from the water through a course canvise, put them into a silver dish and cover them, and set them by, then take 10 or 12 pipins and as many paremains [pearmains], or John apples, pare and slice them cores and all, but not the kernells, put them into two quarts of fayre water, and boyle them untill the strength of the aples be gon into the liquuor, then strayne the liquor through a course canvise; take to every pinte of the liquor a pounde of double refined suger, boyle it and scime it for a quarter of an howre, then put in your sliced oringes, and let them boyle very fast, adding two ounces more of suger; when it is almost enough, which you may know by the cleereness of the sliced oringe, then strayne all the juce from the meat of the oringes, through a peece of course [coarse] lawne; and put it into the jelly; and let it boyle very fast, put in a little bagg with muske, and ambergreece, when it is redy to take off the fire; then put it into glaces.

Pipin jelly with slices of pipins: Mrs Brownes Receipt

pare 14 good pipins, and quarter them, and put them into a pint and halfe of water, and set them one the fire, and let them boyle uncovered, till the vertue [goodness] are well out of the pipins in to the liquor; then put it through a sive and let it runn through a haire-sive, into an earthen basson, and let the sive stand droping all night; put in a peece of Cittron pill to it, asoake all night, and by morning it will be setled; then peere out the cleere of it, and to a pinte of juce, take a pounde of suger, and set it one the fire together, but not the cittron pill; and when it boyleth take some slices of pipins cutt the long way, untill you come to the kernells, and put them in, and boyle them quick, and they will soon be redy; about two fayre pipins will be enough for this quantity, when it is almost boyled redy to jelly, put in the juce of one Lemon, and the juce of one oringe if you please, and let it boyle very fast, till it be enough, then lay the pipins in glaces poureing the jelly one them, to this proportion pare one oringe very thine, and boyle the pareings in a skillett of water, till they are very tender, drye them in a course cloath; and cutt them in long thine slices, and put them into the bottome of the glaces, under the apples, or you may boyle Lemon peele, and put under if you please, some will put canded [candied] oringe, and Lemon peele cut in thine slices into it; but I thinke the rines boyled in water as well, some will cutt the apples the roune way,

[218]

and cutt them as thike as their finger; but I thinke it best to cutt them the long way, and cutt them not so thike, but you may trye both.

Jelly of quince: Mrs Greens Receipt

Take quinces pare and quarter them and put a pound of quince to a quart of water, and let it boyle apasse till it comes to a pinte, keepe it stiring that it may looke payle and clare, strayne it and let it stand till next day then put to a pinte of liquer a pound of fine suger and let it boyle halfe an howre then strayne it through a jelly bag.

Conserves or jelly of Barberys: my Aunt Ryes Receipt

Take your barberys and put them into a pott, and let them boyle in a kittle of water untill they are tender, and the juce will come out, then strayne it and boyle it to a fitt thickness, but first take the weight of it in lofe suger, beat and drye it, and when the liquor is boyled put in the suger, and let it stand to scume, but not boyle, when it is cold put it up.

Jelly of Curants, Rasberys, Goosberys, or any the like fruit: Newtons Recept

When you have drawed out the juce of your fruit by setting it in a kittle of water (as above mentioned in ye other receipt,) run it all through a flanell bagg wch will make it very clare, then to a pinte of that clare juce take three quarters of a pound of suger, set it on ye fire and boyle it apasse scuming it cleane, it will immediately be enough about halfe a quarter of an hower will do it, as soon as you perceive it to jelly on ye back of your spoone or Ladle that you stir it withall it is enough: if you make jelly of goosberys, it must be before the goosberys are ripe whilst they are very green, you must top and tayle them, and give them a slit on ye side, then put them into your pittcher and be sure to peere the juce out as fast as it comes or else it will be too deepe coullered; and to a pinte of goosbery juce put in a pound of double refined suger; but to any red jelly good pouder suger will do, and 3 quarters of a pound to a pinte of red juce will be enough.

[219]

Jelly of Courants or Rasberys or any other fruit: my Mothers

Take your red courents and strip them off the stalks, then put them into silver, or earthen potts, and set them into a kittle of boyling water, with waites upon the lids that no water may gitt in, you must keepe the water boyling all the time, and in an howre or a little more, you may begin to peere out some juce; for you must be sure to peere it out as it coms, and when you thinke you have gott out all the juce, that is to say the clearest of it, without strayneing it at all, then take to a pinte of juce a pounde of double refined suger and some thing more; then wett your suger with eight spoonfulls of fayre water to a pounde of suger, set it over the fire and let it boyle till it be almost canded [candied]; then put in your juce and boyle it apasse, keepeing it clean scumed, it will be presently boyled enough, about halfe a quarter of an howre will do it, you may see when it will jelly by some one your spoone, if you coole it a little, if you make it too hard it is not neere so good; make jelly of rasberys, the same way, or of any other fruit, you may make jelly of the white courents [currants] so; to know when your suger is boyled almost to a candy height [setting point], is when it begins to make a great noyse in the boyleing; and bladers very much, more than it did at first, I believe it may boyle about halfe an howre; but that you must do according to discretion.

To preserve Aprecoks in jelly, or out of jelly, a very quick way: Newtons Receipt: any sort of plums may be don ye same way

Take your Aprecoks [apricots] as soon as they are at theire full grouth and begin to turn of a paylesh yellow before they are quite ripe, take their waite in double refined suger, then stone and pare them, and haveing your suger redy beat and sifted strew some of it on your Aprecoks as fast as you pare them, for if you do not cover them with suger they will change couller, when you have pared them all, then strew on all the remainder of your suger upon them, and so let them stand for 3 or 4 howers, then have in redyness for every pounde of Aprecoks a pinte of pipin water strayne it clare into your preserveing pan and put to it three quarters of a pounde of double refined suger, make it boyle as fast as you can scuming it cleane and so let it boyle very fast for almost a quarter of an Hower, then poure your Aprecoks with all theire suger to it and keepe it boyleing as fast as possibley you can scuming it cleane, and now and then shakeing it round, never stiring it with any spoone; when they begin to be clare and tender

[220]

they are enough, they will be boyled enough in about a quarter of a howers time, then take them off and scume them cleane and put your Aprecoks into potts, and if you thinke ye Liquor will not jelly, boyle it a little more till it will jelly, then strayne it through a sive upon your Aprecoks, and when cold paper them up. If you would not be at the charge of doing your Aprecoks in jelly you may only take their waite in suger before they are stoned and pared, and strew it on them as you pare them and when 'tis pretty well dissolved wch will be in 3 or 4 howres time set them on ye fire, and as soon as all ye suger is well melted let them boyle and keepe them boyleing as fast as you can till they be enough as above mentioned; and then poure the sirup on them when you have layed them in the potts; this quick way of preserveing Aprecoks at once boyleing makes them eate much tenderer, and looke much larger, then those that are 2 or 3 days adoing, you may also preserve ye white pare plum or any other plum this way:

To make the pipin water is as followeth; you must take a douson or more of green pipins, or any other good apple, and without pareing them cutt them into quarters or slices, into a quart of spring water and let it boyle as fast as you can uncovered till it come to a pinte, and that the vertue of the apples be well out, then strayne it and put your suger to it as above mentioned:

observe this for a rule that in ye preserveing of all white sweetmeats you must take a spiciall care to keepe the sides of your preserveing pan often wiped with a wett cloath in ye boyleing of your sweetmeats; or else that wch gathers and sticks on ye sides will be apt to boyle into and discouler your sweetmeats.

To preserve Aprecocks in slices: my first Cousen Clerke's

Take pretty ripe aprecoks, pare them, and cutt them into prety thine slices, as you do for chips, cover them as you pare them with fine searced suger; make your suger into a fine clear candy then put in your aprecoks and keepe them one the fire, till they turn the suger into a sirrop, and the aprecoks grow cleere, in the sirrop, but be sure you do not let them boyle, when they are enough put them up; you must take the weight of suger to the weight of aprecoks; and keepe a little of it, to strew one your aprecoks as you slice them, and the remainder you must boyle to a candy;

[221]

To preserve peaches   Mrs Yorkes Receipt

Take them when they are at there full bigness before they grow soft, pare them and put them into a silber [silver] bason, and put in so much white-wine as will cover them; if you will have them red; you must cover them close, in the boyling, but if you would have them amber couller, then boyle them uncovered, they must boyle gently in the whitewine untill they be tender; then take them out and slitt them, and take out the stones, and to every pounde of peaches, take a pounde of double refined suger beaten small; and halfe a pinte of fayre water, mixe your water and suger together, and set it one the fire, and let it boyle, and then scume it, which being don put your peaches into it, and preserve them gently untill you thinke they are enough.

To preserve white Bullis in jelly: My Lady Howe's Receipt

Take a pounde of white bullis [bullaces], before they be ripe when they begin to change couller, that is to say when they begin to be yellow, scald them tender leasurely, they must be scalding 3 or 4 howres, then take three quarters of a pounde of fine suger, and put to it a quarter of a pinte of fayre water; make the water and suger scalding hott, drye the plums, and put them to the suger, and water, and keepe them warme about an howre, and shake them often in doing, then take them off and heat them twice a day for 3 or 4 dayes, till the sirrop be very thike, then drayne them from the sirrop, and boyle a pounde of double refined suger to suger, againe, then take a pinte of the juce of bullis drayned; as it is for cleere-cakes, then put it to the suger, and when it is melted boyle it very fast, and keepe it scumeing [skimmed], then put in your bullis, and give it one boyle, then put them up in potts, and be sure you have jelly to cover them. If you will drye any bullis preserve them only as you do these, in the first sirrop, and then lay them one glaces in your stove.

To preserve any plums: Mrs Greens Receipt

Take the fayrest and freshest plums you can gitt, wipe them and snip off the knuby part of the stalks, then slit them on one side and take their weight in lofe siger beaten fine, then take an earthen pott off an equall broadeness from top to bottome, about the broadeness of a rowne trencher, strew some of your suger on ye bottom of it and lay a lay of plums and a lay of suger till all be in but the last must be suger, then set them in a pott of seething water let it boyle very softly 2 or 3 howres at least, then take the pott off and let it stand till next day than put them out into a silver dish and boyle them a pretty pace with all clare sirup, then put the plums in glaces and set the glaces in cold water to make them stick together that they may not swim, when the sirup is put to them which must not be till quite cold: if they are well don they will keepe three yare: this is ye best receipt for plums.

To preserve Morellow Cherrys: Mrs Brownes Receipt

Take a pounde of cherys the fayrest you can gitt, take their weight in lofe suger, beat and sift it, cutt your cherys a little one the top; and take out the stones with a pare of sissers; leave a little short tayle to take them up by, then put almost halfe your suger at the bottome of your basson, with foure spoonfulls of water, and the juce that drops from them in the stone-ing, then lay in your cherys one by one, (you must never let cherys lye one upon the other in the preserveing) then put the rest of the sugar upon the cherys, and poure upon them a quarter of a pinte of the juce of red courents strayned; then sett it one the fire, and when the suger is all melted, let them boyle as fast as they can possible, scume them in the boyl-ing, and when they looke cleere take them off the fire, and scume them, and cover them with a linnon cloath for a quarter of an howre, to cleere them, then put them into glaces; and when the sirrop is cold poure it one them. Any cherys may be preserved so, but morellows are the best.

To preserve Cherys in jelly: My Lady Howe's Receipt

Take one pounde and three quarters of suger; and a pounde of cherys, stone them, beat your suger fine; and put to it three quarters of a pinte of the juce of red courents; and a quarter of a pinte of the juce of white courents, set them one a slow fire till your suger be melted, then boyle it up prety fast till they are enough, keepe them clean scumed.

to preserve goosberys rasps or curants I find it best to a pound of each to take a pound and three quarters of suger and a pinte of fayre water wch will quickly jelly with but a little boyling.

To preserve Goose-berys: my Lady Sheldons Receipt

Take Goosberys before they be ripe, stamp [purée] and strayne, them, and to a pinte of that juce, take a pounde of the fayrest goosberys stoned and to them take a pounde and three quarters of lofe suger, put not in all your suger at first, but as they boyle strew in some, boyle them so fast that you cannot see the gooseberys; when they are cleere they are enough, then put them up: your gooseberys must be at their full groth [growth], and before they begin to turn: instead of ye juce of goosberys you may take ye juce of white curants; which will jelly better.

To preserve Gooseberys: for Tartts Mrs Beriges Receipt

Take your gooseberys when they be at their full groth [growth], and redy to turn yellow, cutt off the tops and prick them, take their weight in suger and put in as much water as will wett it, and dissolve it one the fire, and after it is melted, and colde, put in your gooseberys, and sett them one the fire, and do them very gently for fear of breaking them, and when you thinke they are enough; take them up; and keepe them in the sirrop for your use.

To preserve Grapes when they are ripe: My Lady Howe's

Take the fayrest grapes, pull them off the stalks; and stone them and to a pounde, take a pounde of fine suger, beat and sifted, put to it 4 or 5 spoonefulls of the juce of grapes; then put your grapes to it and set them one the fire, but let it be very slow till the suger be melted, then boyle it up fast and keepe it sciming till it looks cleere, and is of a jelly, then put them up.

To preserve Grapes: Mrs Allines Receipt

Take white grapes before they are too ripe, pull them off the stalks, and stone them, and save the juce, and to a pounde of grapes take a pounde of suger, then take a pinte of water and boyle some shread pipins in it, till the liquor be very strong of the pipins; then strayne it out and put your suger to it, and when it is well scumed, put in your grapes and boyle them very fast, and when you see them very cleere; and that the sirrop will jelly, then they are enough; it may be the grapes will be enough, before the sirrop will jelly, than take the grapes out and put them in a pott, and boyle the sirrop a little more, and then put it to your grapes; after you have strayned your pipin water you must put the juce that came from the grapes into it, at the same time that you put the suger into it.

To preserve Mulberys: Mrs Whiteheads Receipt

Take a pounde of mulberys when they are ripe, and a pounde of fine suger beat and sifted; strew some suger under them, and lay a row of mulberys, and a row of suger; till all be in, only leave out some suger, to strew one as they boyle, let them have roome enough, put in 2 or 3 spoonfulls of water, or as much as you thinke will melt the suger; then set them one the fire and keepe them with gentle shakeing them now and then, boyle them as quick as every you can till the sirrop be pretty thike.

To preserve Rasberys: my Lady Sheldons Receipt

Take halfe a pounde of the fayrest rasberys, and a pounde of pure pouder suger, stew some of it in the bottome of the basson, being beat very fine, lay in your rasberys with the holes upwards, and strew some suger one them, then lay another layer of rasberys, and then suger, so do till all be in, then strayne in almost halfe a pinte of the juce of rasberys, with three spoonfulls of fayre water, for that will make them tender, then sett them one a slow fire, till the suger be melted; then let them boyle as fast as you can, be sure you put no spoone in them, but keepe them with sciming, and offten shake them, when they are enough they will shine, then put them up. *Note.* that it is best to boyle the suger and water with ye juce together, and after 'tis scumed then put it in ye rasberys.

To preserve Barberys in jelly: Mrs Ridges Receipt

Take a pounde of the fayrest barberys and stone them, and as you stone them, lay suger one them, then take a pinte and halfe of fayre watter and boyle foure pipins quatered in it; till your water begins to jelly; then take your pipins out, and put in some whole barberys bruseing them, and let them boyle till your water be prety red, then strayne it, and put in a pounde of fine lofe suger; stir it about till it be all melted, then put in your stoned fruit; and let them boyle till they are all of a fine couller; and that you thinke they are enough then put them up.

To preserve Barberys in syrup not to jelly, a good way

ffirst take a little scutcherneel [cochineal] beaten small, tye it up in a rag and put it into some fayer water with some barberys being brused boyle them together very gently untill the water looks of a good red, then strain it out, and to a pound of lofe suger take a pinte of the strained liquor and set it over ye fire in a preserving pan and as soon as it is scalding hott and the suger well melted, put into it a pound of Barberys redy stoned, or a pound of those that are called Maiden Barberys which are without stones, let them heat and boyle gently till the Barberys looketh clear, and when you thinke they are enough take them off ye fire, and cover them close over with a clean sheet of white paper to keep them down in ye syrup, and so let them stand all night, the next day take the Barberys out of ye syrup and put them into glaces or potts that you desine to keep them in, and boyle over the syrup again sciming it clean, and when you thinke it is boyled thik enough (wch it will be in a little time) poure it over your Barberys, which being thus done will keepe good two years or longer. Remember to clip off the blacks on ye tops of your Barberys, and 'tis best to preserve them without their stalks.

To preserve curants in jelly: Newtons Receipt

Take your largest curants and clip them from ye stalks after you have stoned them, and as you do them put them into an earthen thinge strewing some fine beaten suger on them, when you have so picked what quantity you would have, take to a pound of picked curants a pound of fine suger, and a full pinte of the juce of curants, drawed out as you do for jelly to wch you must add three quarters of a pound of suger more, so that to a pounde of curants and a pinte of juce you must have a pound and three quarters of suger, some of ye same suger will serve to strew on them as you stone them, put it altogether and set it on the fire and as soon as your suger is melted let it boyle as fast as it can scuming it cleane, less then a quarter of an hower will boyle it enough, when 'twill jelly it is enough.

To preserve Oringes in slices: Mrs Whiteheads Receipt

pare your oringes extreamely thine, cutt them in halves, and lay the
flatt side downe one a plate, and so cutt it out in very thine slices meat
and all, and lay them in water for eight dayes changeing them every day
in fresh water; then drye them with a cloath gently, then take somthing
more then their weight in suger, and put it in your preserveing-pan, and
as much water as will wett your suger, boyle it up neere to a candy height;
then lay in your oringes gently, all over your suger which will melt it,
then cover it up, and set it upon embers for 7 or 8 howeres, but be very
carefull that it do not so much as simber, but only scalding hott, for if it
be more it will change couller, and be spoyled; when it be enough, the
peele will be tender; and the white next the peele will be delicately cleere,
then put it into your glaces, in order and betweene every laying put some
little bitts of leafe gold;[1] you may fill some of the glaces only with the same
sirrop, which is very fine, and to some of them you may put jelly of pipins
which is as well as if you put sirrop to them; or better.

To preserve whole Oringes in jelly: Mrs Bornfords Receipt: and it is a very excelent one, I have often used it my self

Take the best Sivill oringes and waye them, then pare them as thine as
you can possible, puting them into a pan of fayre water as fast as you do
them, and so let them lye in water for foure days, changeing the water
twice a day; then put them into a large skillit of cold water, and set them
on the fire, and make them boyle as fast as you can, keepeing them close
covered all the time they are boyleing; you must all the time have another
skillit of water redy boyleing, that so you may shift them out of the first
water into that; let them boyle in the first water not halfe an howre because
twill be very bitter, then shift them into the other skillitt of boyleing
water without takeing them off the fire at all; and keepe them close
covered, you may let them boyle a little longer in the second water then
in the first; you must not fayle to have a skillitt by all the while with fresh
boyleing water, for you must boyle them in six or seven fresh waters, in
the three first waters you need not let them boyle so long as in the others,
but in all you may boyle them about six or seven howrs, or longer if
you finde them not tender enough, be sure to keep them boyling very
fast, and close covered all the time, then when you thinke they are tender

[1] Gold leaf, applied as decoration.

enough, take them and cutt out a little round peece at the stalke-end, saveing the peeces to put on againe, at the hole you may take all the seeds out which you must do as cleane as you can, pulling out as little of the meat as is possible, the best way to take them out will be a pare of long sisers [scissors], or a bodkin, against your oringes are seeded, you must have redy a sirrop to put them into as fast as you do them; which must be made as followeth: to every pound of oringes take a pound of sixpeny suger, for that will be good enough; to every pound of suger take a pinte of fayre water; and put your suger to it, then beat the white of one or two eggs, according to the quantity you do; two whites will be enough for foure or five pound of suger, stir them in very well, and set it on the fire stiring it some-times; and when it boyles scume it very cleane, which when you have don, take it off the fire, and as fast as you take the seeds out of your oringes put them into this sirrop; and when all your oringes are in, set it on the fire, and keepe it boyleing for an howre or longer, scuming it as it needs, let them boyle uncovered, let them boyle till the sirrop begins to be somewhat thike, they may boyle indiferent fast; boyle ye bitts you cutt off also, then when you thinke they have boyled long enough, take them out and set them in an earthen pott with their holes upwards, poureing the sirrop over them, and fill the holes full of sirrop, so let them stand till the next day; and when they are cold cover the thinge they stand in, and let them continew so in the sirrop for foure or five days; or longer, every day doing the sirrop over them with a spoone, and filling the holes with it, let the little bitts lye in the sirrop also: how to make the pipin jelly that they are to be kept in: Take to every pinte of fayre water take ten pipins, and ten John-aples, your water being in a large skillitt, pare your Apples and cutt them in good big peeces, puting them as fast into ye water as you do them; pull out the kernells, and put in the cores also, when you have put in what quantity you would; set it on the fire, and let it boyle till all the vertue be out of the Aples, and the water tast very strong of Aples, you must not cover it in the boyleing for the payler it looks the better; let it boyle no longer then whilst it is strong for fear of makeing it too high coullered, but you must be sure to have it strong enough, for then less boyleing will serve it when it coms to have suger; when you thinke it is strong enough take it off the fire; and strayne it throw a haire sive and so let it stand an howre or two to settle; then peare away all the clearest, and strayne it thro a jelly bag of flanell; then to every pinte of this clear liquor, take a pound of double refined suger, put them together; and if you please to have it perfumed tye a very little muske in a cloath and boyle it together, as soone as the suger is all melted; make it

[228]

to boyle as fast as it is possible sciming it cleane; keepe it with fasy [fast] boyleing till it will jelly wch you may know by now and then puting a little into a spoone to coole, if the pipin water was very strong it will immediately be enough; but a little before you thinke it is enough, put in some juce of Lemon; as much as you thinke will give it a tast, let it boyle but a little while after the Lemon is in, when you thinke it is enough take it off; and your orinnges being redy drayned out of their sirrop wch they must be an howre or two before; set every orinnge severally in a gally pott [gallipot]; or deepe glace; with the hole upwards, and so poure the jelly on them; filling the orinnge with it, and let the pott, or glace, be so full of jelly as will cover the orinnge; and when they are cold put the little bitts on the hole of your orinnge; and then cover them with papers, and keepe them in a drye place; the'll keepe good all the yare, be sure to boyle a little muske in the jelly if you have it, for that gives it a very fine tast, but take care of puting in too much, for a very little will do: you must not cover the jelly at all in the boyleing.

To preserve *Wallnutts: my second Cousen Clerkes Receipt*

your wallnutts must be green, tender, and not too ripe, and to trye whither they be fitt for your use, take a needle and runn it through them in divers places, especially in the steam [seam] where the shell is joyned; and if the needle go in easily, and gently, and they seem not hard, then they are for your use, then put them into water 4 or 5 howres, and boyle them in that water halfe an howre, then poure away that water and boyle them awhile in another, so change them till the water wherein they boyle is clear, and the blackness, and bitterness, of them be boyled away which will be seen by the cleereness of the water, then to every pounde of wallnutts, take a pounde of suger, and halfe a pinte of damaske-rose-water, boyle all these together, till the liquor become to a sirrop some-what thike; then put them up in a pott with the sirrop, and when they are cold cover them close. One of these being eaten fasting, and a little of the sirrop drank after it, will mildely and gently, purg malencholy, windes and coller, and also good for the wormes.

To preserve *Wallnutts: my Aunt Franckline's Receipt*

Take green wallnuts, and lay them in soake in fayre water three dayes, shifting them every morning, then boyle them in water, and salt, and when they are tender take them out and peele off the skine, and to every pounde of wallnutts, take two pounde of suger, and a pinte of water, then boyle them to a sirrop, and then put them up, and keepe them for your use, these are very good for those that hath a costive body, and a little consumtive.

To keepe Goosberys all the yare for Tarts: Packsons Receipt

Take your Goosberys when they are at their full bigniss before they are ripe or begin to turn; top and tayle them, and put them into a cleane drye glasse bottle; let ye bottle be filled with them; then corke your bottle very close and tye a leather over it; then dig a hole in the grounde and put the bottle into it, and cover ye earth over it, and when you have occation use them; some will onely set ye bottle in a seller [cellar] and they say yt will keepe them well enough; but you may trye both ways if you please.

To keepe plums all the yare for Tarts: Mrs. Charltons

Take your plums when they are ripe; but not over ripe; wipe them, then take new long pots; yt will holde about three pounde a peece; put in your plums, and to every pounde of plums put in about a quarter of a pounde of suger; and when ye bread is drawne, and the heat of the oven be a little over put ye potts in being close covered with paper; so let them stand in the oven an howre; but you must watch diligently that ye oven be not too hott to crack their skins too much for yt will spoyle them; they should be plumped but their skins kept as close as may be; then take them out of the oven, and when they are cold, take a pounde of butter and melt it; and poure it into the pott all over them; so cover your pot close with thike paper, and set a trencher upon the paper, and set it into the seller or some prety damp place; but not too damp; and when you see any molde on the sides of the pott wipe it off; and keepe them for your use; damsons will do very well this way, and so will ye white bullis [bullace]; and also ye damoisen; or the black pare-plume; or the musell plum; thus you may drye plums puting them into ye oven just as you do those to keepe; some will use dryping instead of butter, and says it will do very well; so yt you may trye both ways; you must not put any of their liquer into your tarts for yt will make them tast ill; you must take them clear from their liquor and put them into your tarts, with a little suger; when you have begun to breake a pott; you must use all yt are in it, for they will not keepe well after the butter is taken off; you may keepe plums thus if you please till Easter.

To keepe Goosberys or plums all the year for Tarts

Take goosberys when at their full groweth before they are ripe or begin to turn, gather them drye, and top and tayle them, then put them into clean drye glace bottles fill them, and corke them downe close, and set them into an oven after bread is drawn, and the oven a little coole, let them stand till they are codled, but take great care the oven be not so hott as to crack the goosberys in the least for that will spoyle them; when you thinke they are all codled, take the bottles out of the oven, and rosin the corks very well to keepe all manner of aire from them, then set them in a drye and coole place, and use them as you have occation, you may keepe plums this way, but your plums must be done when they are ripe tho not too ripe.

To Bake pares very Red

Take about 40: good bakeing pares [pears], you must pare them and put them into an earthen pott with halfe a pound of suger, and as much scutcherneele [cochineal] beaten to pouder as will lye on a shilling, and a quart or three pintes of water, and a few cloves, and some quinces if you like them, then tye the pott down close with double brown paper, and bake it with household bred and let it stand in the oven after ye bred is drawn for 2 hours, and so keepe them in the liquor for your use.

To preserve red Rose Leaves: my Mothers Receipt

Take the leaves of the fayrest buds halfe a pounde sifted cleane from the seeds, then take a quart of fayre water; and put it in an earthen pipkin; and set it over the Fire untill it be scalding hott; then take a good many other red rose leaves and put them into the scalding hott water untill they begin to looke white, then strayne them out, and thus do till the water looks very red, then take a pounde of lofe suger, finely beaten and put it into the liquor, with the halfe pounde of red rose leaves, and let them seeth together, untill they be enough, which is to be knowne by

[231]

takeing some up in your spoone; and when the sirrop begins to be thike, and hang upon the spoone, they are enough, then when they are cold put them up, and keepe them very close.

Sirop of Violets, or Clove gillyflowers, or any other flowers: my Mothers Receipt

Take a pinte of water and make it scalding hott, or you may boyle it, then take your flowers and cutt of all the whites, and poure your water scalding hott to them, you must make your water extream thike of flowers, so thike that you may set a spoone an end in it, then cover it close and let it stand 24 howres, then set it one the fire and make it scalding hott; but be sure it do not boyle, then strayne it, and if in the strayneing it growes cold set it over the fire and make it scalding hott; and poure it one fresh flowers as you did before; and let it stand 24 howres, then set it one the fire and make it scalding hott then strayne it, and if you thinke it not strong enough of the flowers you may add fresh the third time if you please; after you have made it off what strength you please strayne it, and to a pinte of liquor put two pounde of double refined suger, or fine pouder suger; then set it over a slow fire and let it be thorow hott and then let it simber a quarter of an howre; but be sure not to let it boyle for that will spoyle it: made thus with double the weight in suger will be extream rich; and it will keepe 3 or 4 yare very good, but for present use you may make it with less suger, that is to say a pounde of suger, to a pinte of liquor, but then you must be sure to make the liquor extream strong of the flowers, and also boyle the sirrop gently for halfe an howre, thus you may make any sirrop, that is made of any kinde of flowers, as roses, couslips, or any others: you must not put your sirrop up in bottles till it is quite cold.

Sirop of Violets: my first Cousen Clerke's Receipt

Take the violets when they are picked, and take double their weight in lofe suger, then wett the suger about halfe a pinte of water to a pound of suger, is enough, then boyle it, in the mean while stamp the flowers, you weighed, and when the suger is boyled to a sirrop put in the flowers; let it not boyle after the flowers are in; but let it stand over coles stiring it about halfe an howre; then strayne it hard out; and when it is cold put it up in your glaces; I fear halfe a pinte of water to a pounde of suger will be of the most; but you may guess that according to your discrestion, some says this is a better way to make this sirrop then [than] by infusion.

Syrrop of Violets, Clovejellyflowers [clove gilliflowers]: or any other flowers

your flowers being redy picked heat some water scalding hott, and poure it to them, make your water extreame thike of flowers and keepe it on hott embers all night; ye next morning strayne it, and to a pinte of liquor put two pounde of suger, set it on ye fire and make it scalding hott; but not to boyle nor simber, only so hott as to rayse the scume which take off very cleane: by that time it has stood so long as all the scume that riseth is taken off it will be enough; then strayne it and when 'tis cold put it in bottles: for farther directions to make this sirup read to the bottom of this leafe: in case you cannot gitt a great quantity of violets together you may as you can gitt them pick them and put them into any sort of cold still [distilled] water, that hath little smell or tast, as Burage, or Baume, or any such like water, and so you may let them steepe in ye water till you have gott as many as will make ye water very thike of flowers so that a spoon may stand up an end in it, if they lye in ye cold water a weeke together it being in stilled waters it will be never the worst, still putting in the violets as you gitt them; and when you have put in what quantity you intend, strayne ye flowers out, and heate the liquor scalding hott and poure it on the flowers againe; and so keepe it close covered and by the fire untill ye next day, then strayne out ye flowers and to a pinte of ye liquor take two pound of good suger, and make it into a syrup as above directed.

Clovejellyflowers sirrop in sack

put some sack into a bottle and put to it enough of clovegellyflowers (the whites being cutt off) to make it very thike of flowers that it may be strong of them; stop your bottle close and set it in a pott of boyleing water, and there let it boyle till you thinke all the vertue be out of the flowers; then strayne it out and to a pinte of liquor put in a pound and halfe of suger; set it on ye fire and keepe it scalding hott untill you have taken off all the scume that riseth; let it not boyle nor simber; when you thinke it is enoygh take it off and strayne it, keep it for your use, it is a very cordiall and pleasent surrop.

[233]

To make sirrop of Diacodian: with the vertues of it

Take of white poppy heads with their seeds, gathered a little after the flowers are fallen off, keepe them in the House after they are gathered three days, then take 2 pound of them and steepe them in eight quarts of water 24 howres, then heate and press them gently and boyle it till it comes to 3 quarts, then strayne out ye liquor and put to it 6 pound of suger and boyle it gently to a syrup keepeing it scimed:

this syrup is rare good for any coughs, and thisicks [tisick],[1] and also most rare good to cause sleepe in any illness; two spoonefulls of it being mixed in any cold stilled water warme it a little, and take it going to bed at night, you must not exceed two spoonefulls of it to a growen person at once, and a spoonfull or less to children is enough at a time; for it is a great provocative to sleepe therefore must be given with caution; if for a cough take it 3 nights together; it is also of a bindeing quality and if given in a loosness will stop it, and if it be given in a fitt of the colick it will cause them to sleepe and give ease of ye paine.

To make syrup of Diacodian: Mr ffletchers Receipt

Take a pound of dryed white poppy heads, and halfe a pound of dryed black poppy heads, Boyle them together gently in six quarts of water till it cometh to four quarts, then strain it and put to it ten pounds of pouder suger and Boyle it gently till it be a syrup keeping it scimed: This is the way that the Apothicaryers make it, the vertues of it you may see in the above Receipt.

Concerves of Roses, or any other flowers, or of any sort of herbes: Leeche's Receipt

Take a pounde of rosebuds pull them and cutt off all the white, then take three pounde of lofe suger beat very fine, then strow a handfull of your roses in a stone morter, and strow a handfull of the suger one them, then strow another handfull of roses, and one that another handfull of suger, so do till the morter be full enough, to beat, then beat it very well, and so do till you have beat it all, then make it up in a lump and lay it in a silver thing so let it lye a weeke, then beat it over againe, and in 3 or 4 days beat it againe very well; then put it in potts for your use; and set it in a drye

---

[1] 'Asthmatic condition or shortness of breath.' (*OED*)

place, that is not too hott; you may make conserves of any flowers this way, and also of any herbes, but off them you must remember to pick off the stalks, and the great strings.

Conserves of Hips: given me at Mountpelier in France: by the Ablest Apothecary there

Take hips when they are thorow ripe cutt off their stalkes and tops, and take out all their seeds, and prickles, both within and without, then put them into a puter [pewter] dish for 3 or 4 days, sprinckling them every day with a little rose water, then beat them very well in a stone morter, and then pulpe it throw a haire sive, with ye back of a spoone; to every pound of the pulpe take a pound of fine pouder suger beat fine, mingle them very well together in a stone morter; beating it till it be well mixed, then put it up in potts close covered for your use: the hips that grow wilde in Hedges will do as well as those that grow on sweetbryers in gardens: this is rare good for a loosness; eating some of it at any time: if any on[e] yt hath a consumtion attended with a Loosness this is good for it.

Surrop of Lemons

Take some Lemons and squeese out their juce to a pinte of which put in a pound and three quarters of good pouder suger; stir it well together that the suger may dissolve; and being close covered let it stand 24 howres, then scume it very cleane and strayne it and so bottle it up; it will keepe 2 or 3 yare very good; you must not set it on ye fire as you do other surrops, for that quite takes away the tast off the Lemons: Let the juce of Lemons stand 24 howres to settle, then poure of all the clear liquor and put your suger to it.

Sirop of Mulberys, or Black-Berys: Leeches Receipt

Take some mulberys and breake them with a spoone, till you have gott a pinte of juce, to which add a pounde of lofe suger, or fine pouder suger, then boyle it gently for an howre, if you would make this sirrop very rich put in two pounde of suger to a pinte of juce, but then you must let it boyle but simber for halfe an howre, or longer as you see occation; thus

[235]

you may make a sirrop of blackberys, which is rear good for sore-throughts, and so is sirrop of mulberys.

Sirrop of Garlick: my first Cousen Clerkes

Take three heads of garlick and peele of the upper skine, then boyle them in a little whitewine whilst the strength of them be something abated, then take two quarts of whitewine, one handfull of red sage; as much of heartshorne [hartshorn], and as much of unset Isopp [hyssop], then take your garlick pick every clove that the strength may come forth, put them altogether into the wine, so let them boyle gently untill they come to a quart, then take a pounde of the best honny and put to it, affter the honny is in let it but just boyle up that so you may scume it, then strayne it all, this sirrop is rear good for a Tisike [tisick],[1] and for a colde, and a cough, take of it one spoonefull at a time, (or two if you please) in ye morning fasting, and at foure of the Clock in the affternoone, and at going to bed at night; this sirrop is also good for a consumtion.

To preserve Garlick: Mrs Gills Receipt

Take three score cloves of large garlick, and put them into a pinte of spring water, and set it one the fire and let them boyle halfe an howre, then take them out, and put them into another pinte of water made redy scalding hott, and let them boyle in it halfe an howre; then take them out of that water, and put them into another pinte of scalding water, and boyle it as before, then take them out haveing your sirrop redy made, to put them into immediately as you take them out of the water, and so boyle them in your sirrop gently, till your sirrop coms to the height [setting point] of other preserves; make your sirrop to preserve them in as follows, take one pounde of the finest pouder suger, and put to it halfe a pinte of spring water, and six spoonfulls of unsett-hisop [hyssop] water, and 3 spoonfulls of the best whitewine vineger, then set it over the fire, and let it boyle, and scume it, then put in your garlick and preserve it as before directed, then keepe it for your use, this is very good for a cold, or cough; let the party take all this quantity at times, let them take three cloves of garlick every night, and a spoonfull of the sirrop after it, and so let them do till they have taken it all out.

[1] See note 1, page 243.

[236]

Sirop of Turnops: Leeches Receipt

Take some turnops [turnips] and slice them; and put them in an earthen pott and set them in the oven to bake with household bread, cover your pott very close, when it is baked strayne it, and to a pinte of juce take a pounde of lofe suger finely beaten, and so boyle it up to a sirrop, this is very good for coughs, and coles.

Sirrop of Verjuce, or Vineger, Chapmans Receipt

Take a pinte of verjuce, and put to it a pounde and a quarter of pouder suger, set it over the fire and boyle it very gently till it is a sirrop, stiring it all the while it boyles with a licorish stick, sirop of vineger is made the same way, the sirrop of verjuce is very good for a consumtion, and a cole [cold], and good to cutt flem; the sirop of vineger is good for the same, but not for a consumtion.

Sirrop of Coltsfoot: my first Cousen Clerkes Receipt

Take colsfoot at the spring, wipe it, cleane then stamp it, and strayne it, take a quart of the juce and set it one the fire boyle it, and scume it then put in a quart of honny; and take two handfulls of the leaves shread very small, and put them to the sirrop with halfe a pounde of suger; so boyle it up to a sirrop; this sirrop is very good for the consumtion of the longues [lungs].

A Rare sirrop of Coltsfoot: my second C. Clerkes Receipt

Take of coltsfoot halfe a peck; horehowne [hawthorn], peneroyall, meadenhaire [maidenhair fern], scabious, cinquefoile, hyssop, of each a handfull, liquoris, one ounce and a halfe, sweet fenell-seed, anniseeds, heartshorne, of each an ounce, figgs a quarter of a pounde, raisons of the sunn a quarter of a pounde, Iceingglasse [isinglass] a peneworth, steepe all these in spring water over night, and in the morning set it to infuse about six howres, then strayne it and make it into a sirrop this will make 3 quarts if you put water soficient; this sirrop is excelently good for a consumtion, and any cough, or for any stoping at the stomack, being offten proved.

[237]

Sirop of Femetary: Leeches Receipt

garther your femetary [fumitory] in may, beat it and strayne it till you
have got a pinte of juce, then boyle it and scime it, boyle it very gently
and there will rise a great scume, which you must take off cleane; then
take it off, and put to it two pounde of double refined suger, or good
pouder suger, then set it one the fire—and let it simber for halfe an howre,
then keepe it for your use, this sirop is good to clense the bloud, and to
coole the liver, also good for worms in children: thus you make any
sirrop that is made of hearbs; for it is a very good way.

Sirop of Howrehowne [Hawthorn] or any other sirop that is made of herbes: Leeches Receipt

Take a pounde of horehowne [hawthorn] in maye, and bruse it a little
with a pestell, then put it into a quart of water and boyle it very gently
for two howres being close covered, putting into it an ounce of Licorish
sliced, then take if off and let it stand 24 howres, then set it over the fire
againe and let it simber till it coms to a pinte, then streane [strain] it and
put to it two pounde of suger, then set it one the fire and let it simber for
halfe an howre, then keepe it for your use; this sirop is good for a consumtion cough, or for coles; if you can get horehowne enough you may make
this sirrop as you do sirrop of femetary [fumitory], you may make any
sirrop of herbes this way, by infuseing them in water, but if you can
gitt herbes enough to take onely the juce, as you do off femetrary that will
be much the better.

Sirop of Wood-sorill: my second Cousen Clerke's

Take your sorrill [wood sorrel] leaves and stalks, stamp them and strayne
them, then clarify the juce with the white of an egge, then to a pintte of
juce take a pounde of suger and boyle it to a sirrop; this sirop is very good
in a favour.

to pickle all sorts of herbs & flowers

PICKLES

PICKLES

to make vineger, and to pickle mushroms, to make Anchoves, and to pickle all sorts of herbs, and flowers, or any other thing of that nature

To pickle Mushroms: Mr Calcott's Receipt

Take those that are cleane without wormholes, peele the skine off of the outside, and cutt off the cups of the insides, cutt them into peeces as big as a wallnutt, the stalks also are as good as any, but be sure there be no holes in them, then scoure them well with water and salt, then set them over the fire with water and salt, boyle them well, till they are very tender, then strayne them from the liquor, and let them stand till they are cold, then take good whitewine-vineger and water a like quantity, put them together with some nuttmeg, cloves, mace, white peper grossly beaten, according to the quantity of your mushroms; boyle them altogether with a handfull of salt, till they tast well of the spice; then let them stand till cold; then put the pickle and mushroms into a deepe pott, and tye them up close with a cloath over them, and in a weeks time you may eat of them; be sure you take them that are cleere from wormholes for they are as bad as poisson.

To pickle Mushroms: my first Cousen Clerkes Receipt

Take little mushroms of a nights growths, which must be a pure white on the outside, and a fresh pinck within, peele them and throw them into fayre water, then drayne them drye, and put them into a kittle with a handfull of salt; and some water, let them boyle a quarter of an howre, then poure that water from them which will be very black, cleanse the kittle and put them in againe, with a quart of whitewine-vineger, a quart of water, some salt, some oynions, a race of ginger, cloves, and mace, bay leaves, and Lemon peele, then let them boyle one howre, then poure that away, and put in some whitewine-vineger, fayre water, fresh oynions, and mace, ginger, cloves, Lemon peele, bay leaves, and a little horse-redish, let them boyle halfe an howre, and keepe them in that pickle all the yare.

To pickle and dress Mushroms: my second Cousen Clerke

Take the mushroms and put them into water, and rub them over with a woolin cloath which will take away all the furr, and soyle off of them, then wash them well in fresh water, and to a quart of mushroms put 2 spoonfulls of salt, and boyle them in a pipkin with water over a quick fire, if you will stew them to eat hott let them boyle till they have stewed their liquor almost all away, then poure away that and put in a pinte of clarett, a bundle of sweet herbes, a whole oynion, 2 or 3 blades of mace, as many cloves, halfe a nuttmeg grated; about tenn whole peper corns, and with all these let them stew or boyle a quarter of an howre, then take out the spices and all that was boyled with them and dissolve 2 or 3 anchovies in the liquor, and put in a little gravie, boyle it up, put some butter and grated bread to them, and some persly shread if you like it, so serve them up hott: but if you would pickle your mushroms put a little vineger to the aforesaid liquor, and boyle it up with some searced cloves and mace, and whol peper.

To pickle Mushroms

Take small mushroms of a nights groweth, wch must be of a pure white on the outside, and a fresh pink within, peele them and throw them into water as you do them, then drayne them and put them into a kittle of milke and water and boyle them, till they are tender keepeing them scimed, then drayne them through a cullender and lay them on a clean cloath to drye till they are cold, then put them into pickle made as followeth: Take whitewine, and vineger of each a like quantity and put to it of cloves, mace, ginger, nuttmeg, and whole peper about halfe an ounce alltogether, and a peece of Lemon pill, boyle it together about a quarter of an hour, and when it is cold poure it to your Mushroms being cold also, when your mushroms and pickle are together cover the top of the glace or pott they are in with the best oyle 3 inches thike, they will keepe thus very good a year.

How to make a pickle for mushroms

When your mushroms are boyled, cold and made every way redy to be put into pickle (according to the severall receipts in this booke) let them be put into the pickle made as followeth:
Take of Rape vinegar[1] or any other vinegar what quantity you please and put to it a peece of Lemon pill, and an oynion if you like it, and of cloves, mace, ginger, nuttmeg, and peper all grossly brused [bruised] what you think fitt, and still [distil] it altogether in a common still, and then poure the distilled water to your mushroms, and keepe them close

[1] 'Vinegar from the stalks of grape clusters or the refuse of grapes from which the wine has been expressed, Wine vinegar.' (OED)

covered: the pickle so made keepes them good all the year and makes them looke whiter and finer then any other pickle that is not stilled wch. makes them looke yellow.

To pickle any thinge greene: my second Cousen Clerke

Boyle a pickle with halfe vineger, and halfe water, with salt and nuttmeg sliced, cloves and mace, boyle it in bell metell,[1] and when it is cold put in either cucombers, pursline [purselane], stone-crop, lupines, turnops [turnips], or carotts cutt in slices, and what else you please to pickle; for the first moneth they will be yellow, but afterwards they will turn greene.

To pickle Colleflower: Newton's Receipt

Take the whitest and closest Colleflowers [cauliflowers] you can gitt, cutt them from the leaves and part them in little bunches, then lay them in an earthen pott and strew on them a good handfull of salt, them boyle some water with a little milke in it scuming [skimming] it well, and poure it boyleing hott on your colleflowers covering them pretty close, and so let them stand till the liquor be almost cold, but before it be quite cold you must take them out or else it will make them stinck; then lay them in the pott againe and strew on some more salt on them, and poure some cleane boyleing water on them covering them close and so let them stand all night; then the next day take them from that water and strew some more salt on them, and poure more fresh boyleing water on them, covering them and let them stand till next day, then take them cleane from the water and salt, and poure your pickle boyleing hott on them; your pickle must be whitewine vineger with some whole cloves, mace, peper, ginger, and clove-peper, just boyled up together, cover them close and keepe them for your use.

To pickle Collyflowers, to eat like Mushroons

Take the whitest colyflowers you can gett, and cutt them into little bunches like Elder Budds, you will find they grow in little bunches but do not cutt them too bigg, take away all the green leaves that grow

---

[1] 'An alloy of copper and tin, the tin being in larger proportion than ordinary bronze. Used for making bells, thus "bell metal".' (OED)

between them, then lay them in a gallypott [gallipot] and strew a little peper and sliced ginger and a little gemacoe [Jamaica?] peper and a blade of mace, then boyle some vineger and pour it on them hott, you must not put in any salt at all: cover them close and they will eat like mushroons.

To pickle Cucombers: my second Cousens given by Mrs Jackson

Take a good glassed [glazed] earthen pott which you do intend to pickle them in, let your cucombers be new gathered, and wiped very cleane, lay them into the pott and here, and there, some dill and fenell; and mace, and cloves, and when you have filled your pott with cucombers, then fill it up with the pickle boyleing hott; which must be made thus: take two quarts of whitewine vinegar, add to it as much fayre water, and a good handfull of bay salt; and a good handfull of dill, then put it over the fire, and boyle it halfe an howre, then fill up your cucombers with it boyleing hott; then stop it up very close whilst it is hott, after the pickle is in cover them with a dousen of vine leaves; or more, and tye the top of the pott with some leather, or any thinge else.

To pickle Cucombers: Newton's Receipt, and it is an excelent one

Take some salt and water and a good quantity of bay salt, let ye bigest quantity be bay salt; ye water must be so strong as to bare an egg, then just boyle it up and scume it, and haveing your cucombers redy placed in an earthen pott, poure the brine boyleing hott to them, and immediately cover it very close with cloaths double, and then a plate and a borde over that, and another double cloath over all and round ye pott that no steame may gitt out; so let it stand till the next day, then poure out the brine and boyle it up againe scumeing it and poure it boyleing hott to your cucombers againe, covering them close as you did before; and so you must do the like ye next day againe; and in 3 times doing so you will finde they will be very green, then drayne your cucombers cleane from the brine in a coullender; when so don place them close in your pott you desine to pickle them in, and lay on them a little dill, fenell, and vine leaves, putting in also a peece of rock allom and a bitt of shineing salt peeter, then for the pickle take two quarts (or more according to your quantity) of wine vineger and put to it a nuttmeg sliced, some cloves, whole mace, whole peper, 2 races of ginger sliced, just give it one boyle up scuming it

[245]

and immediately poure it boyleing hott on your cucombers; covering them exceeding close as you did in the brine, that no steame come out, and if you thinke they are not greene enough you may at any time poure out ye pickle from them and boyle up, and poure it boyleing hott on them againe; for the offtner you do so the greener they will be; you may keepe ym all ye yare, boyling ye pickle sometimes.

whereas this receipt mentions the scalding of ye cucumbers but once a day note that it is much better to scald them twice a day that is to say morning and night for then the liquor will not be cold wch. will make them much greener and in 2 days you will scald them 4 times wch. will green them enough before you put the pickle to them.

To pickle kidney Beans an Exelent way

gather young kidney Beans at the latter end of the year, do not string them, neither top nor tayle them, put them into an earthen pott, and cover them with spring water, put to them salt enough to make it a strong brine so let them stand 8 or 10 days in a coole place, and if any froath rises scim it off, then poure all the brine from them and wash them well with fresh water, and put them into a brass skilet just scoured cleane, fill it up with water enough to cover them, and set it on the fire again covering it with a brass cover, keepe them simbering for almost an hour till they become green stiring them sometimes and at last you may let them boyle a little, when you thinke they are green enough take them off the fire close covered about a quarter of an hour, then take them clean out of the water and lay them on a cloathe till they are drye and quite cold, then put them into an earthenpott, and take as much vineger as you thinke will cover them boyeing it with a little salt and scim it, then put in whole peper, and jemeco-peper [Jamaica pepper?], and quartered nuttmeg and some dill, and after it hath boyled a little put it into an earthen pott to coole and when it is quite cold poure it to your beanes covering them close with double paper, be sure take care that they are always covered with pickle and keepe them in a drye place.

To pickle red Beets: Mrs Green's Receipt

Boyle your Beets roots till they are a little tender but not too soft then cutt them into what fasshon you please, and put them into a pipkin or pott with pickle made with whitewine-vineger, peper and salt.

[246]

To pickle Broome-Budds and Elder-Buds; Mrs Whiteheads Receipt

make your pickle of ye best whitewine vineger, and bay salt, make it prety strong of the salt, to your tast, stir it well together till the salt be dissolved, then strayne it, and let it settle till the next day; then poure it from the dregs of the bottome, then rub your broome buds very drye in clean cloaths, and put them into your pickling-glasse, and poure your pickle to them; and stir them once every day till they are sunck under pickle; Ashen keys, and elder budds are don the same way.

To pickle Nostation Berrys: Newton's Receipt

gather your Nostation-Berys [nasturtium seeds] and put them into a pott, and boyle water and salt with some bay salt in it, and poure it boyleing hott on them, covering them close as you do ye Cucomber in ye former receipt, and so scald them 3 times as you do those, then after the third scald when they are cold strayne out the brine from them, and have redy boyled some whitewine vineger with cloves, mace, peper, clove-peper, and ginger, boyle it just up together and poure it boyleing hott to your berys, keepeing them close covered; these berrys will not be very greene.

To pickle Wallnuts: my Aunt Ryes

garther them at mitsemer [midsummer] or a little before; put them into cold water and set them over a gentle fire untill they are scalding hott; then shift them into another warme water, and so set them one againe; and let them stand till they are scalding hott, then take them up and let them stand till they are cold, then peele them, and put them up with vineger and salt, they will keepe untill lent [Lent].

The Best way for ye pickling of Wallnutts to keepe all the year: Mrs Salmons Receipt

gather your wallnutts before they have any shells when a pin will go thro' them, and put them into water and salt for a month shifting the water twice a weeke, the water must be made very strong with salt, then drayne the nutts well from ye water and rub and wipe them very drye, then put

[247]

them into the following pickle. Take of whitewine vineger as much as is requisite putting into it of cloves, mace, clove peper, black peper, and ginger, what you thinke fitt, and 2 or 3 cloves of Garlick, a little Mustard seed, a little peece of Allom [alum] with a little salt boyle all together for an quarter of an hour, and when it is cold put it to the wallnutts and keepe them for use.

To pickle quinces: my first Cousen Clerkes

pare your quinces and core them, then take water, and about a quart of whitewine, which quantity will serve for about a hundred quinces, you must put your pareings and cores, into the liquor with some other small quinces that are not fitt for use; cutt them in peeces, put in also as much salt as will season porige, boyle these together halfe an howre; cover up your quinces to keepe them fresh till your pickle be redy, which you must make as much hast as you can, when the pickle is cold put it into your pott to your quinces; cover them with the pareings and cores, that was boyled in the pickle; put a borde upon them to keepe them downe, and another boarde upon the top of the pott, then past [paste], or clay, it up close, to make them take pickle till you spend them.

To pickle little hard green figgs: Mrs Westons Receipt

Soke them in water 24 howres then put them into cleane cold water and boyle them till they be a little tender; take them out and let them lye upon a drye cloath till they be cold, then have redy your pickle which must be boyled with spice, some whole peper, and a little salt; the liquor must be white-wine-vinegar, and beere, halfe one and halfe the other; power [pour] it hott upon the figgs, let them stand so covered 24 howres, then powre it from the figgs and boyle it againe a little while, and when it is quite cold put it to the figgs, cover them up close and keepe them for your use; the time of doing them is best a little after Micklemas.

To make Mango's a very good way

Take Millions [melons] when almost at full groeth and quite green leaveing a little of stalks on, then cutt off a round peece on the top and take out all the seeds and pulp very clean, then put into each millon two cloves of peeled garlick and a nuttmeg quartered 2 or 3 bitts, and a little whole peper with some beaten peper, and a little mustard-seed brused, when all is in put on the top again and tye it on with a packthred so fast as not to come off; put them upright into an earthen pott and cover them all over with whitewine vineger, and put in 3 or 4 cloves of garlick, and whole peper, and quartered nuttmeg, and some mustardseed brused with a little salt, and so let them stand covered with paper for 4 or 5 days, then boyle the liquor in a brass skillet and poure it boyleing hott upon them and cover them up close and so let them stand ten days, then boyle ye same liquor again and poure it on as before adding more vineger if there be not enough to cover them, so let them stand ten days more, then put the millions and the liquor all into a skillet and boyle them gently till they are green keepeing them close covered, boyle them till a little tender, then take them from the fire and let them stand close covered a quarter of an hour, then put them upright into an earthen pott poureing the pickle on them and cover them with double paper, and when you use them take one at a time and cutt it the long way and scrape out all that was put into it, the wch you may put into your pickle.

To pickle any Flowers: my first Cousen Clerkes

Take halfe whitewine, and halfe water, and to a pounde of flowers take neere a spoonfull of bay salt, for that is the best, but for want of that take white salt; but off that you must put in more, boyle a good quantity of the smallest sort of flowers you intend to pickle the more the better, boyle them in the pickle about halfe an howre; and when it is cold strayne out the flowers, and put the pickle into the flowers you intend to pickle, which must be put hard into your pott, then tye them up close, when you use them, eat them with vineger and suger.

To keepe rose-buds all the yare: my first Cousen Clerkes

Take first some blone [blown] roses, boyle them in vineger, buttermilke strayne them out, and when it is cold take a little of it and put into a pott, then lay a laying of butter, thine, and stick in rose-buds close one by the other, then poure on some pickle enough to cover the roses, and then lay another laying of butter, and stick more rose-buds as before, so do till

[249]

your pott be full, laye a laying of butter uppermost, tye it close and keep them for your use, they are very good to garnish dishes withall.

To pickle clove-gilly-flowers, or Couslips: Mrs Beriges Receipt

garther your flowers and pick them, and strew a row of them in the bottome of a pott, or glasse, and then a row of suger, and then another row of flowers, and then a row of suger, and so do till all be in, but let the last row be suger then poure on as much vineger as will wett them, then cover them close with paper, or Leather, that no aire goeth in; and so you may keepe them all the yare.

To make Vinegar of Goosberys

Take goosberys when they are at their full groth before they are ripe, to every gallon take two gallons of water, and two pound of suger, pound them and put them to the water to steepe: 8 days covering it close and stiring it every day; then strayne it out and put your suger to it, and a browne tost [toast] spred with a little yest to worke, the next day tunn it up into a vessell that is fitt for it, and when it hath don working, stop it up close for three quarters of a yare or longer ye better.

To Make Anchovies of Sprats: my Lady Sheldons

Take a deepe earthen pott and strew some bay salt in the bottome of it then lay a row of sprats being clean wiped with a cloath, upon them lay a row of oynions thine sliced, with as much oringe cutt with the peele on as the quantity of the oynion was, some 3 or 4 slices will do it, then lay more salt as at the first; and more sprats with the rest of the things, so doing till the pott be full, but let the row of sprats be double; then fill it up with red wine; and vineger, of each a like quantity, lay more salt on the top and so keep them close, and in a moneth they will be redy.

[250]

to drye Aprecoks, peaches, plums, goosberys, apples, wallnutts

CONFECTIONERY

CONFECTIONERY

—◦◎◦—

all manor of suger jumbells and other suger things; for all sorts of Biskitts: makerons, jumbells, almond cakes and marchpaine, and wafers; all manor of fruite jumbells and puffs made wth. fruiet; All sorts of pasts of any fruite and coullering for pasts; to drye and candy oringes and lemons, and to drye all manor of other fruit, and chips and anjelaca; to candy any flowers and herbs

[253]

Puff cakes or Egg Shells: Mrs Whitehead's Receipt

Take halfe a pounde of double refined suger; finely sifted, the whites of foure eggs beaten to a froath, with 3 or 4 spoonfulls of rose-water, steep 4 graynes of ambergreece [ambergris], and one grayne of muske, in your rose-water, all night, then put in almost all the froath of the egg, into your suger, and beat them together an howre: then do the plates with a little butter very thine and set them into a temperate oven, to bake, you must drop it in little cakes one the plates.

Rashers of Bacon: Mrs Whiteheads Receipt

Take marchpan [marzipan] past [paste], and role it up in red-sanders,[1] or juce of barberys, till it be red, then take three peeces of that, and foure of white, marchpan, and so lay a white, and a red, till all are layed, cutt them through, and drye them, they will be like rashers of baccon.

Eggs and Bacon made with suger

Take some gumdragon [tragacanth] and steepe it in rose water with some muske, then take some lofe suger, beat and sift it extreordnery fine, devide your suger into three parts: one for white; one for yellow, and the other for red: then take one part of your suger and put it in by digrees into a stone morter with some of the gum being redy strayned, beat it well together till it be a past [paste]; a little of the gum will wett it enough to make it a past; when you have made it a very fine past take it out and role it up for your use. Then take some of the strayned gum and couller it with saffern [saffron] being dryed and poudered, put in enough to couller the suger as deepe as you would have it wch when so don put it into your morter and put to it by digrees another part of your suger beating it to a fine past, then take that out and role it up as the other for your use. Then take some more of the strayned gum and put into it some red sanders enough to make it as red as you would have it, then put it into your morter and by digrees put in the other part of your suger beating it to a past as the others then role it up for your use. Make the eggs as followeth, take a peece of the white past as big as an egg and role it in your hands with a little sifted suger (to keepe it from sticking) into a rounde Ball, then take a

[1] 'A red dye obtained from an East Indian tree, pterocarpus Santalinus. It was used as a colouring agent in cookery.' (*OED*)

little of the yellow past and role that into a lesser round Ball, when so don make a hole in your white ball and put your yellow Ball into it, and so close your yellow ball within ye white that non off it be seen, and role it in your hands till it be rounde; then cutt it into foure quarters and laye them adryeing in the sun, or before the fire till they are drye, then keepe them in Boxes for your use. To make the rashers of Bacon take a peece of the white past and role it out thike, then take a peece of the red past and role it pretty thine and then lay it one the white past, then role out another peece of white past as before and lay that upon the red, and then another peece of red one that, and so continue laying one roe upon the other untill you have layed on five roes that is to say three of white and two of red, the white past must be at bottom and top, you must not let the red past be roled out neare so thike as the white past; when you have made it of five roes thikeness then cutt it downe the sides in thine peeces like rashers of baccon off what length you would have them: lay them before the fire or in the sun to be dryed: both these rashers of Baccon, and the eggs, will keepe good seven yares.

Jumbells: my Mothers Receipt

Take a pounde of lofe suger sifted, and a pounde of butter, and eight yolks of eggs, six spoonfulls of rose-water, and as much flower as will make it into a past, put in what seeds you please either carewey-seeds, or coleander-seeds [coriander], then make them one flowered paper, off what fasshon you please, prick them and bake them upon pye-plates, halfe an howre will bake them, they must not be coullered [coloured] at all, nor your oven must not be too hott: you must not lay ym too close one by the other for they will run together.

Jumbells, or knotts, off all coullers, my Aunt Rye's Receipt

beat fine suger and sift it, soke some gum-dragon in the juce of Lemon and then mix it with your suger, but make your suger no wetter with it then [than] to make it into a past, worke it well together, and so role them into what fasshon you please; if you would have them coullered [coloured], you may take what coullered flowers you please, and take the juce off them, and couller it with that, but then you must put in the more gum-dragon; set them a dryeing, but with a small heat, if you do them in the oven.

[256]

Jumbells like Trees: my Aunt Ryes Receipt

Soake gum-dragon in water, when it is dissolved, mix it with a little suger then with the back of a spoone do it through a haire sive, and lay it in what fasshon you please, you may make them of what couller you please, if greene then the juce of spinage, or sorill, if yellow then the juce of mare-golds, if red then the juce of any red flower, if blue then the juce of any good blue flower, or the blue bottles [cornflowers] which grow in the corn, mix any of these juces with that is soaked, and so lay them adrying as before directed, for the other jumbells.

Suger of Roses: my Aunt Rye's Receipt

Take red roses before they are bloone [blown] out, cutt off the white part and drye them, beat them to pouder, and wett it if you please with the juce of a Lemon, then boyle some lofe suger to a candy height, then put in the pouder of roses, and stir it over the fire untill it be redy to cand [candy], then drop it one a plate.

Suger cakes of any Flowers: my Mothers Receipt

Take what quantity of double refined suger you please being finely beaten and siffted, drye it over coles [coals] very well, then do but just wett it with a little fayre water, then set it over some coles and keepe it stiring till the suger be very well melted, but be sure it doth not boyle for that will quite spoyle it; after you have kept it so a good while without simbering [simmering] or boyleing, put your flowers in being redy cutt, as for the quantity you may put in according to your owne discrestion, but I thinke it best not to put too many in, after the flowers are in set it one the fire againe, and there keepe it stirring as before without boyleing or simbering, for above a quarter of an howre as you see occation, and when you thinke it is enough, drop it with the poynte of a knife in little cakes, upon puter [pewter] plates, being strewed over with suger to keepe them from sticking, so let them stand till they are cold, and then lay them up; in a drye place or else they will runn about; you must not let them touch one another, but lay them one by one upon papers: if you please you may make them with the juce of the flowers, which if you will, it is but takeing the juce of what flowers you please, and instead of the water

[257]

put that into the suger, and do them just as you do the others with the flowers but into these you must not put any cutt flowers, but let them be made only with ye juce, and for veriety they will do very well, to mix with the others; you may also make them with the juce of Lemon, or oringes, which will eat very well.

Past of any Flowers: Mrs Whiteheads

Violets, Couslips, Maregold, Burage, Buglos, flowers pickt curiously [carefully], and beat severally, then beat refined suger, finely searced, and take some gum-dragon being steeped, put your suger, and gum, together, and make it into a past [paste]; if you would have it like marble lay it thine roled one upon the other, make it in balls cutt it a thrawt and then roule it, you must mix your flowers with the suger and gum.

Drop Cakes of Angelico: my Lady Howes Receipt

Take angelico [angelica] stalks when they are young, in the begining, or midle of may, and set it one the fire in a skillet of water close covered, and so let it scald but not boyle; as soon as they will peele, take them out, and peele them, then put them in the water againe, and keepe it close covered, and after it hath stood so some time, boyle it till it be very tender, then beat it very fine in a morter, and take the weight of it in lofe suger, boyle it to a candy height, then put in your pulp, and drop it as you do other cakes made of flowers.

Ratafie cakes

Take halfe a pound of apricock [apricot] kernells beat them very fine with oring-flower water, and mix with them the whites of three eggs well beat, and two pound of single refined lofe suger beat and sifted, worke them into a past and lay them in round bitts upon tinn plates flowred, set them into an oven not too hott for they will soon bake: instead of Aprecocks kernells some will make them of Bitter almonds blanched.

[258]

To Make Melindes: a french Receipt: given me by Monsieur le Marqui Achiolier

Take halfe a pounde of lofe suger beat very fine, and three whites of eggs, put them with the suger into a copper or silver skillitt, then with a wooden spoone stir it till it be as white as snow, then set it over a few hott embers till it becoms like pap, keepeing it stiring and not leting it boyle; take it off and put to it a good halfe spoonefull of oringe-flower-water, then set it over the fire againe, that the humedity of the water may be dryed, be sure not to let it boyle, then lay it upon white paper (strewed with suger) in what fashon and bigness you please to have them, then bake them in a temporate oven that is not too hott, I thinke the best fashon to make them in is rather longesh, that is to say about an inch and halfe longe, and almost an inch broade.

Pastillas [pastilles] the best Spanish way: Mrs Lords Receipt

Take a pound of lofe suger finely searced, a quarter of an ounce of amber-greece finely ground; halfe a quarter of an ounce of muske ground small mixe them altogether in a morter, infuse a little gumdragon 24 howres in 2 or 3 spoonfulls of rose water, of this gum use no more then will bring it to a stiff past, then beat it together till the whole mase be made up fitt to worke into cakes wch make as big as three pence: halfe a cake will sweeten and perfume a whole bottle of wine:

Very fine Cakes: Mrs Whitehead's Receipt

Take halfe a pounde of fine flower dryed in an oven, and a pounde of searced suger; and a pounde of march-pane-stuff [marzipan] finely beaten, one nuttmeg grated, a grayne or two of muske, a thimblefull of grated Lemon peele; the yolks of foure eggs, beat all these to a past in a morter, them bake them one plates; and when they are baked ice them with rose-water; and suger, they will be quickly baked.

Suger Cakes: My Lady Howe's Receipt

Take 4 yolks of eggs; 4 spoonfulls of thike creame; 4 spoonfulls of suger, a spoonfull of rose-water, and a pounde of sweet butter washed in rose-water, stir your eggs, creame, and suger, together, breake your butter in little bitts, beat it small with a spoone amongst the eggs, then strew in as much flower by little, and little; as will make it a past, roule it into cakes; cutt them with a glasse; and print them with the teeth of a combe, bake them in a cleane oven, pricking them with a pinn, the oven must not be too hott; bake them one buttered plates.

Suger Cakes: my first Cousen Clerkes Receipt

Take halfe a pounde of butter from the cherme [churn], wash it in rose-water, put to it a pounde of suger, one yolke of egg beat with a spoonfull of rose-water, and as much sack, worke in as much fine flower as will make it a stiff past, or else it will runn about the oven; if they be too limber [soft], they will be immeadiately baked enough, the butter must be in bitts, it must not be kneaded, but worked in.

Shroesbery Cakes: Mrs Burnford's Receipt

Take a pounde of flower, a pounde of butter, and a pounde of suger, grate a nuttmeg and a halfe into the flower, with a few beaten cloves, then mix your suger in your flower, then rub in your butter very well, till it coms to a past, and when you are redy to put them into the oven, put into it the yolks of 2 eggs very well beaten, with 2 spoonfulls of Creame, and 2 spoonfulls of oringe-flower, or rose-water, when you have mixed all these very well together make them in thyne cakes, and in what fasshon you please, put them upon flowered papers, and prick them, put them into an oven that is no hotter then for Custards, you must not let them be coullered at all, about a quarter of an houre I beleive will bake them, when they are stiff at the bottome they are enough, for they will be soft atop when they come first out of ye oven, but when they are cold the'll harden.

Cracknells: My Lady Howes Receipt

Take a pounde of flower well dryed, and a pounde of suger dryed and sifted, foure eggs, and one of the whites, 2 spoonfulls of rose-water, and 2 ounces of butter, rub your butter in the flower and suger, mix all well together putting in some coreander [coriander] seeds, about 2 spoonfulls will be enough, make it up into a past, and roule it out very thine and cut it out into cakes, prick them, and bake them in an oven that is not too hott some will bruse [bruise] the corender seeds a little, but if you please you may put them in whole, and when they are going to the oven, some will wash them over with the yolke of an egge beaten with cold water; but if you please you may bake them without it. you must rowle your cakes as thine as paper; and prick ym very much.

Shell-Bread: given me at schoole

Take a quarter of a pounde of lofe suger sifted, put to it a spoonfull of flower, or the yolks of 2 eggs, and one white, beat this together to fine batter with 2 or 3 spoonfulls of creame, and a grayne of muske and a thimblefull of dryed Lemon peele, put also to it a little searced annyseeds [aniseeds], and a little rose-water, affter you have made it in a very fine batter, take mustle shells and rub them with butter, as thine as you can, then pour the batter into the shells, but not too full, but poore them thyne, then lay them one a gridiron in the oven and when they are baked take them out of the shells, and ice them with rose-water, and suger, this is very fine; it is called the Italian-Mussell, you may keepe them all the yare, and in rayny weather put theem into the oven.

Jumbells of any fruit: my Lady Sheldon's Receipt

Take ripe aprecoks and scald them in fayre water till they are soft then take the pulp from the skines, and stones, and do it through a haire sive with the back of a spoone, then set it over coles in a silver thinge, and let it stand till it be very drye, then take some lofe suger and sift it, and put a little of the dryed fruit to it, and beat it in a marble morter for 2 or 3 howres; then roule it upon a cleane table with battledores, and so turn them into what fasshon you please, you must not roule them biger then the small end of a toobacko-pipe, let them drye upon papers. Thus you may make it of quinces, or black pare plums, you may couller some of your aprecoks with blue starch, you must be sure when you drye your fruit not to let it boyle, nor simber, but only heat.

Oringe jumbells: Mrs Whiteheads Receipt

pare your oringes very thine and put the peeles into a morter, and beat them as fine as possible, and put double refined suger to them as you please; beat them together till they are a fine past, then take it out of the morter, and role it in what formes you please, lay them one papers, and drye them, before the fire, or in a stove, and when they are drye, take more fine suger mingled with rose water, pretty thike; then with a feather spread it over the jumbells, when one side is drye spread the other, the suger and rose water must be beaten together.

Lemon jumbells: my Aunt Rye's Receipt

Take the peeles of Lemons and boyle them very tender, then beat it very fine in a stone morter, and set it over coles, scald and drye it awhile, then worke in as much lofe suger sifted as will make a past, then make them into what fashon you please or print it if you will, lay them upon a borde for 2 or 3 days where they may have some small heat.

Almond jumbells: my Lady Sheldon's Receipt

Take halfe a pounde of Almonds, and as much fine suger, blanch your almons and drye them in a cloath, beat them very finely with rose or oringe-flower water, but no more then will keepe them from oyling, when they are finely beaten put in some ambergreece and muske, then beat and sift your suger, and worke it into your almonds, then take some more suger to rowle them up withall, roule them upon papers with suger, which you must strew over it as flower for past, roule them into long roules not too big, turn them into what knots you please, you must then have your stove hott that they may drye a passe [apace]; as fast as you do them upon papers put them into the stove, you must be sure to suger the papers, when they are all don, take the white of an egg and some double refined suger, sifted, worke it together a good while to make it look white, then with your knife lay it on one side of your jumbells, and so set them in the stove, when that side is drye, slide them on cleane papers, and with the top of your knife do the other side, when they are drye box them.

Almond jumbells: my Lady Sheldon

Take to one pounde of almonds beat very fine with rose-water, take a pounde of fine suger sifted, the whites of six eggs, beat to a froath, then mingle them with the almonds, and three quarters of the suger, leave the other quarter of a pounde to make them up withall, then set a dish one a chafendish [chafing dish] of coles, and put it all in, and stir it continually, with the back of a spoone, till it is so thike that it will make up in rowles, they must not be rouled till it be cold, then take oyle of sweet almonds and anoynte the papers, so lay them one and bake them, the oven must not be too hott.

Hollow jumbells of Almonds: Mrs Whitehead's Receipt

Take a quarter of a pounde of Almonds, blanched in cold water, beat them small with the white of an egg, then take halfe the peele of a Lemon pared thike and boyle it in water, changeing the water 3 times, then beat it small with the almonds, add to it a pounde and a halfe off lofe suger, beat it altogether till it coms to a past, then roule it into little long stripes and turn it rounde, leaveing a hole in the midle, lay it one double papers, and undermost a browne one, halfe a quarter of an howre will bake them.

Aprecock puffs: my Lady Sheldons Receipt

Take a quarter of a pounde of the pulp of aprecoks, grinde it in a stone morter, and as you do it, very often put in a little of the froath of the white of an egge, and a quarter of a spoonfull of double refined suger, and keepe it grindeing rounde the morter, puting in suger, and egg, till it looke very white, then lay it one waffer papers in little roune [round] drops, put your papers one pye-plates, so bake them in an oven, after household bread be come out, they may stand all night.

Quince puffs: my Lady Sheldons Receipt

Take a fayre quince and boyle it very tender, then take the pulp of it, and double the weight in lofe suger, beaten and sifted, then take the white of an egge beaten to a froath, put the pulp of quince into a marble morter,

[263]

grinde it rounde with the pestell, be sure to grinde it all one way, and let one often put in some white of egg, and strew in some suger, a little at a time, till all be in, beat it till it looks white as snow, and rises to the top of the morter, then drop it out with a spoone upon plates, and put them in the oven, just when any thinge is taken out, for the oven must not be too hott, be sure to keepe them in a drye place.

Oringe or Lemon puffs: Mrs Whiteheads Receipt

grate the outside of the oringe, or Lemon, and grinde, or worke, it well with some white of egge beaten to a froath, and taken of with a spoone as it riseth, stir it well together with a spoone with some refined suger enough to make it of a prety stiffness; then role it one paper with suger one it, cutt them in little peeces, and make them flatt and roune, make them the bigness of a farthing, bake them in an oven immeadiately after the pyes have been drawne [withdrawn]; but if you thinke the heat too flatt, a very little more will do it.

Almond puffs: my Lady Sheldons

Take halfe a pounde of blanched almonds beat them very fine with a little rose-water, then mingle them with a quarter of a pounde of suger, and the whites of 2 raw eggs, make them into little rounde cakes, set them one buttered white papers, and bake them in an oven, as hott as for manchetts [bread], when they looke white draw them and put them into a dish, then poure upon them rose-water, and butter, scrape upon them good store of suger, and set them into the oven againe, till they be canded to the top, then draw them and serve them to the table.

To make Marchpane: Mrs Lord's Receipt

Take 2 pound of jordin Almons blanch them then beat them in a stone morter till they come to a fine past puting in now and then a spoonfull or two of rosewater to keep them from oyleing; you must have redy a pound and halfe of fine searced suger three parts of wch suger must be beaten with the almons, and when it is all beaten to a past take it out and worke it with the rest of the suger, then make it up in what shape you please, if you like it you may make your marchpane in a sheet as big as a charger and cutt it rounde and set an edge about it as you do about the bottome of a tart, and have a bottome of waffer under it, then bake it in a coole oven, or in a bakeing-pan, and when it is hard and drye take it out and ice it wth rosewater and suger being made as thike as batter for fritters, spread it on wth a brush or feather and put it into the oven againe and when you see it rise a little and browne take it out and gild it, if you do not like gilding of it you may let it alone.

Almond Cakes Iced one both sides: my Aunt Rye's Receipt

To a pounde of jordin almons take a pounde of double refined suger, beat and sift it, then blanch your almonds by putting them in hott water, till the skins will slip off, and as they slip off put them into cold water, when they are all blanched, drye them in a cloath, and then beat them to a fine past, putting in sometimes a little rosewater to keepe them from oyleing and turning yellow, then put to them halfe the suger, then make it into little cakes, with a little of the suger, to keepe them from sticking to your hands, and the paper, then mingle the rest of the suger with damaske rose-water as thike as you stir a puding; then with your feather Ice your cakes on one side, and set the lidd of a bakeing-pan over them, covered with wood coles, and let it stand till the Iceing is hardened and begins to blister, when the cakes are thorow cold, turn them upon fresh papers, and Ice the other side, in the same maner.

Almond Cakes: my Aunt Rye's Receipt

Take halfe a pounde of almons blanched, and beat them very fine with a little rosewater to keep them from oyling, then put to them half a pounde of lofe suger, siffted, mix them well together, then put in 2 whites of eggs redy beaten, put to it also 2 spoonfulls of white starch sifted, stir all well together, then set it over the fire a little while, and stir them well, then put in the whites of egg for it was a mistake in saying they must be put in before, stir the egg well in, then have sheets of wafers redy and durst [dust] them over with fine suger, lay your cakes one, and set them into the oven, but let it not be too hott, they will quickly be enough: lay your wafers one plates, and drop your cakes one them, dust ym with suger.

[265]

Fruit Biskets or drop Cakes of fruit: Mrs Aline

Take goosberys when they are greene, and scald them, then pulp them
through a sive; but not too neare the stones, then to a pounde of pulpe
take a pounde of double refined suger, mix them together, and beat them
together in an earthen bason, with a silver spoone for 3 or 4 howres; but
be sure all the time to beat it one way; then take pye plates and butter
them very thine, and drop them one it in very small cakes about the bigness of a new shilling, then set them in the oven but be sure the oven be
not too hott; in halfe an howre they will be enough, you may know when
the pulp is beaten enough by the thickness of it; for it will thicken in beating very much, thus you may make cakes of aprecoks, either when they
are ripe or green, some will put the white of an egg into the pulp as they
beat it; for that will make it quite difirent from the others, so that for
veriety you may make some both ways; when you make these cakes of any
greene fruit, you must scald your fruit in a skillet of water, and then pulp
them through a haire sive, with the back of a spoone; but if you make
them of ripe fruit, you must put your fruit into an earthen pott covered
close, and set it in a kittle of boyleing water, and there let it stand till it
be redy to pulpe; you cannot make these cakes with the pulp of courents
or raspes [raspberries]; therefore you must only take the juce off them,
wch you must do; by puting them in an earthen pott and seting it in a
kittle of water as before mentioned; and as the juce comes peere [pour]
it out, and to a pinte of juce take a pounde of suger, and so beat it as you
do those that are made of goosberys before mentioned, but into these that
are made of juce you must be sure to put the white of an egg in, or else
they will not do, so you may make them of what juce you please, puting
in the white of an egg; which must always be put in when you make them
of any juce; there are but few that will make these cakes with green
aprecoks; but instead of them, will take green plums, which will do a
great deale better; you must green your plums and then plump them,
but the goosberys you need only scald for they will not looke green, the
fruit that one generally makes these cakes off, is green goosberys at their
full-groth, and green plums, and ripe aprecoks, and ripe courents and
rasberys, those that are made of goosberys will be of a brounish couller,
and those of plums green; and those of aprecoks yellow, and those of
courents and rasberys red; you must be sure to keepe those that are made
of juce in a drye place, and if they should agine [become soft] put them in
the oven againe, and let them stand till they are drye, and so do those also
that are made of the pulpe; if you make a pounde at a time you must put

[266]

in above 2 whites of egg; but to halfe a pounde I beleive one white will be enough, halfe a pounde will make a great many cakes, so that you had not best make any more at a time, for if you do, 3 or 4 howres will not be enough to bake them; if you see that halfe an howre will not drye them in the oven then let them stand longer, but be sure your oven be not too hott, but let them drye by digrees.

Drop cakes of Lemons

Take of the juce of Lemon one spoonfull and make it thike with fine lofe suger, and let it simber [simmer] but not boyle; grate in ye peele of a Lemon also, then when it is enough, with the poynt of a knife drop it on sheets of paper to drye.

Oringe or Lemon Cakes: Mrs Whiteheads Receipt

Take as many oringes, or Lemons, as you intend to make cakes, then rub them very cleane and put them into a bell skillit; full of spring water, and let them boyle till a straw will go through them; then take them up and put them into a sive, and bruse them through with the back of a spoone, and squese it all through with the back of a spoone, then put as much suger to the puls [peels] as will make it very sweet; then set it over the fire and when it is redy to boyle take it off; and beat the white of 2 or 3 eggs, according as you make and beat them to a froath, then put your froath to your oringes or Lemons, and beat it an howre, till it is as white as a cloath then suger paper, and drop it in little cakes, and let them stand in the stove till they are drye.

Oringe Cakes: my first Cousen Clerke's Receipt

Take your oringes cutt them in halves, and squese out all the juce then take out the meat, boyle them in severall waters, till the bitterness be boyled out, the water you shift them into must be prepared very hott, take their weight in suger, and boyle your suger till it is almost drye, your oringe pill must be redy minced and put into it, you must not set it one the fire after the oringe pill is in; put in as much of the juce of oringe as will give it a tast, to your likeing, then drop them one a plate, the bigness

[267]

you would have them, put them into a stove till they are pretty drye, then [take two and] clap both the wett sides together; drye them one day in the stove after they are clapt together, and then lay them up.

Oringe Cakes: my Aunt Ryes Receipt

Boyle your oringe pills in 2 or 3 waters in a cloath; till they are very tender, then clear [clean] them with a knife and squese out the water from them, then beat them in a stone morter, and to a quarter of a pounde of it, put to it halve a pounde of the pap of pipins, then with the back of a spoone do it through a haire sive, then drye it a little over coles, to a pounde of pulps put in a pounde and more of lofe suger, finely beaten, wet your suger with a little water, and boyle it high, then put in your pulp, and give it one boyle, then put in some juce of Lemon; and heat it a little more, but not boyle for fear of roaping [becoming thick and stringy], and so put them into your coffins to drye.

Oringe Bisquets: my first Cousen Clerkes Receipt

cutt your oringes in halves, or quarters, take out the meat and soake the pills in water 24 howres or more shifting the water 2 or 3 times; if you please you may pare the pill of the oringes, but if you do they must be pared as thike as may be; else the pill will be tuff, and not so good coullered; then boyle them in severall waters till the bitterness be out as you would have it, then beat the pills in a morter to a fine pap, then take double the weight in lofe suger, and enough of the juce of the oringes to mix it a stiff past [paste]; then put it upon a trencher, or what you please, set it in a stove, or coole oven, for a day and a night, you will finde it to cand one the top; it must be beat out square upon the trencher, when it is thus drye; you must cutt it into little long bisquets as you please; and when they are drye enough lay them up.

Aprecock Cakes, or any other fruit: my Aunt Ryes

Take aprecoks before they are too ripe; scald them in fayre water very tender, but do not cover them that they may be the paler, then with a knife take the pulp from the skins, and stones, save all the juce that coms

[268]

from them in the skining, and put it into the pulp; break your pulp very fine with the back of a spoone, then take the weight of it in double refined suger beaten, sifted, and dryed over a chafindish of coles, then stir it into the pulp, and set it over gentle coles that it may only scald, but not simber, nor boyle, at all, keepe it with stiring untill it be indiferent thike, then put it into your glaces, or cofins, of tinn or paper, and when they are thorow cold drye them in the sun, or stove, or oven; but be sure the oven be coole enough, or else they will be too deepe coullered, for the payler they are the better, and the best cakes are made of the paylest aprecoks; as soon as they cand turn them, that they may cand one the other side, when they are drye enough put them up in boxes, with papers betweene them; you may if your please poure your pulps upon glace plates, or earthen plates, if you finde they will make them thike enough, and so when you turn them you may cutt the cakes into what fashon you please; som will make them only roune, others will make them three corners. And as you please you may make cakes of any plums, quinces, or pipins, after this maner, red plums you may do with couser [coarser] suger.

Thine Aprecock Cakes: my Lady Sheldon's

Take ripe aprecoks cutt them in halves, stone them and pare them, then put them into a deep pan, tye a paper over them prick it full of holes, set the pott in a kittle of water, let it boyle one howre, then put the fruit into a canvis strayner, the liquor that runs from it set by itself; with a spoone drive as much of the fruit through as will go, then do the like of the greenest goosberys you can gitt, put the two pulps together, but twice as much aprecoks as goosberys; take their weight in lofe suger mix it with the pulp in a skillet, and boyle them almost halfe an howre; then put a spoonfull in a place in 2 or 3 places of a new trencher; so knock the trenchers upon a table to make it spread abroad, let it stand all night, the next morning strew searced suger upon them; rub it gently one with your hand, then blow it cleane, and with a knife sliped under it, slip it off from the trencher, suger that side as the other, if you have prints you may print them, lay them one paper for a day or two, to drye, then box them, and keepe them for your use, the liquor that runed from them will make cleere-cakes.

Note. For a Memorandum

That in the makeing of Rasbery cakes and all other sweetmeat cakes, you must be sure to keep the pulp of the fruit warm untill you put it into ye canded suger, and that will make them drye the better, you must also observe not to drop the cakes out so soon as you take it off the fire but let it stand till it be almost cold, and then drop them out as big or as small as you please, in so doing 'twill prevent their runing.

pipin Cakes: Mrs Brownes Receipt

Take pipins and pare them, and quarter them, then boyle them untill they are tender in fayre water, then rub them through a haire sive with the back of a spoon, and to a pounde of pulpe, take three quarters of a pounde of suger, then boyle the yellow peele of a Lemon in water untill it be very tender, shread it very small and mixe it with your suger and apple; stir it well together, and set it one the fire, and make it scalding hott, but let it not boyle nor simber, then put it one plates and set it in an oven, that tarts hath been drawne out off, and let them stand till next morning, and then cutt them into what fasshon you please, and so drye them, you may put in a little juce of Lemon when you mixe them, if you please.

An Exelent way of makeing Rasbery Cakes, or any other cakes of fruit

Take some Rasberys and break then all to mash with a spoon, then put to it some juce of red currants to make it a little sharp, if you like it, boyle it over a fire till the liquor be all wasted and that it becometh almost drye, then way [weigh] it and to a pound thereof, have redy a pound of lofe suger finely siffted and dryely wetted with a little water, and boyled untill it cometh to suger again, to which put your boyled Rasberys stiring it well together till it becometh a little thike, but be sure not to let it boyle nor the least simber; when you thinke it is thike enough then with a spoon drop it into little cakes on a puter [pewter] dish and drye them in the sun, or in an oven the next day after bred is drawn for if they are putt into an oven too hott they will not cand, they will not require any turning in the dryeing. That after the same maner may be made cakes of aprecoks, quinces, or any such like fruit, being first boyled tender in water and afterwards pulped thro a hair sive.

[270]

Clear Cakes of Courents, or any other fruit: my Aunt Rye's Receipt

Take your courants and strip them from the stalks, then put them into a skillet without any water, and set them over a very gentle fire, and as the juce coms out take it up in a spoone, and when you have gott out what juce conveniently you can without squesseing the courants too much for you must have a care of that, if you squesse them very hard it will make the juce thike, and of a mudy couller; strayne your juce and waye it and to a pounde of juce, take a pounde of suger, set your juce one the fire and let it boyle up and scume [skim] it, let it boyle no longer then whilst you can scime it, then take it off the fire, and your suger being beaten in good bigg lumps, and dryed over a chafindish of coles; put it into the juce then set it over a very gentle fire, and cover it close, so let it stand till all the suger be very well melted, stiring it now and then, you must be sure it do not boyle, nor so much as simber all ye time, for if it doth it will be quite spoyled, some will put the suger whole into the juce without beating it at all; when your suger is very well dissolved in the juce, take it off the fire; and put it into glaces, and fill them of what thickness you please to have the cakes; or you may put it into paper coffins, then set them in the sun, or stove, to drye, and when they are canded enough to turn, you must turn them; and if you will not have then rowne, then cutt them into what fasshon you pleased, for affter both sides are canded they will crackle so that you cannot cutt them; therefore cutt them when but one side is canded, thus you may make clear cakes of plums, or aprecoks, or goosberys, but you must gitt the juce out of any such fruit, by puting them in an earthen pott covered close, and set it into a kittle of boyleing water, and as the juce coms out; peere [pour] it out, and when you have gott what quantity of juce you would, order it just as you do the juce of your Courants for clear cakes, some will fetch the juce of their Courents out so, and I beleive it will make the juce clearer then the other way; onely puting them in the skillet is the quicker way, some will onely strip their courents and bruse them with a spoone, and so strayne their juce from them; if you would make cleere-cakes of quinces, or pipins, pare, core and quarter them, and boyle them in water till they are tender enough to crush; then strayne them hard by one at a time, then take the weight of your juce in lofe suger; and order it as above mentioned; one of these ways you may gitt out juce off any fruit for cleere cakes.

Clear Cakes of quinces, and pipins, together: Mrs Beriges

Take some quinces, and as many pipins, pare core, and quarter, them then boyle them in fayre water cores, and kernells, altogether till the water be slippery, and well jellyed, then strayne out the water but let not the pulp of the aples come through, take to a pinte of that water a pounde of suger, then dryely wett your suger and boyle it to suger againe; keepe it stiring all ye while; when it is come to a suger take it off ye fire, & when it hath don boyleing put in your apple water, and stir it together, and then set it one the fire, and scald it a little, then put it in glaces and drye them.

Cleere Cakes of Oringes, and Lemons: my Lady Sheldons

Take oringe, or Lemon, pill being rasped [grated], watered, and boyled, as you do them to preserve, but tenderer, then strayne them through a peece of canvis, then mingle that pulp with twice as much off the liquor or water of quinces such as you make jelly of, mingle it so as that it may cast a little thicker, then that you make jelly withal; but let it not be too thike; for then it will not be clear; then take the weight thereof in lofe suger, boyle it to a candy height, then put in the liquor, stir it together, and immeadiately take it from ye fire; when it is but warme put it into glaces and set them in a stove till the top is canded, then turn them upon sheets of [or] glaces till they be dry.

Past of Aprecoks: My Lady Howe's Receipt

Take a pounde of aprecoks when they begin to turn an apple yellow, scald them very tender; take out the stones, and then stamp your aprecoks in a morter till it be very fine, and looke white, then put to it a pounde of double refined suger dryed, beaten, and sifted, mix it well together, till the suger be all melted, then put it into your glaces, and put it in your stove.

Past of quinces: my Lady Sheldon's Receipt

Take the fayrest quinces newly garthered off the tree; let them boyle in fayre water; and be sure to keepe them under water all the while with a ladle; then take them up, and pare them, and take the pulpe; but not neere the core, be sure you leave no lumps in it, then take the weight in double refined suger, and boyle it to suger againe, whilst this is doing beat your quince in a silver basson, with a silver ladle; to make it looke white, then poure in your pulp to the suger and keepe it with stiring upon the fire, till all the suger be melted, but be sure it do not boyle, then drop it out into what fasshon you please, drop them upon plates, set them into a stove, when they are drye on one side, turn them one the other sides upon cleane plates, let them not stand too hott, for that will make them tough: you must boyle your quinces very tender.

Past of plums. white or red: my first Cousen Clerkes Receipt

Take your plums put them in fayre water, let them scald till they will peele, then scrape them from the stones, and to a pounde of that puls [pulp], take a pounde of lofe suger, wett it dryly and boyle it to suger againe, then put in the puls, and let it scald till there is no tast of rawness in it, but do not let it boyle; then put it into glaces; and set them in a stove, when it is prety drye, cutt it out, and keepe it with turning, till it be quite drye.

Past of oringes: My Lady Howe's Receipt

Take eight fayre John apples, pare them pretty thike, and cutt of the specks, slice them very thine, but not neere the core, into a bason of water, then put them into a skillet with a little fayre water set it one the fire and keepe it boyling, and stiring, till it be very soft; then put it in a morter and stamp it, very fine, then take a pounde and a quarter of lofe suger dryed, and sifted, then take halfe a pounde of the apple pulp, and put it to the suger, then boyle a pounde of oringe peele very tender till the bitterness be pretty well gon, then stomp them very fine in a morter, then mingle it with the apple, and suger, and strayne in the juce of 2 or 3 oringes, mingle them well together, stiring it in the morter till it looks white, then put it in cleere-cakes glaces and set them in a stove to drye.

Green coullering for any past, Mrs Chapmans Receipt

Take 3 or 4 good handfulls of spinige, or green beech which you can gitt, put it into a stone morter and pounde it, then strayne it, and take the juce of it, and put it into a skillet, and sett it over the fire, untill it be redy to boyle, then there will rise a green curde, then take it off the fire, and drayne all the liquor from the green curde very clean; then take the curd and beat it very fine; so that no lumps remaine in it, and with this you may couller your past as you thinke fitt.

How to make Bisquitts: Newtons Receipt

Take a pound of the finest flower drye it well, and then grinde it in a morter with a pestell that ye clumpers [lumps] may breake, then have redy a pound of fine suger beat and sifted, mingle it with your flower, and take six eggs leaveing out 3 of the whites, beat them well with a little rose, or orangeflower water strayneing them that ye treadles may not be in them; put them to your flower and suger and put it all into a stone morter and keepe it beating well with a wooden pestoll for an hower or longer till it be very white and thike; then bake them on buttered plates or in little pans buttered, but you must be sure to put but very little into each pan for fear of makeing them too thike; for they will rise mightily; keepe downe the oven lid all ye time they are abakeing, let not the oven be too hott, to couller [colour] then, when you take them out of ye oven lay them upon papers for a day or two, for if you lay them upon puter [pewter] without papers that damps them, in a day or two boxe them up.

To make Bisquitts: Mrs Marshes Receipt

Take a pound of butter wash it in water working it with your hands, and after you have done so wash it in rosewater, or oringe flower water, leave about a spoonfull in the thinge and worke it in with ye butter, let the butter be worked in a pott with your hand for a full hour, and take 12 eggs leaving out 4 whites let them be well beat, then put them into the butter spoonfull, by spoonfule, and after they are all in beat it with your hand another full hour, then take a pound of flower well dryed by the fire and sifted, and take a pound of double refined suger beat and sifted, mix the flower and suger together, and twopeneworth of mace, and a little sinomon [cinnamon] beat together and mix it with ye suger and flower, and shake it into the butter a handfull at a time continewing beating it all the time, then fill your pans and put them into a pretty hott oven; let them be well baked for then they will keepe the better.

[274]

Biskits: my second Cousen Clerkes Receipt: we make it by this Recept

Take a pounde of fine flower drye it, and searce it through a tifiny [tiffany] sive, take also a pounde of fine suger beaten and sifted; then take six eggs and 3 of the whites, but be sure to take non of the tridles; beat with your eggs foure spoonfulls of rosewater till they are enough, then put your suger in by little; and little, at a time till all be in; keepeing it beating all the while; and always one way, for an howre by the clock, as fast as you can, but when you first go abeating put fire into the oven, for you must not stay for that, make it as hott as for white bread; be sure to have it hott enough, when you have clensed it very well you must take a mop wetted and wipe the top, and sides, of the oven, then shutt up your oven a little while, when your oven is redy put your flower into your suger, and eggs, keepeing it stiring till you put it in your pans, which you must have redy buttered, and put them in the oven as fast as you can, first trying with a paper if it couller not too much, keepe downe the lid all the while they are in, take them out when they are enough which will be before they are coulered, you must be sure not to stay for your oven, for that will spoyle them quite; when they are don, take them out of the pans, and lay them one a cloath with their bottoms up, for a day or two till they be drye; if you have not pans to put them in, you may drop ym upon plates buttered, and that will do as well: insted of rose use oringeflower-water wch is much better, 4 spoonfulls is enough.

The Countisse of Waricks Biskitts: my Lady Sheldon's Receipt

Take one pounde of lofe-suger, sift it and put to it the yolks of eleven eggs, with 4 of the whites, and nyne spoonfulls of rose water, beat all these together till they are white, and thike; when the oven is hott stir into these things aforesayd, twelve ounces of flower well dryed; the plates being buttered, drop them on, and put them in ye oven as fast as you can, if you please you may put in some careway [caraway] seed, you must beat them with a whiske.

Suger or Italian Biskits: given me at schoole

Take a pounde of lofe suger beaten and sifted, then take some gumdragon [tragacanth] steeped in rosewater, and a grayne of muske, and another

[275]

of ambergreece, mix all these together with the white of an egg, and beat it in a stone morter till it coms to a puff past, then take halfe an ounce of anny seeds [aniseeds], being rubed and dryed; then take it out of the morter and rub ye seeds into it, lay them upon marchpan waffers and bake them in a hott oven; they will be as white as snow.

Suger Biskits: Mrs Whiteheads Receipt

To every 3 ounces of double refined suger finely searced, take the white of a new layed egg, beaten with a whiske till it turn all to froath, put it in a stone morter to ye suger, and stir it together with the pestell and to one egg put as much gumdragon [tragacanth] steeped as a hasell-nutt, mix your egg, and gum, together before you put in your suger, then stir it a quarter of an howre together, then put in a few careway seeds, first rubed in a canvis cloath, put also some ambergreece [ambergris] in, then drop it one cards, and bake them.

Biskitts with Almons: My Lady Howe's Receipt

Take a pounde of almons, and blanch them in cold water, and take halfe a pounde of lofe suger, beaten and sifted, beat the almons very fine, put to them in the beating the whites of three eggs, beaten to froath with 4 or 5 spoonfulls of rose-water, when the almons are beaten enough, put in the peeles of two Lemons grated, a little muske, and ambergreece, and the juce of a Lemon, mix all these together and role them, and lay them one paper, strowed wth suger, bake them in a slack oven, there was a mistake in saying but halve a pounde of suger, for you must take to a pounde of almons, a pounde and halfe of suger.

Almon Biskits: or makerons [macaroons]: Mrs Whiteheads

Take a pounde of the best jordin almons, blanch them in cold water, beat them very fine with rose water to keepe them from oyleing, take a pounde of suger searced, the whites of 4 eggs beat very well, a quarter of a pounde of fine flower dryed, beat all together till they are very well mixed, butter the plates and set them into the oven; as fast as you can; sift suger one them, as you set them in, so you may make makerons, only you must not put so much flower in them.

[276]

To make French Makerons: given me at schoole

Take a pounde of jordin almons, wash them in 2 or 3 waters to take away the redness off the outside, then lay them in warme water all night, and ye next day blanch them, and drye them with a cloath, and beat them in a stone morter, till they are very fine, then put to them a pounde of fine suger finely beaten, beat them together till it coms to a puff past, and put to it six spoonfulls of rose-water, and a grayne of muske, and 3 grayns of ambergreece [ambergris], when you have beaten all this together, drye it one a chafendish of coles, untill you see it grows stiff, and white, then take it off the fire and put in the whites of 2 eggs beaten to froath; stir it well together, and lay it one wafers, in the fasshon of long buns, bake them in an oven as hott as for manchetts [bread], but you must let the heat of ye oven pass over first, when you see them rise up and very white, take them out of ye oven, and put them into a warme place, and then afterwards you may put them into ye oven againe, and let them stand 2 or 3 howres: and they will keepe all ye yare.

Honey-comb Cakes: Mrs Whiteheads Receipt

Take halfe a pounde of double refined suger, two ounces of almons blanched, in cold water, the white of an egg beat to a froath; take halfe a spoonfull of it, and a spoonfull of rose water, and so put them in by digrees in this maner, beating them exceedingly well to a past, till they be all in, in a stone morter, then roule them in thine cakes and bake them one papers.

Naple[s] Bisquets: given me at Schoole

Take a pounde of refined suger beat it and sift it, then take a quarter of a pounde of almons blanch and beat them very well, then strayne them with 4 or 5 spoonfulls of creame, and 2 or 3 spoonfulls of rose water; then take the suger, and 2 graynes of muske, and 4 graynes of ambergreece, and so mix it altogether, and put into it 3 or 4 spoonfullss of flower, so beat it with a spoone, in a silver bason, then put it into long coffens [coffins], and bake them in the oven; and then turn them out of ye coffins, and put them into ye oven againe, in a dish to drye.

[277]

To clarifye Honey, or Juces: Mr Smiths

Take Honey and put it in a gally glasse [jam jar] and let it stand in hott water almost to the Brim, and the worst part of the Honey will rise on the top: and this way you may clarifye any strained juce.

How to Boyle suger to a candy High: Newtons Receipt

Take what quantity of suger you please beat it very fine and dryly wett it with a little fayre water, set it on the fire and boyle it apasse [apace] keepeing it stiring all the time, and when it comes to almost a candy high it will make a great noise in the boyleing and blader very much more then it did at first; and when it begins to be at a full candy high, it will grow very thike and make a broyleing noise like frying which when it doth so, it will immediately candy and turn all to suger againe.

To keepe the Couller of red sweetmeats: my Lady Sheldons

when you preserve Cherys, or red plums, or make sirrop of gillyflowers, or violets, or any thinge you would have looke cleere; put in 2 or 3 drops of spirett of vittreal [vitriol], and it will keepe it from looseing the couller.

To drye (or candy) Aprecoks, peaches, plums, goosberys, apples, wallnutts: oringe, Lemon, and sittron [citron] pills: Mrs Sandfords Receipt

Stone your aprecoks and pare them, put them in cold water as you pare them; then take to a pounde of aprecoks, a pounde of suger, and almost a quart of water, melt the suger in the water and scume [skim] it cleane, and in the mean time scald the aprecoks in hott water till they are very tender, then put them into the sirop whilst it is very hott; but be sure it doth not boyle, neither must you cover them, then set them by till the next day, and heat them every day morning and evening; for eight or nyne days, till you see they begin to candy; one the top; then take them out and lay them one glasse plates, (or other plates) to drye them in the sun, thus you may do any plums, or peaches, but to them you must not make your sirrop with so much water; because it is a watrish fruit, thus

[278]

you may do the little jenneting-apple which the comferters [makers of comfits?] do greene, which must be first scalded, and peeled, and then put into the water againe, and they will green in it, if you keepe them warme, and under water; then put them into such a sirrop as the aprecoks are, with their weight in suger, and so heated every day: great goosberys may be canded so to, and oringe, and Lemon peeles, but the very outside must be a little rubed off upon a bread-grater; for that is tough, and harde, and will not boyle tender; the water must boyle before you put them in, and so shifft them 2 or 3 times and when they are tender put them into such a sirrop as above directed, and thus you may do sitterne pills [citron peel] which are very cordiall, and thus you may do wallnutts before they have shells, but they must be boyled pretty tender in severall waters to take away the bitterness of them; then have redy such a sirrop as for the aprecoks, and pare them and put them in it, and so heat them twice every day as hott as may be, but be sure they do not boyle for then they will never candy; they must be offten taken off the fire and shaked together gently; and turned that they may heat all places alike, thus you candy pare plums or musselle plums, which you may stone; but not the pare-plums, you must scald them pretty tender before you put them into the sirrop, thus you may candy white plums before they be thorow ripe, but when they are scalded there will be a little skine; which must be scraped off; and then put into watter againe; and they will be green, if kept warme in the water; then put them into the sirrop as the other things; when any of these things begins to drye; and are turned one drye plates every day; then put some double refined suger in a peece of tifiny [tiffany], and shake one them, still when you turn them, but some thinke [thick] white suger candy beat fine and put in a tifiny doth better, these things will all looke much better if they are don with double refined suger, the aprecoks must not be over ripe for then they will be apt to fall a peeces, and to looke with too deep a couller; this receipt is to candy the fruit.

Chips of Aprecoks: my Aunt Rye's Receipt

Take aprecocks pare them, and slice them thine, to a pounde of aprecoks take three quarters of a pounde of suger, beat it, and sift it, and strew it all over your chips, and let it stand till the suger be melted, then set it one the fire; and let it scald for two howres, and then boyle them quick, and you shall see them cleere, in a little more than a quarter of an howre; then take them off and let them stand untill the next day, and then take them out of the sirrop, and lay them one by one upon sives, and so drye them in a stove, or the sun; or the oven; turning them somtimes, so when they are drye put them in boxes betweene papers.

To drye all sorts of plums: my Aunt Ryes Receipt

Take a pounde of suger 2 or 3 pounde of plums, wett your suger dryly with water, it may be about a pinte of water may serve; then prick the plums, and set them over a very gentle fire, and make the sirrop but bloud warme; and so let them continue a little while; scuming them cleane; then take them off the fire, and lay a paper upon them, to keepe them downe in the sirrop, so set them by till the next day, and then set them one the fire againe, and keepe them scalding, but not boyle for above an howre, poureing the sirrop upon them with your spoone; then set them by till the next day, and then do as you did the day before; they must not be above halfe preserved in all; for if they are don thorowly they will never drye well, some will stone them, you had best either stone them, or slitt them, if you stone them take out the stones as hansomly as you can and close them well up againe; small plums are best not stoned, then lay them adrying upon glaces, or plates, damsons or any black plums lay adrying upon puter [pewter], to make them hold their couller, and when they are almost drye you may lay them upon glaces if you please; but as for any other coullered plums you may drye them quite upon glaces, when they are almost drye enough take boyleing water and dip a cloath in it, and wring it out quick and wipe your plums very quick with it; then lay them adrying againe, but do not let them be too drye, you may drye them in the sun, stove, or oven, but let not the oven be too hott; if the sun be hott enough that will drye them best; if you drye them too much you will quite spoyle them.

To drye plums: Mrs Allins Receipt

Take the black or white pare-plume, or the great red pare plum, or the musell plume, put them into an earthen pott, and to every pounde or plums, put in a quarter of a pounde of suger, then cover your pott close with browne paper, then when bread is drawne that the heat of the oven be not too hott, put them into the oven; and so let them stand in the oven an howre, but watch diligently that the oven be not too hott, to crack their skins too much, for that will spoyle them; they should be plumped but their skins kept as whole as maybe, when you have taken them out off ye oven, and they are almost cold put them one the bottoms of sives, one by one, and set them in the oven for about two howres or longer, then put them one cleane sives and set them in againe, and so turn them every 2 or 3 howres, you may either do them in ye sun; or stove, you must be 3 or 4 dayes adrying of them; and if you do drye them in the oven, you must heat it a little every day; but it must be but a very little, for too much heat spoyleth them; you must shift your sives offten espicially at the first; let not your plums be over ripe, and wipe them clean before you put them into ye pott.

To drye or candy pipins, Aprecocks, or plums. My Lady Sheldons

Take fayre yellow pipins, pare them, and bore a hole thorow them, then put them in an earthen platter, or pott, and strew fine suger one them, being finely sifted, then sprinckle them with rose-watter, and bake them in an oven, as hott as for manchets [bread], and stoped up; let them stand halfe an howre, then take them out, and lay them one by one, upon a haire sive, or one a letise [lattice] of wire; or biskitt bakers reeds, and so drye them in a warme oven; in 3 or 4 dayes they will be thorowly drye; you may if you please drye them in a stove; you may do aprecoks or plums this way, but the pare plum is ye best: you must give them a cutt to the stones; and if you lay glaces over them like marmelett boxes, they will sooner be canded: don this way makes them as cleere as amber.

To drye Cherrys: my first Cousen Clerkes Receipt

To a pounde of cherys take a quarter of a pounde of suger, stone your cherrys, and wett the suger dryely, with the juce of cherys which must be gott out either in an earthen pott, over the fire, in a kittle of boyleing water, or by bruseing them; boyle them quick halfe a quarter of an howre; let them lye in the sirrop till the next day, then lay them upon glaces to drye in the sun, stove, or oven, but let not the oven be too hott, the sirrop that is left will do more.

To innamell [enamel], or Candy, Courants; Mrs Allens Receipt

Gerther the largest bunches of Courents you can gitt, then beat some
white of eggs to a froath and take it off, and dip your bunches of courents
severally one at a time in the white of the egg, that is to say in the froath
you tooke off; then have redy some fine lofe suger beat, and sifted,
extreamely fine, and as you take your bunches out of the froath; rowle
them severally very well, all over in the suger; and then lay them bunch
by bunch, upon a puter pye plate, do not let them touch one another, then
if the sun be very hott set them in it to drye; but if not then sett them at
a distance before the fire; and when one side is drye turn the other; and
when they are well dryed, put them in boxes, and keepe them in a drye
place, they will keepe good above two moneths, courents don thus eats
very pretty.

To candy quinces or figgs: my Aunt Ryes Receipt

Scald your quinces and peele them, make a sirrop with fine suger that hath
halfe the weight of the quince in it; when it is boyled, and scumed, put
your quinces into it, being tyed up severally in tifiny [tiffany], and let
them boyle as fast as they can untill they are tender, then have some suger
that hath been boyled to a candy, and take them out of the rags, and put
them into the candy, and let it stand over the fire till it melt againe; but
not to boyle; this do some times, and betweene every time, they must
lye 5 or 6 howres at least, that so the candy may go into them, then take
them out and lay them upon glasse plates, searce some suger one them:
thus you may do figgs, but you must not do them in water, but only in
the sirrop, and the candy, and lay them out one puter disshes, to make
them looke blew.

To Candy Oringes whole with jelly in them: Mrs Whiteheads

Pare, water, and boyle, them as you do those, you preserve, to a pounde
of oringes, a pounde and halfe of suger, wett your suger then let it boyle
almost to a candy height [setting point]; then stir it in your skillett till it
cools and it will come thiker, and thiker, and before it be too hard put in
your oringes; and set it one embers, and it will turn thine againe, so let
them preserve softly in the sirrop till you thinke they will come drye, and

the suger candy, but not too hard, when they are hott fill them with suger [based?] jelly, and put one the toples, drye them in a stove.

To Candy Orange Chips

Pare your Oranges as thine as you can putting the rines into water as you do them, then Boyle them in a skillet of fresh water and then change that water and boyle them in another, and after that boyle them in a third water till they are tender, then draine them thro' a cullender very drye, then take to every pound of chips one pound and a quarter of suger puting to it a quarter of a pinte of fair water, boyle and scim it very well and when it is a syrup put in your chips, first drayning them well out of ye water and so keep them boyleing till it be almost a candy hight [setting point] then turn them out into a sive and stir them with two sticks till they are cold; you must remember that as soon as you have drayned your chips from their boyling water and wayed them, to be sure to put them into clean cold water out of wch you must drain them again just before you put them into ye syrup to Boyle.

To Candy Angelica: my Aunt Rye's Receipt

Take angelico stalks, when they are very young, at the latter end of Aprill, or begining of may; set them in a skillet of water one the fire being close covered; let them scald gently, and be sure not to let them boyle, as soon as they will peele, take them out and peele them, and then put them in the water againe, and keepe it covered, and after it hath stood so some time; boyle them a little, till they be tender enough then take them up, and drayne them from the water, so take their weight in lofe suger, or good lump suger, then in a dish lay alaying of suger, and then alaying of angelico, and so do untill it be all layed in, but let the last laying be suger, and so set them by untill the suger be melted very well; then do them just as you do the chips of oringes, when you drye either them, or these, you must spread them, and turn them offten, or else they will cloder and hange together.

To Candy Roses, or any other flowers in their owne coulleurs: my Lady Sheldons, and Mrs Whiteheads Receipt

Cutt off a little of the stalks of your flowers, lay them one by one upon a sheet of paper, then take some white suger-candy, and beat it very small, and wett it with rosewater, or fayre water, no more than will just wett it, then spread your flowers with it, and so let them drye before a cleere fire two howres, and the suger will grow fast one them, when that side is drye turn up the other side, and do it as the other, then keepe them in boxes.

To Candy sweet-majerom, or any flowers, my Aunt Rye's Receipt

Soake gumdragon [tragacanth] in water, then put in your herbes, or flowers, with the stalks to them; and wett them well in it; then jumble them well in fine suger beaten and sifted, and to make them cand the more, take some beaten white suger-candy and strew over them; so set them in the sun, or stove, adrying upon puter-plates.

A slite way to drye any flowers presently: my Aunt Rye's Receipt

Take jelly-flowers [gilly flowers—wallflowers], mary-gold-flowers, or burige-flowers [borage flowers], the white cutt off, then put them into a silver basson; and strew some fine suger one them, being first beaten, sifted, and dryed, very well, keepe your flowers, and suger, well stired over the fire till they grow scrispe [crisp]; you must set them over a very gentle fire, and so let them drye by digrees; and be sure to keepe them stiring well all the time, for else they will burn too, you must not put any water, nor no licked [liquid] thing to them, onely suger, and put good store of that to them, and yt will make them very scrispe, and drye, and when they are so, keepe them for your use; they are good to eat drye, or in a sallet [salad] haveing some vineger put to them an howre before you eat them.

To Candy any flowers, or branches of herbs: Mrs Beriges Receipt

Take the whites of egg and beat them to a froath; and throw that froath away then take your flowers or herbes with long branches and dip them in the thine of the egg; and when they are threwly wett let them hang downewards to draw away some of the white of the egg, then cast some white suger one them, with your hands so long till the wettness be covered, and dryed up with suger, then stick them in a peece of past, and set them in the sun to drye; or in a warme oven, then keepe them for your use, they are fitt to stick either in marchpints [marzipan] or in tarts, or in boyled waters, or in milke; or in boyled meats or in any other thinge to stick in severall collers, as red, blue, and yellow, you may candy this way buglace [bugloss], burige [borage], couslips, or marygolds, or rosemary; or any other flowers whatsoever, or any herbes: but remember to gerther your flowers with long branches, and with flowers and leaves, and also gerther your herbes with long branches, you must mingle the suger with white suger-candy.

all sorts of wines, and other pleasent drinks

DRINKS

DRINKS

for all sorts of Mead and metheglam: Alle and strong Beer, and to fine sider and all sorts of wines, and other pleasent drinks

A fine small Mead: Swanells Receipt

Take six gallons of water and put to it six pounde of Honey by waite, put in a small handfull of sweetbryer a sprig of rosemary a little sweetmajerom, one nuttmeg quartered, 3 or 4 blades of mace and twenty cloves, let all boyle together for one hower keepeing it cleane scimed [skimmed], then set it acooleing and when it is almost cold make 2 or 3 browne tostes [pieces of toast] and spread them hott with yeast all over on both sides and so set it aworkeing for 24 howers, then strayne it through a haire sive and put it into a vessell fitt for the quantity, and put into it a quart of whitewine, or renesh [Rhenish] with a quarter of a pinte of syrup of cittern [citron] stired in it and when it hath don working stop it close and in a moneth bottle it.

To make White Mead: Mrs Whitehead's Receipt

Take six gallons of water and put to it tenn pounde of honny, and two pounde of pouder suger, set it over the fire and as it boyles scime it cleane, then put into it a small handfull of these herbes: sweetmajerom, sweet-bryer, muscovie,[1] and a few violets if the season affords them; put in 4 blades of mace, a dousen (or more) of cloves, and a nuttmeg sliced, let it boyle in all halfe an howre, then set it acooling, when it is almost cold make 2 or 3 browne tostes spread them hott with ale yeast; and put them to ye liquor, then take 2 or 3 spoonfulls of yeast and 3 or 4 ounces of sirop of Cittron, or Lemons, mix it well together and put it into the liquor, cover it warme for 24 howres, that it may worke according to [your] dis-crestion [discretion], strayne it, and tunn it into a vessell fitt for the quantity, when it has done workeing stop it close, for 3 weekes, if it be clear draw it into bottles, puting into the bottles a lump of lofe suger; as big as a wallnutt, in a fortnight you may drinke of it, it will keepe a quarter of a yare or more.

To Make Mead: Mrs Renols of Aston's Receipt

Take 3 gallons of water, warme it over the fire, then take it off, and put into it of cleane honny six pintes so much as being stired, and dissolved,

---

[1] 'A species of cranesbill or geranium erodium moschatum, so called because it smells sweet like musk.' (*OED*)

will make the water bear an egge, almost to appear, and no more, least it be too strong and too sweet of the honny; then set it over the fire againe and let it boyle so as to scume [skim] it, then put in a bundle of these herbes following, of sweetmajerom, and rosemary, of each a little; of sweetbryer one handfull, and 2 or 3 bay leaves, then take a little bag and put therein a little ginger, a little mace, a stick of cinemon [cinnamon] a nuttmegg, a few cloves, being brused a little in a morter, then let it boyle altogether for above halfe an howre; then set it acooleing, and when it is coole poure it out into another thinge for the settlements, takeing out the bag, and herbes, put in halfe a spoonful of yeast, and so let it stand 12 howres then tunn it up, and after a moneth in the barell bottle it; the honny after haveing taken froast[1] is much the better.

Metheglam very strong: my Mothers Receipt

Take two gallons of water, and one gallon of honny; set it over the fire and if it will bear an egg then it is strong enough but if it will not put in more honny; let it heat and keepe it scimeing, then let it boyle halfe an howre, then put it into a tubb and let it stand till next day; then set it aworking with browne tost spread thike on both sides with ale yeast, cover it close yt it may worke, so let it stand 2 dayes, then take out the tost and put the liquor into a vessell, but leave a little vent for 2 dayes, then stop it close, and in 2 moneths bottle it, and within a moneth or six weekes you may drinke it, it will keepe good a yare.

The Best Receipt for Sider [cider] that I know off is this, and by which I used to make my sider, which always prov'd good and mightily liked off

After your aples are gathered let them lye in a heap to mellow about a moneth or five weeks, or longer, then stamp and strain them, and tunn up the liquor into your vessell, and only lay a single paper loose over the bung-hole, not stoping it at all, so let it stand about ten days or not so long sciming off the froath and scume as it riseth every day with a spoon out of the Bung-hole, then draw it off into tubbs clean from the thike leese [lees], and let your vessell be renced well wth the leese then poure

---

1 After having been exposed to a frost.

[292]

them clean away, and having redy dissolved six ounces of isinglace [isinglass] strain it, and poure it by degrees into your tubbs of liquor stiring and beating it all the while you poure it in, and after you have so beat it well together, tunn up your liquor again into your Hogshead, laying a paper over the Bung-hole and so let it stand 4 days close-stoped, then draw it off again through a sive into the tubbs all as is very clear of it, for you must take great care not to let any of the thike run in, when so done put to it an ounce of scutcherneele [cochineal] being redy boyled in some sider, which will give it a fine couller, stir and beat it well together, then rence your Hogshead extraordinary well with the leese, and afterwards with some of the clarer liquor, and wipe it with a cloath as far as you can, when you have thus cleaned the Hogshead very well from all the leese, tunn up your liquor into it again, and having in rediness three linnon Bags put into one fifeteen pound of raisins of the sun, or malagos [raisins] being first picked and stamped pretty small, and into the second Bag put in fiveteen pounds of good pouder suger, and into the third bag nyne pintes of wheat, allowing the wheat-Bag roome enough for the wheat to swell in, let each bag be tyed up and let them hang in ye Hogshead by a string on some nayles so as not to touch the bottome, then bung it up very close and let it stand a moneth and no longer, then bottle it up, and in a fortnight it will be redy to drinke.

The Isinglass you are to use is to be dissolved in the maner following; put into a skillet about two or three quarts of your sider, and let it boyle up so as to scime it clean which will make it very clear, then to a Hogshead of sider put in six ounces of Isinglace, being first beat and pickt a broad, and so let it stand on a gentle fire five or six hours, a little simbering [simmering] till it be dissolved, then strain it through a hare sive, you may keept it 3 or 4 days before you use it, but then you must set it over a few coles again just to dissolve it, and then mingle it with a quart or two of your sider and poure it by degrees into the whole quantity beating it up and down as you poure it in, and then tunn it up into the Hogshead as before mentioned in ye Receipt.

The scutcherneele you are to use is to be ordered as follows, take about three pintes or two quarts of your sider and boyle it in a skillet till all the scume be taken clean off, then put into it one ounce of scutcherneele being beat to a fine pouder, and so let it simber and boyle gently for almost halfe an hour, then strain it through a fine cloath and when cold put it to your sider as before directed in the Receipt. Take care not to make it too high a couller for then it will not looke naturall, therefore it you see that this quantity of scotchnerneele be too much, leave some of it out.

[293]

I generaly made my sider of Golden Runetts allowing 28 Busshells for a Hogshead, which made about five gallons of liquor above the Hogshead, and that served to fill up what was wasted in leese: it is best to make sider all of one sort of aples, and not to mix two or three sorts together, next to the Red-strak, the golden pipin, the Golden Runett, and paremains, are the best aples to make good sider withall.

When I made a Kilderkin (that is to say twenty gallons) of sider I had ten Busshells of aples, two ounces of Isinglace, and one third part of an ounce of scutcherneele, five pound of raisins, five pound of suger, and three pintes of wheat.

If once fineing it with Iseingglace do's not do, then fine it down again a second time, before you put in ye coullering and other things, and be sure to stop it down close in ye fineing. Note: That whereas in ye begining of this Receipt for cider it is mentioned to let it stand ten days and to scim off the froath with a spoone, insted of so doing you must be sure as soon as ever you perceive it begins to fermint and to froath imediately to draw it off from the thike Leese, for as soon as ever cider fermints it thikens it all: and the Leese will mingle amongst it again, therefore neglect not to draw it off as soon as ever you perceive the least froath begining on it.

To make sider: Mr Daniell Sheldon his Receipt

As for the fineing of sider to drinke presently my way of doing it is thus, as soone as you have prest your apples, put the liquor into some tubb, or barrell, if the tubb be broader at the top then bottome 'tis the better, and if a barrell let the bung be very large twice or more as big as the bungs of barrells use to be and let it be open not stop'd; when the liquor is in either tubb or barrell you must watch it, and if you finde it begins to firment or worke, and shewes any white froth, draw it imediately off into another tubb in which you may either keepe it, or with a pale or large bowle put it into another barrell, and so watch it again, and be sure as soone as it begins to throw up any white froth draw it off again, and so perchance you must do 3 or 4 times before it will be quiet and not firment, when tis quiet let it stand a day or two, and then draw it off again, for the oftner you draw it off the sooner it will be fine, but the weaker ye sider will be.

But if you would save yourself all this trouble, and desire to have the sider perfect fine, tho' not strong nor lasting, take some Isinglace and dissolve it in some whitewine over a fire, then let it coole and mix some with about a quart of wine, poure this into your bowle with some of the liquor of the aples and mix it well in the bowle first, then pour it by degrees into the tubb where all the liquor is stiring it all the while you pour it in, and afterwards stir the liquor with your bowle in the tubb very well, that the desolved Isinglace may be well mixed with the liquor, then let it either stand in the tubb or put it into a barrell, and so let it stand a day, or if it be quiet and do not firment let it stand two days, if then you thinke it is not fine enough, you may fine it downe again with Isinglace as you did before, and at twice fineing it will be as clear as Rock water. You must be sure to keep it from firmenting, and always when the brown cap begins to breake, and it throws up a white froth, draw it off imediately. I have find sider this way with Isinglace at once very cleare, and the sider so ordered will drinke very pleasantly but will not last. You must take notice that tis not possible to make sider looke cleare imediately but it will be whitish for 2 or 3 days, but that find with Isinglace will in that time or a weeke at most be very cleare and in a fortnight be fitt to drinke.

March Beere: my second Cousen Clerke's Receipt

if you would have it strong, take twelve busshell of malt, one peck of wheat, halfe a busshell of oates, one gallon of peese, or beans; spelch [?] your beere corn every sort by it self, and when you mash put halfe a busshell of malt to it; and wett it with your liquor no thicker than your mash-rule will stand up in it, and when you mash, put your beer corne together on one side of the mash-vatt; your liquor must boyle halfe an howre before you put it into the malt; and be sure you wett all the malt; then let it stand an howre and a halfe, or two howres, before you let go the first that runns; you must cast into the vatt 2 or 3 gallons untill it be cleere; to a hoggshead of the first runing of this beere you must take 3 pounde and a halfe of hopps, and 2 quarts of the corne of malt, let the wort, with the hopps, and malt, boyle a full howre, it will wast very neere nyne gallons, therefore you must gather so much above a hoggs-head, worke it up coole, and let the watch runn very slow, let it be a weeke in workeing in the vatt; be sure you fill the vessell you put it into, and when you bung it up put in a bagg 2 or 3 handfulls of hops, a pinte of cornes of maltt, a handfull of bay-berys brused, and a little cinemon, and ginger, with a few cloves, the wortt must be as strong as an egg may swime in it, before it boyles keepe 3 peck of malt out to cover it withall when you have masht; and if you would have it peale in couller cast in 4 or 5 gallons of cold water before you cover it with malt; after you have

[295]

drawne off your hoggshead of beere, you may draw 8 gallons of good alle, with one hott liquor, and then two hoggsheads of table-beere.

An Almond Caudle. My Second Cousen Clerkes Receipt

Boyle your Ale and scime [skim] it; then put in cinemon, cloves and mace and a sprig of Rosemary. Boyle it well; then let it coole, having saffi-cient quantity of Almons blanches and beaten exceeding small with a little rose or oringe flower water to keepe ym from oyleing then put some of the liquor to it and strayne ye rest of your liquor and put to it and stir it together, sweeten it to your taste; Drinke it cold or hott.

How to order made wines of any sort

1710: Remember when ye goosberry, or curant wine is made, to let it run through a flanell, bay or a hair sive just before you put it into the Barell, and after it hath stood 5 or 6 days in the Barell unstoped, only with a paper over it, draw it off into bottles, covering them only with a paper, or cork loosely in, and in 2 or 3 days you may peere [pour] off ye clare from ym, then bottle up ye thike again, and as fast as you see it settle peere of ye clare into clean bottles wch. corke well for use:

30:pound of curants
10:quarts of water
10:pound of suger

this quantity just fills my five gallon vesell.

To make Courant Wine: my second Cousen's given by Mrs Turner

Take three gallons of fayre water and put to it six pounde of lofe suger, or the best pouder suger, boyle it together halfe an howre or better, and as the scume riseth take it off, then poure it out and set it to coole, when it is almost cold take a little yeast beat it well with six ounces of sirop of Lemons, or cyttron [citron], beating it well too and againe with a dish in the liquor for a considerable time; then take a gallon of red Courents bruse them a little with a spoone only to break them, then put them to the liquor and let them worke 2 or 3 dayes; then strayne it forth and put it into a caske just big enough to holde it, when it hath don workeing stop it close; then about three weeks or a moneth affter bottle it; puting a peece of suger into every bottle; your vessell must be new or else a sack cask; put your bottles into the coolest place you can; this wine will keepe good three yare.

Courant Wine: my Lady Sheldon's Receipt: also goosbery or rasbery wine

To every three pounde of Courents white or red, take a pounde of suger, and a quart of water, bruse your fruit in a stone morter and steepe it in the water 24 howres, somtimes stiring it, then let the clear liquor runn through a haire sive, to which add the suger then put it into a runlett [wine cask], or a steane pott, according to your quantity, stop it close and let not the vessell be too full; let it stand till it be very clear, which may be in a moneth's time; then bottle it; this will keepe above a yare your bottles being very well stoped and tyed down; you may let your sive stand droping all night least you loose some of your liquor; so you may make goosbery wine or rasbery wine. Stop not up ye vessell till it hath don workeing; and keepe some to fill it up as fast as it wastes in working for it will worke like bear [beer].

To make curant Wine with black cherrys in it: Mr Cox his Receipt

Take to every gallon of currants, take halfe a pound of black cherrys, two quarts of water, and three pound of suger, when you have brused your currants, and cherrys, put the water boyleing hott to them, and let it stand about two hours then strain it of and put ye suger to it, and let it stand tel ye next day, then put it into the vessell leting it be full, and let it worke over if it will, and when it hath dome workeing wch you will know by it's not hissing if you lay your Ear to the cask, then draw it into a clean cask, and let it lye in it tel it is fine, and bottle it off.

To make currant wine with rasberys in it

To 20 pound of currants redy picked from the stalks take five pound of Rasberys, bruse the currants well with your hands, and the Rasberys a little, then put to them three quarts of water and stir it well together for a good while, then strain it thorow a flanel bag and put to it five or six pound of suger then put it into a Barell which must be but three quarters full, shake it well when it is in the Barrell doing so many times in 24 howers, then stop it up leting it stand about a month, and if you find it sharpe put more suger to it and bottle it, but fill the bottles only to the necks.

To make Aprecock wine, Lady Danvis her Receipt

Put into three quarts of Water three pound of lofe suger Boyle and scime it, then put to it six pound of aprecoks [apricots] after they are pared and stoned, let them boyle gently till they are very tender, then strain them out, and when the Liquor is cold put it into a large bottle that will hold it all, and tye a paper over the mouth of the Bottle, you will see that it will have a great scume on the top when it hath stood a while, therefore you must not stir it till that scume be sunke to the bottom, then peere [pour] it into small bottles from the leese [lees], and corke them close, it will be fitt to drink by Michaelmas.

Goosbery wine: or Rasbery, or curant wine: Mrs Green's Receipt

To every three pound of goosberys when they are full ripe and cleane picked and stamped take a quart of water and a pound of suger, strayne it through a canviss and then stir in the suger, and after 2 or 3 days put it into a vessell fitt for ye quantity and when it is very clare bottle it wch may be will be in a moneth or longer, do not bottle it too soon, neither stop it too close in the barell at first: as soon as your fruit is stamped put your water to it and after 24 howrs straine it on the suger, it will worke in the barell like bear [beer].

Rasbery or Strabery wine: my Mothers Receipt

Take a gallon of new gathered Rasberys, or straburys, and put them into a great glace [glass] with a wide mouth, and put to them a gallon of the best canery, then stop it up close with a neat blader [ox bladder], and set it in the seller for two dayes, then strayne it through a haire sive, and put to it a pounde of double refined suger, and when it is dissolved bottle it; corke it close and tye it fast, you may make it of whitewine, or any other wine if you please.

Rasbery Wine: Mrs Whitehead's Receipt

Take 3 quarts of fresh Raspes, and put two quarts of spring water to them, that hath been boyled but cold againe let it stand in an earthen pot close covered 2 dayes, then strayne it, through a thike cloath and ring it hard then put to it 2 pounde of lofe suger, and let it stand 2 or 3 dayes more, then let it run through a jelly bagg and bottle it up, puting into each bottle a knob of suger; if you intend to drinke it quickly set the bottles in water, tye the corkes downe; and keepe them in a coole seller, this will keepe 4 or 5 moneth: put no wine into it.

Red Chery Wine: Mrs Whitehead's Receipt

Stone your cherys and breake them in the stoneing with your fingers as much as you can, put them into a deepe tub and cover them very close all night, in the morning press them through a haire bag till they are very drye, then to every gallon of the liquor put a pounde and a little more of good dryed suger, then tunn it, and when it has don workeing stop it very close, and in 3 weekes you may bottle it; if it be not sweet enough put in more suger as you bottle it.

Red Chery Wine: my Mothers Receipt

Set 3 gallons of water one the fire and let it boyle halfe an howre and as it boyles scume it; then stone and shread 3 pounde of raisons of the sun; and stone 4 pounde and a halfe of cherys, and take one pounde and a halfe of suger, and one Lemon and a halfe, pare the whole Lemon and slice it, but slice rine [rind] and all of the halfe Lemon, mix all these together in a pott, and put your water boyleing hott to them; cover your pott very close and stir it twice a day for 3 dayes; then strayne it through 2 or 3 sives one finer than another, so bottle it up, corke it close and tye it fast; fill not the bottles too full; you may drinke of it in a weeke.

[299]

Black Cherry Wine: My Mothers Receipt

Take what quantity of black cherys you please pull of the stalks, and breake the Cherys all to mash, then strayne them very hard through a strayner pressing out the juce as much as may be, and if there be a gallon of juce put to it a pounde of suger; but if the cherys should not be very ripe then put in a pounde and halfe of suger, then put it into a bottle that is very strong, or else it will breake it, do not fill your bottle too full, corke it close, and tye it down very hard, then set it in the seller, and let it stand till September, then poure it from the Leese into glasse bottles, and stop them up close, and keepe them in a seller, it will keepe good a yare or two; it is rare good for convoltion fitts or any other fitts, or vapers, give a childe not above a spoonfull at a time, and an older body give 3 or 4 spoonfulls; that which you strayne from the juce if you breake the stones and distill it, it will make a good black chery water.

plum wine: my second Cousen Clerke's Receipt

Take the violet plum which is the best, pick them from the stalks and put them into an earthen pott, and poure over them as much water as will just cover them, then tye a paper over it, and when bread is drawne put it in the oven for a night, the next morning poure out the liquor, and vessell it with halfe a pounde of suger to a gallon, and when it is clear bottle it ading more suger to it.

quince wine: Mrs Mar. Westons Receipt

Take your quinces, when full ripe, and wipe them very well with a cloath but do not pare them, only be sure to pick out all the specks very cleane then grate them one a bread grater; and as fast as you have grated any little quantity strayne it through a canvise cloath; squeseing all the juce out as hard as you can; and when you have gott what quantity of juce you would, measure it, and to every gallon take a pounde and a quarter of lofe suger, then put in a little of the suger in a pott, and put your juce in a cotton-bagg made picked at one end, such as you strayne other things withall, and so hang it up and let it drop into the pott you put some of the suger into; and when it is all strayned through, put the rest of the suger to it, and so let it stand being close covered 24 howres;

[300]

then bottle it, and tye it downe fast, and in a moneth or six weekes you may drinke of it: you must be sure to strayne your juce as fast as you grate any little quantity; or else it will be not so cleare: if you put it into a vessell and let it stand 5 or 6 weeks before you bottle it, 'twill be the clarer and much better.

To make Mulbery Wine: or Aprecock Wine

To every gallon of Mulberys take 3 quarts of water, bruse your mulberys and steep them all night in ye water, then strayne it and put to every gallon of liquor three pound of suger, mingle it well together and put it into a vessell and in a moneth bottle it up; you may make wine of Apre-cocks the same way, gathering them when they are full ripe, pare and stone them, and to a gallon of pared Aprecocks take three quarts of water; bruse your Aprecocks and steepe them in ye water in an earthen thinge; and order it just as you do ye mulbery wine, only it need not stand so long in the Barell, you may bottle it up in a weeke or ten days time.

Orange Wine

Take 4 gallons of Water and put to it Ten pound of ordinary pouder suger, and the whites of four eggs well beaten, Boile all together and scime it till it be very clear, then have in redyness the Rines of four dou-sin of sivil [Seville] oranges pared so thine that none of the white remain on them, let them be put into a clean Tub with all the juce of the oranges, and poure your water and suger Boiling hott to it, and let it stand till it be almost cold, then worke it with yest puting in 3 ounces of syrup of cittern [citron], and let it worke two days, then put it into a vessell with halfe of the rines, and let it stand ten days before you Bottle it.

To make Elder Wine: Jos. Pen's Receipt

Take Elderberys when full ripe and pick them off the stalks, and to 20 quarts of berys take 40 quarts of water and boyle them together about an hour, then strayn it through a hair sive and let it stand droping all night; putting in 12 pound of suger, and a quart of hony, and a handfull of rose-mary sciming it cleane, let it stand in ye tub till it be pretty coole, and worke it with about a quarter of a pinte of yest as you do bear [beer] for

[301]

two days, then put it in a barill and when it hath done working stop it up close, and let it stand 3 months before you bottle it, and if you please you may put a little suger into each bottle.

Elder Wine: Sister Kerstemans Receipt

Take of the juce of Elderberys one quart and 3 quarts of water boyle them together for a small space scimeing it, and to every gallon thereof put in 3 pound of suger, and boyle them together a little while scimeing it clean, then worke it coole 24 hours and put it into a barill; and in 3 or 4 months bottle it.

To Make White Elder Wine: J.B. [Jos. Pen]

Take a quantity of white elderberys full ripe, press out the juce, and to every quart of juce take 3 quarts of boyleing water, put it to the juce and let it stand all night close covered, the next morning strain it, and to every gallon of liquor put in three pound of white suger, let the suger and liquor boyle together till it be clear from scum, sciming it as long as any scum riseth, then putt it in a tub and when it is cold worke it with yest as you do Ale; let it be put in a barill fitt for it, and let it stand in the vesell halfe a year if a small one, but if it be a large vesell let it stand a year and then bottle it.

for the filling my 4 gallon vessell with Elder Wine, take as followeth viz.

take 12:quarts of water:
take 12:pound of ordinary suger:
take 4:quarts of juce:

Note: that my great Bell mettle pott holdeth 4 Gallons and two quarts of water.

To make Rayson wine [Raisin]: Lady ffranklin's way

Boyle four gallons of water and put it into a tub leting it stand till it be but bloud warm then put to it 16 pound of Raisons of the sun, or 20 pound of malegoes well choped, stir them together for a quarter of an hour so let it stand 7 or 8 days stiring it 2 or 3 times every day, then strain it and put it into a vessell with the bottom of a halfepeny lofe tosted and spread with ale yest, wch will set it aworkeing like ale, and when it hath done working put in a sprig of seedy wormwood which will fine it down, stop it down with a cork and if you please slice a Lemon into it, in two months time it will be fine to drink or to Bottle, be sure you give the vessell vent else it will burst; make this wine in temperate weather and after 'tis in the vessell set it in a coole seller, and keepe it a good while in the vessell before you bottle it.

Note: That it is best not to put any wormwood in at all.

To make Grape Wine

When your grapes are full ripe gather and pick them from ye stalks, bruse them with your hands that the ruffness of the stones and stalks may not make the wine unpleasant, strain out all the juce hard throw [through] a thine cloath, and to a gallon of juce put in two pound of ye fatest and whitest pouder suger, stir it well together and put it imeditely into a vessell; it will worke and fine itself, and when it hath done workeing stop it up close the vessell being full, and let it stand 3, 4 or five months according to ye quantity, before you bottle it.

If you would have your wine like high country whitewine let your grapes after they are brused lye 24 howers before you strain the juce out, and put to it the fatt sort of browne suger.

If you make your wine of red grapes, and desire it should be red wine, the liquor must lye on the huskes [grape skins] two days before you strain it out, and the suger not to be too fine.

If you desire your grape wine to be small, like renish wine, after you have strained all the juce out of your grapes, put in as much water to the huskes of your grapes as will cover them and let it stand tell the next day sometimes stiring it, then strain it out hard, and put it to the juce that you strained out the day before, put to every gallon two pound and halfe of fine fatt white suger, put into a vessell that 'twill fill, and when it hath done working stop it close, leting it stand three months then bottle it: if you put in three pound of suger to a gallon of liquor it will be ye better.

Clove-gilly-flower-Wine: my second Cousen Clerke's

Take a glasse that will holde about 2 quarts and put into it a quart of renish wine, or whitewine, and as much water, then put in as many

[303]

clove-gilly-flower-leaves [petals] as will couller it well, cover it close and let it stand a day or two, then strayne it and sweeten it with suger, and so bottle it up; the same way you make rasbery wine.

Couslip Wine: Mrs Masons of Stradford's Receipt

Take 3 gallons of faire water, put to it six pounde of pouder suger, (or lofe suger if you please) boyle it together halfe an howre, or better, as the scume riseth take it off, then take two gallons of picked couslips, bruse them in a stone morter and poure your liquor one them hott from the fire; when it is almost cold take a spoonefull of yeast and beat it well with six ounces of sirrop or juce of cittron; brueing it up and downe with a dish in the liquor, let it stand 2 or 3 dayes then strayne it and put it in a barell fitt for the quantity; stop it close, and when it is 3 weekes or a moneth old bottle it, and in every bottle put a lump of lofe suger; for want of the juce of Cittron I put in a quart of whitewine.

Couslip Wine: my Mothers Receipt

Take to every gallon of water halfe a peck of picked Couslips, bruse them in a stone morter, put likewise to every gallon 2 pounde of white suger; mix them altogether and set them one the fire and when it has boyled a quarter of an howre, take it off, and when it is as cold as milke from the cowe put into every gallon the meat of 2 Lemons, and the peele of halfe a one, put in also as much ale yeast as you thinke will set it a workeing, poure it into a narow vessell to worke and when it has worked 2 or 3 dayes puting downe the Lemon and flowers under the liquor, put it all into a close barell, and when it is clear which will be in about three weekes bottle it.

Sage wine: Mrs Greens Receipt

Boyle 24 quarts of spring water till it comes to 12 quarts, then take it off the fire and when it is but a little more than luke warme put to it a peck of sage stript off the stalks, with 12 pound of malago raisons shread, and rubed with a cleane cloath, when it is well mixed put in a poringer of good all [ale] yeast and let it stand for 7 dayes stiring it once every day, then strayne it through a haire sive and put to it a pinte of malego sack, then put it into a runlett and when it is clare bottle it with a lumpe of suger in each bottle.

To Make Frontiniac Wine

Take 6 gallons of water, 12 pound of white suger, 6 pound of raisons of the sun cut and stoned, boyle them together one hour, then take Elder flowers when they are falling and redy to fly off, and rub them gently, the quantity of halfe a peck, put them in when the liquor is cold and the next day put in 8 ounces of syrrup of Lemons and 4 spoonfulls of good yest, 2 days after strain it and put it into a firkin that may be full with it, and when it hath stood 6 weeks or longer bottle it off.

A Water to perfume Wine: Mr Smiths: viz

Take ambergreece [ambergris] 24 grains, and of muske foure grains, or any other quantity, only observe to take 6 or 8 of ambergreece to one of muske, then grind them severally as small as dust, which is done by mixing a little white suger candy with it, or else they will not be brought to pouder, then put it into a glace, and put to it halfe a pinte of the strongest spirit of wine, set it in the sun well stoped for six days, shakeing it foure times a day, and when it is well settled poure off the clare yellow, and then you may poure in more spirit to the grounds to draw out more of the vertue, one drop will perfume a great quantity of wine.

To make Cherry Brandy

To a gallon of Brandy put foure pounds of cherrys, two pounds of suger, halfe an ounce of Cinnamon, one ounce of cloves, seting it in the sun a fortnight or better in bottles close corked.

A pleasent drinke called shrobb [shrub]: the Lady Desmon's Receipt

Take a galland of the best brandy put it in a large pipkin, then take 12 lemonds and slice them thine with the rines on, leaveing a peece underneath to make the slices hang together, put them into the brandy and let it infuse 4 or 5 days; then take out the lemons and press them betweene two trenchers one by one as hard as you can; then strayne the brandy through a sive, and take two quarts of the best whitewine and if you would have ye shrobb but weake put to it a pinte of water, then take as much fine suger as your wine will dissolve and beat the whitewine and brandy together and bottle it up for your use.

To make shrobb wch is a ready thing for makeing of punch, viz

put into a stean [stone] pott 4 quarts of Brandy, one quart of Lemon or Orange juce strained, with two ounces of the rines [rinds] pared thine, and a pound of ye finest lofe suger, stir it well together, and so let it stand close covered covered for three weeks or a month keeping it stiring once a day all the time, except 2 or 3 days before you bottle it that so it may be clear, then Bottle off the very finest by it self corking it close. For the makeing of it into punch take a pinte thereof and add to it a quart of fair water, but in case you would have ye punch small then add three pintes of Water to one pinte of shrob and if it be not sweet enough add more suger to your likeing.

Hippocrass: my Lady Sheldon's Receipt

Take one gallon of sack, and 2 gallons of whitewine three ounces of cinemon brused, tenn ounces of ginger, halfe an ounce of nuttmegs; a few cloves, a few coreander [coriander] seeds, three pounde of suger, a good sprig of rosemary, a Lemon sliced peele and all, the seeds taken out, and one quart of milke, bruse not your seeds, nor spices, too small for fear of spoyleing the couller of your wine; infuse your spice and suger in some of your sack one the embers all night, in an earthen pott; then poure it to the rest of your wine, and stir it in the milke then runn it through a cotton bagg, and when it hath runed a little put it into the bag againe; in twice or three times it will be clear; and if you would have it red; couller it with red wine, and keepe it in bottles; and it will not loose ye couller a good while.

To make punch

Take two quarts of water and put to it three quarters of a pound of fine suger, and the juce of 12 Lemons and when the suger is well dissolved strayne it, and put to it a quart of Brandy, and if you please grate in some nuttmeg: you may either drink it presently or keepe it in bottles.

To make a coole tankett

Take a quart of Renish wine, or whitewine and put to it a pinte of fayre water, and 2 Lemmons, sweeten it to your likeing with good suger, and put on it some Burage [borage], Baume, and Burnett [burnet saxifrage], if you please. Yet ye Lemon pill be cutt hansomely some to be in ye wine and some to hang on ye tankett.

A pippin water very pleasent to drinke: Mr Smiths

Take 3 quarts of water, slice into it 12 pippins the pareings, cores and all, and boyle it till it comes to a quart, then strain it thro' a fine sive, slice in a Lemon, and sweeten it with suger, and syrup of citrons.

Pipin Water: A very pleasent drinke: My Lady Howes

Take twelve large pipins, wipe them, and splitt them, in halves, then put them into 5 or 6 quarts of water, let it boyle till 3 parts be consumed, then put in the rine of an oringe; and one rine of a Lemon, and halfe an ounce of whole cinemon; when the cinemon has been in a little while take it off ye fire, and put to it six ounces of suger, and the juce of oringes, stir it well together, and strayne it through a bolster bag, and when it is cold bottle it up, with a few fenell [fennel] seeds if you like it.

Sherbett of Lemons: my Lady Sheldons Receipt

Take foure large Lemons, pare of the yellow rine, as thine as you can, shread it very small, squeese out all the juce into a preserveing-glasse, and put the shread rine into it, let it stand two dayes, then strayne it, and put to it a pounde of suger, then sett it upon a chafindish of coles, in a basson, let it be so hott that it do smoake, but not boyle, then take it off, and put it in a gally-pott [gallipot], and keepe it for your use, when you put the suger to the juce put in muske, and ambergreece, to your likeing; a spoonefull of this put into a glasse of water and stired about till it be dissolved in it, is a very pleasent drinke for the sumur, and some will squeese in some juce of Lemon because it should not be too sweet: Let ye muske and ambergreece be ground to a powder and tyed up in a thine cloath.

To make Chocolate: Newtons Receipt

Take a pinte and halfe of water and let it boyle till it comes to a little more than a pinte, then take it off the fire and put in two ounces of chocolate brooke in little bitts, mill it well and set it on the fire againe and let it boyle up as fast as you can; you may mill it a little as it boyles, it need not boyle very long after the chocolat is in; then take it off and haveing in redyness [readiness] the yolks and whites of 2 eggs well beaten with a spoonefull or two of the boyled water put them in and mill it extreordenery well, when so don set it on the fire just to boyle up after ye eggs are in, then take it off and put suger enough to sweeten it to your likeing and mill it extreordinery well, and then poure it into your cupps, laying some of the froath with a spoone on every cupp; and some like to have it made with milke in it, wch is made just the same way only by takeing halfe milke and water together instead of all water.

To make chocolate without milke or eggs in it

Take a pinte and a halfe of water and let boyle till it comes to a little more than a pinte, then take it off the fire and put in 4 ounces of chocolate, mill it well, and set it over the fire againe and let it boyle up as fast as it can, then take it off againe and let it boyle a little longer milling it over the fire for some time, then take it off and put in suger enough to sweeten it to your likeing, and mill it extreordnery well, and so poure it out into your cupps laying some of the froath upon it with a spoone; you must not let it boyle after the suger is in.

To make chocolate the Lady Howards way: whch is the best

To a pinte and quarter of water, break or slice in foure ounces of chocolate, set it on the fire, stiring it sometimes, as soon as it boyles take it off ye fire and mill it well, then set it on again and if it will carry a good froath, it is enough, if not, boyle it longer and when it is well boyled sweeten it to your tast with fine suger and then mill it very well poureing 3 or 4 spoonefulls at a time in your cupps and when you have almost filled a cup, scim some of the froath with a spoon off as you mill it and lay it on the top of your cup, and if it begins to be cold before you have filled all your cupp, heat it over the fire again.

Note: that it is best to make chocolate the day before you use it wch will make it the thiker and froath the better when it comes to be heated again.

MISCELLANEOUS

Note. That in ye boyleing of yellow peese [peas] 'tis best to soake them in warm water for about an hour, and then tye them very loose in a cloth or bag, and put them into boyling water, you must be sure that the water boyles before you put them into it or else they will never be tender, and as soon as you find that they are swelled pretty much, beat them in ye bag with something, and then tye them up very tyte and boyle them till they are enough. If you observe this rule, in 2 or 3 hours they will be boyled very soft and eat well.

To boyle Spinage green

Pick your spinage and put into a skilett with a little handfull of salt only; cover it close set it on ye fire and so let it boyle of itself without any water in it and it will be extraordinary green, and eat much better this way than any other.

To thiken sauces without ye yolks of eggs

Note: That if you take a little fine flower and mix it well with the back of a spoon into a peece of butter and so put it into your sauce, stiring it well over ye fire, twill thicken better than [with] eggs.

To Order the Bakeing of Tarts

As soon as your tarts are in the oven get up the lid till they are as much covered as you have them; then take down your lid again before the liquor of your tarts boyles up or elce all their liquor will run over; you need not get up the lid again, three quarters of an hour will bake them.

To wash currants for Cakes, Pyes or any use

First rub your currants well with flower till all the little stalks are off, then put them into a cullender to sift out all the soile; then turn them out

[313]

and pick them over and then wash them clean, and drye them with a cloth.

Note: That when you are to beat cinomon [cinnamon] 'tis the best way to just wett it with water and then beat it as fine as you would have it; the wetting of it makes it beat fine immediately.

The best way for the washing of windows is as followeth

Heat about a quart of water scalding hott then put it into a pan and put in a handfull of salt and as much whiteing as the bigness of a walnutt, and, when all is disolved, take a woollen cloath and dip it therin and rub your windows therewith pretty well and, before they are drye, rub them over with a dryle linnen cloth, and afterwards rub them over with another drye Linnen cloath to clear them.

For the scowering of Plate do as followeth. Viz

First wash your plate in a strong lye with flanell cloaths then rence it in clean water with whiteing in it, and set it by the fire to drye, and then rub it clean with a drye linnen Cloath.

A perfume to Burn: Mrs Beriges Receipt

Take 8 ounces of Benjamen [benzoin] beat it small, and lay it over night in rose or oringeflower-water, then take a pounde of damaske rose leaves, the white being cutt off; beat them very fine, and take the Benjemen it being beaten with the rose water till it coms to a past [paste], then mix with it a quarter of an ounce of muske, and as much scivet [civet], being finely beaten, beat all this into a past with as much rose or oringe flower water as will make it so; then molde them together with three ounces of double refined suger, searced; and make them up into little cakes; and lay them severally betweene two rose leaves to drye, you must drye them in the shade.

A pouder for sweet-baggs my second Cousen Clerke

Take one pounde of orris, a quarter of a pounde of calamus [calamine?], benjemen [benzoin] and storax, of each halfe a pounde, Lignum, and Aloes, of each one ounce, rose-wood, one pounde, muske, scivett [civet], and ambergreece [ambergris], of each a quarter of an ounce, oyle of oringe flowers one ounce; of Labdanum [laudanum?], and Cypress, of each two ounces, beat all these severally by themselves, and then mix them together, and to a pounde of these pouders [powders] take a pounde of damaske roses dryed, the budds that are well growne will be the best to drye; mix them together, and put them into baggs for your use.

A pouder for the haire: my Cousen Wheatlys Receipt

Take a pounde of white starch, beat it and sift it, then set it over coles [coals] in a puter [pewter] dish, and so let it stand till it is as drye as you can possible make it, then beat halfe an ounce of storax, halfe an ounce of Benjemen [benzoin], one ounce of orris, a quarter of an ounce of cloves, halfe an ounce of oringe peele dryed and beaten to pouder; beat all these together very fine and sift it, then mix with it a graine of muske, and a grayne of scivett [civet], then set it over a very slow fire between 2 puter dishes, let it stand 2 howres just to keepe it warme, then keepe it for your use; but if you will not have it so rich put in more of the white starch, some will make this pouder of rice, saying it will not rott the haire so much as starch if you make it of rice you must beat your rice very fine, and put it in instead of the starch.

A Sweet Water to Wash with: my Cousen Wheatly's receipt

Take of oringe-flower water one quart, and of the best damaske rose water one quart; of Benjemen 2 ounces, of storex [storax] one ounce, and a halfe, of wood of Jurneper [juniper] one ounce, of ambergreece three graynes, and of muske two graynes; bruse all these together and mingle them together, then put it into a glasse bottle and stop it very close and waxe it, in a moneth you may use it.

A sweet Watter to Wash with: my first Cousen Clerkes

Take halfe a Busshell of roses when they are picked, put them into a pott, or glasse, with as narow a mouth as you can conveniently stur them in, because they may the better be stoped close, put to them one handfull of Lavender tops; one handfull of bay leaves, two handfulls of sweetmajerom, and two ounces of cloves; beat the cloves, and shread the herbes, and roses, then tye them up as close as you can, and set them in the sun nyne, or ten, dayes; sturing them 2 or 3 times, in that time; then still them in a cold still.

GLOSSARY TO THE RECEIPTS

ALMOND—*Prunnus amygdalus (Amgdakys communis)*
The almond tree is a native of the eastern Mediterranean regions and has been cultivated in southern Europe and the Middle East for many centuries. There are many varieties of almond but the main distinction is the difference in flavour between sweet and bitter almonds.

Sweet almonds were used by medieval cooks who made a subtle flavouring called milk of almonds. Marie-Antoinette preferred a drink called 'lait d'amandes' to any other. Sweet almonds are used to flavour many Eastern sweet dishes.

Bitter almonds have a strong taste and are used in flavouring sweet dishes and many kinds of cake and biscuits. There are also ratafias made from bitter almonds or the fruit kernels of plums, peaches, cherries and other similar fruits. These fruit kernels are known as 'noyau'. Besides 'oil of bitter almonds' there was also 'sweet almond oil', used both in confectionery and as a wash for the complexion.

The seventeenth-century housewife made almonds into a paste with sugar and rosewater for 'marchpane' (marzipan), or mixed them with flour, eggs and sugar to make macaroons or simply covered them over with sugar to make comfits.

ALUM—*Alumen*
White transparent mineral salt. Pliny and Dioscorides both describe the uses and varieties of alum.

AMBERGRIS
Fatty substance, grey in colour and veined like marble, formed in the intestines of the spermaceti whale. Usually found in warm climates. Highly regarded as a flavouring in the kitchens of the sixteenth and seventeenth centuries. Essential in perfume-making.

ANCHOVY
Probably from the Basque *anchua*, a dried fish. This tiny fish, a member of the herring family, is caught in Mediterranean waters. It develops its special flavour only after curing. Anchovies were often used to stuff fowl or as a sauce for meat dishes and also to make anchovy butter.

ANGELICA—*Angelica sylvestris*
A giant member of the parsley family known also as the 'root of the Holy Ghost'. It was introduced into Europe from Syria at the beginning of the fifteenth century. It has cordial properties and assists the digestion. The young stems are candied but all parts of the plant are used for some purpose in cookery.

ANISE—*Pimpinella anisum*
Known also as sweet cumin, anise is a native of the Levant used by the

[317]

ancient Egyptians, Greeks and Romans. It reached southern and central Europe in the Middle Ages. Anise is used in flavouring sweets and creams, cakes and cordials (Pernod, Berger, etc.).

APPLE

All apple trees are descended from the Wild Crab by having been grafted on its stock.

The Custard, the Nonpareil, the Oslin and the Arbroath are among the earliest apples cultivated in England and most of these came from France. Pippins (Pepins) were introduced from France in the reign of Henry VIII and were so called because they grew from seed instead of being grafted.

The Codling was an apple of long tapering shape. Jenneting (Pomme de St Jean) was a variety of early apple which was ripe for picking in June.

John Evelyn, in his Calendarium, listed the following varieties of apples: Kentish, Kirton, Russet, Holland, Pepins, Deux-Ans, Winter Queeing, Harvey, Pome-Water, Pome Roy, Golden, Doucet, Reineting, Lones Pearmain, Winter-Pearmain, etc.

Lord Scudamore at Holme Lacy in Herefordshire introduced the Red Streak Pippin, from which the choicest cider was made.

APRICOT—*Prunus armeniaca*

Reached England by the thirteenth century, probably with returning Crusaders. Tudors called this fruit 'apricocks'. In 1620 John Tradescant the Elder brought a new specimen of apricot known as the 'Barbary' apricot and many other varieties home from an expedition with the fleet against Algiers pirates. Parkinson in 1629 mentions many kinds already growing in England and says the fruit was eaten as a dessert between courses or preserved dried or candied.

ARTICHOKE

Referred to by Rebecca as 'Hartichoke'.

Name given to two different vegetables: (a) The globe artichoke, *Cynaria scolymus*; allied to the thistles; native of the Mediterranean regions and the Canary Islands; introduced into England *circa* 1548 from Italy. (b) The Jerusalem artichoke, *Helianthus tuberosus*; related to the sunflower; a native of South America; introduced into Europe by the French from Canada and for this reason first known as 'potatoes of Canada'. They only later acquired their present name because the root when boiled resembled the globe artichoke in flavour. Both varieties were well established in England by the early seventeenth century.

ASPARAGUS—genus *Liliacease*

Best known species is the common asparagus (*Officinalis*), a native of the sandy seashores of Europe including Britain. First cultivated in Britain in the sixteenth century. The heads of the green shoots were much

[318]

esteemed as a vegetable, boiled and eaten with butter, vinegar and pepper.

BALM—*Melissa officinalis*
The sweet-scented lemon balm was introduced by the Romans. The whole plant is scented and imparts its lemony flavour to salads. It was drunk as a cordial and for its soothing effect on the heart. The leaves are used to make potpourri and as a cooling drink for feverish complaints.

BARBERRY—*Berberis vulgaris*
A shrub of the genus berberis or barbaris. The red, acid berry of this tree was used pickled for trimming fish and meat dishes and in broth. The leaves were used to make a sour sauce for meat as an alternative to sorrel.

BAY—*Laurus nobilis*
A small tree usually grown as a bush. The leaves were used fresh or dried as a culinary herb. Bay was used as a flavouring in creams and custards. Prized as a decorative wreath by the ancients.

BAY SALT
(i) A variety of 'spiced salt' made at home. Various herbs, including dried bayleaf, pounded and mixed with sea-salt.
(ii) The best sea-salt was also known as bay salt. It came from Portugal and was obtained by evaporating sea-water in pits by the natural rays of the sun. It was much esteemed for its flavour and preservative powers.

BEER
Most households made beer for their own consumption. There were two chief sorts: double beer was the stronger at 3d. per gallon; small beer cost only 1½d. per gallon. Every good housekeeper kept a 15-gallon kilderkin or at least an 8-gallon firkin in the house. This was constantly refilled.

Wheat, barley, maize, rice and millet were used for the making of home-made beer. In Rebecca's day, beer was flavoured with aromatic or bitter herbs, such as costmary, ground ivy, nettle, dandelion or mixed herbs.

BENZOIN—*Styrax benzoin*
Gum benjamin, aromatic resin from the *Styrax benzoin*, a tree of Sumatra and Java, was first mentioned by Ibn Batuta at the beginning of the fourteenth century. He refers to it as Java frankincense. Used as incense and in cosmetics. It has astringent properties.

BETONY—*Betonica officinalis*
Formerly used as a substitute for tea and as a flavouring for various herb beers. It was listed as an essential in Tudor herb gardens.

BISCUIT
The first commercially produced biscuit known in England was the Bath

Oliver, introduced in 1735 by Doctor Oliver, physician to the Bath Mineral Water Hospital.

BLOUDSWORTH—*Lapathum sanguineum*

A member of the dock family used as an important pot-herb in the seventeenth century.

BLUEBOTTLE—*Centaurea cyanus*

Popular name for the cornflower. Used in the seventeenth century as a cooling cordial and as a remedy against the plague and the poison of scorpions and spiders.

BORAGE—*Borago officinalis*

Introduced to Britain by the Romans, this plant grows on the chalk downs of southern England. The flowers are used both for decoration and for candying, and the leaves in salads and cooling drinks.

BOUQUET GARNI

A bundle of sweet herbs or a fagot of herbs. Rebecca's version of a 'bouquet garni' included marjoram, pennyroyal and thyme. The classic 'bouquet garni' is made up of three stalks of parsley to a small sprig of thyme and a bayleaf. Many other herbs can be added or substituted, according to the individual taste of the cook.

BREAD

Each loaf had to be stamped with either an 'H', to indicate to housewives that this was brown bread, or a 'W' for white or wheaten. They were also stamped with the baker's seal which had to be registered with one of the two bakers' companies, enabling bread which was defective to be traced at once to its manufacturer.

It will be noticed that in several of Rebecca's receipts one is advised to use slightly larger quantities of London bread. This was because country loaves were supposed to be a penny in the shilling heavier than London loaves to compensate for the country bakers' not having to pay the 'scot and lot' or local rates which the City bakers were obliged to pay. There had been a long tradition of country bakers bringing their loaves into the city by cart to sell in the markets.

BROOM—*Cytisus scoparius*

The original name *plants genista*, was the origin of the name of the Plantagenet kings. A sprig was worn by Geoffrey d'Anjou as he rode into battle, and his grandson, Henry II of England, adopted it as a badge. Broom buds were used as a condiment, much as we use capers today. They were preserved in vinegar and eaten as a relish.

BULLACE—*Prunus insititia*

A wild plum, larger than a sloe, smaller than a damson, sharper in taste and ripening later. It was dried in large quantities and sold by grocers as French prunes.

BURDOCK—*Arctium lappa*

In the seventeenth century the common name for the burdock was 'Happy Major'. In the Middle Ages it was called 'bandons'. The French still call it *bandane*. Its stem was used as a vegetable, candied or as a salad.

BUR MARIGOLD—*Bidene tripartita*

'Water agrimony' is the old name for this plant which is common in England and grows by the edges of ditches and ponds. Used in domestic medicine.

BURNET SAXIFRAGE—*Pimpinella saxifrage*

The burnet saxifrages, the greater and the lesser, grow in damp meadows and chalky districts throughout Great Britain. One of the oldest of the cordial herbs. The seeds used to be made into sugar plums like caraway comfits. A classical ingredient in many butters and sauces.

BUTCHER'S BROOM—*Ruscus aculeatus*

The young shoots of this plant can be eaten like asparagus and concoctions of the root are good for pulmonary diseases.

BUTTERBUR—*Petasites vulgaris*

Grows throughout England in marshy ground. Found by streams and rivers. Used in domestic medicine as a tonic, stimulant and disinfectant. Was also used to give coolness and fragrance to wine cups.

CABBAGE—*Brassica oleracea*

The word 'brassica' comes from *bressic*, the Celtic word for cabbage. It still grows wild in certain parts of Britain.

CANDY, To

To coat or preserve with crystallized sugar. Many flowers as well as citrons, orange peel and lemon peel were candied for the table.

CAPSICUM—*Capsicum minimum solanceae*

Known too as cayenne African pepper, cliver's and bird's pepper. Its natural habitat is Zanzibar. The part used is the fruit, ripened and dried. Used with stews, eggs, oysters and many other dishes. Introduced into Britain in the middle of the sixteenth century.

CARAWAY SEEDS—*Carum carui*

Useful in cooking, salads and in domestic medicine. Important in cookery from Elizabethan times. Used in cakes and bread. Roast apples were always served with caraway seeds and Falstaff was invited to 'a pippin and a dish of caraways' by Master Shallow (*Henry IV*, part ii).

CARROT—*Daucus carota*

In the seventeenth century, carrots were mainly used for adorning dishes, cut into 'scutchions', arms, birds or beasts.

'CASE YOUR HAIR'

i.e., skin your hare. A misunderstanding of this word by her printer, no doubt unfamiliar with cookery terms, led to the famous misprint in Mrs Glass's cookery book which was recorded as 'first *catch* your hare'.

[321]

CAUDLE

Hot drink prepared from mulled wine or ale thickened with bread and sugar and various spices. It was drunk out of a squat, round-sided vessel with two handles, a lid and spout not unlike a small teapot.

CHAFING DISH

A vessel for making anything hot. Could also be a small, portable grate for coals.

CHEESE

Rebecca has several receipts for more exotic cheeses, such as slipcote and sage cheese. She describes in detail how she went about making her own cheeses. 'The last Water Cheese I made I had six cowes, and ordered ye milke as followeth:- I made the first cheese on fryday night with thursday nights and friday mornings milke, then on saturday morning I made the other cheese with fryday nights and saturday mornings milke so that in the two cheeses there were four meales milke, and milke of 24 cowes in ye whole cheese which made it very thike and hansome.'

'CHENEY CUPS'

The secret of manufacturing china as opposed to pottery had not yet been discovered in Europe in Rebecca's day and this refers to the small handleless bowls of Kiang Hsi porcelain. These were very expensive as they had to be specially imported from China.

CHERRY—*Cerasus*

Small member of the plum family. The first cherry orchards in Kent were planted about Sittingbourne by a gardener of King Henry VIII.

CHESTNUT—*Castanea vesta*

Fruit of the tree genus *Castanea*. The edible Spanish or sweet chestnut was introduced to Great Britain, possibly by the Romans. John Evelyn in his *Sylva* refers to a 'great chestnut' at Tortworth Court in Gloucestershire as having been known as the Great Chestnut of Tortworth in the days of King Stephen. The horse chestnut *Aesculus hippocastaneum* belongs to another species and is not edible.

CHIVES

A member of the genus allium. Native to the cooler parts of Europe, including Britain. Used since antiquity. Probably not cultivated until the Middle Ages.

CHOCOLATE

From the Aztec word, *chocolatl*. See Introduction.

CINNAMON—*Cinnamomum zeylanicum*

Of spices obtained from bark, cinnamon bark occupies a position of paramount importance. Cassia (known in many countries as Chinese cinnamon, *canelle de chine*) is one of the oldest of all spices. Both cinnamon and cassia come from small evergreen trees or bushes. The spice is in the bark peeled from the branches and sun-dried into quills. The flavour of cinnamon is more delicate than that of cassia. It is used in sweet dishes, biscuits and cakes and to spice creams and wines and hot drinks.

CITRON—*Citrus medica*

A fruit, larger than a lemon, less acid and thicker in rind. It appeared in Europe in the middle of the first century AD. Used to make candied peel. Oil used in liqueurs and perfumery.

CIVET

A resinous musky substance obtained from the anal pouch of the genus *Viverra*. Used in the making of perfumes.

CLARET

A wine drink made with honey and spices and grapes and strained before serving.

CLARY—*Sclaree*

The name given to *salvia sclaria* and also to several labiate plants of the genus *Salvia*. A garden pot-herb. Clary water or clary wine was a cordial compounded of brandy, sugar, clary flowers, cinnamon and ambergris.

CLOUTED CREAM

Cream produced in clots on new milk when simmered.

CLOVES—*Eugenia aromatica*

The clove is the most important of all the 'flower spices'. Cloves are the dried, unopened bud of the beautiful evergreen tree, belonging to the natural order *Myrtaceae* or myrtle family and native to the Molucca Islands. The English word 'clove' is derived from the French nail or *clou*. Cloves were used in China as early as the third century BC for perfuming the breath. They were imported into Europe during the Middle Ages. Cloves owe their aromatic properties to the volatile oil of which they contain a high proportion. Cloves were much used in domestic medicine and were also greatly prized by cooks, especially in confections made with apples. Cloves stuck in oranges and sun-dried, were considered a valuable protection against the plague.

CLOVE GILLI FLOWERS—*Dianthus caryophyllus*

The old-fashioned clove carnations had the spicy, aromatic scent of cloves. Deep crimson in colour, they were used in syrups, sauces, soups and cordials. The flowers were candied and preserved and were used to make vinegar and to decorate salads. Carnation syrup was a soothing and pleasant concoction.

CODLINGS

Green apples for boiling. Long and tapering in shape.

COFFIN

A certain kind of pie-dish shaped like a coffin or coffer from French *coffret* (basket-shaped), or sometimes the pastry case itself.

[323]

COLTSFOOT—*Tussilago farfara*

A coarse-leaved yellow-flowered weed formerly much used in salads and in domestic medicine.

COLUMBINE—*Aquilegia vulgaris*

Plant with five-spurred flowers. Used in home medicine for mouth and throat.

COMFIT

Richly-flavoured and strongly-scented sweetmeat taken after drinking or smoking or to remove any undesired lingering taste of over-spiced food.

CORIANDER—*Coriadrum sativum*

Japanese or Chinese parsley, now native to southern Europe and the Middle East. A very ancient herb. Both green leaf and seed are used. The seed is scented and tastes like tangerine skin. Used in bakery, liqueurs, condiments and as a pickling spice.

COSTARD APPLES

Cooking apples which kept throughout the winter, and were large and green.

COSTMARY—*Tanacetum balsamits*

This plant was introduced into England from the Orient in the sixteenth century and from that time onwards was used to perfume linen, to strew floors and to flavour dishes and ale.

COUCH GRASS—*Triticum repens*

A tiresome weed with underground creeping stems. Used in domestic medicine. The root is so nutritious that it was made into bread when corn was scarce.

COWSLIP—*Primula veris*

Native of Europe and western Asia. The flowers have a sweet, delicate flavour and were used in salads and as decoration and candied as sweet-meats. Cowslip wine was also much appreciated in Rebecca's day.

CUCUMBER—*Cucumis sativus*

A trailing plant, native of the Orient. Its fruit is used extensively in salads and for pickling. It was also used as a cooling medicine.

CURRANT

    (i)   'Raisins de Corinth'. A dwarf, seedless grape—dried—from the Levant.

    (ii) Black, red and white currants of the genus *Ribes* which were brought to Britain from the Island of Zante in the reign of King Henry VIII.

CUTLINS

Oatmeal grits used in the making of hog puddings.

DATE

Any species of the genus *Phoenix*, common in north Africa and Asia

[324]

Minor; red-brown fruits with a sweet pulp surrounding the stony seed. Dates are highly nutritious.

ELDER—*Sambucus nigra*

Used for making elder vinegar and elder wine. Originally elder trees were planted near dwelling-houses to protect them from the evil work of witches. Every part of the tree, from the bark to the berries, was used in cosmetic lotions and washes, to cure sunburn and remove wrinkles. Making elderberry wine and mixing elderberry flowers with fruit were part of the housewife's seasonal programme.

ERINGO ROOTS—*Eryngium maritimum*

Sea holly. The roots were often candied. Used in domestic medicine. Mentioned in Gerard's *Herball*.

FENNEL—*Faeniculum vulgare* and related species

Fennel is native to southern Europe. The Romans used it and introduced it into Britain. Wild fennel is slightly bitter and does not have the anise flavour which is so prized in sweet or 'Roman' fennel *Faeniculum dulce* or *officinalis*. Fennel was used in English cookery before the Norman conquest. Indissolubly linked with fish, it was used in a sauce and also as a spice. Fennel was one of the flavourings of sack.

FIRKIN

Used originally as a measure of capacity, the fourth part of a barrel or half a kilderkin. Later commonly used to describe small wooden casks used for butter, tallons, fish, liquids, etc., and varying in capacity according to the commodity.

FLORENTINE

A kind of pie or tart. Especially a meat pie without undercrust.

FLUMMERY

A food made of oatmeal or bran boiled to a jelly; a kind of blancmange.

FRUIT

Cheap sugar from the New World wrought an enormous change in the eating habits of the English and above all accounted for the sudden increase in the second half of the seventeenth century in the popularity of fruit. As a writer remarked in 1684, '. . . apples, pears, plums, gooseberries currants none of which would be made food and so advantageous to us if they were not mixed with such sweets'. New improved strains of apples, raspberries, currants, strawberries, gooseberries and cherries were introduced from Holland and America. Oranges and lemons became plentiful for the first time, but all fruit was still extremely expensive by today's standards and prices varied erratically with supplies. Even the cheapest home-grown apples and pears were several pence a pound and oranges and lemons from Spain commonly cost a penny or twopence each.

FRUMENTY

A dish made of wheat boiled in milk and flavoured with spices.

[325]

FUMITORY—*Fumaria officinalis*

Had a great reputation both as a cure for freckles and as a syrup, mixed with syrup of roses or syrup of peach flowers. Comes from America, parts of Asia and South Africa. Grows like a weed in England. Country folk called it 'vapour beggary' and 'wax dools'.

FURNACE

Equivalent to a modern copper. It was very large and could hold fifty gallons.

GALLIPOT

Earthen glazed pot or glass jar used for preserving until the advent of modern jamjars.

GARLIC—*Allium sativum*

Cultivated since the days of the ancient Egyptians. Used as a flavouring in everyday cookery and salads. Has many excellent medicinal properties.

GINGER—*Zingiber officinale*

The root is the part of the plant used. The best ginger root comes from the West Indies. It is said that Francisco de Mendoza brought the plant to Europe from the East Indies. Used as a flavouring, candied and in cooking. Was used against the plague. Used extensively in curries, gingerbread, crystallized and preserved.

GINGER, WILD—*Asarum canadense*

Belongs to a different family from *Zingiber officinale*. It is an aromatic plant used in medicine, and was once used in perfumery.

GLASS, JELLY

Conical in shape with a small straight-sided bowl set directly on a foot, 4″ or 5″ in height. Eight to a dozen were usually set in a circle on a glass salver (this would have had a stem and a foot and would have looked not unlike a Victorian cake-stand) around a single tall sweetmeat glass made in a dish or saucer form with a stem, rather like a modern champagne glass, containing candied or preserved fruit, chocolate or nuts. These appeared at the closing stages of a meal and to invite attention required to be attractively served and displayed.

GLASS, OLD FASHION DRINKING

This would have been a glass with a tall, conical bowl such as was fashionable in the 1660s, which would have provided the suitable pyramid-shaped mould.

GOOSEBERRY—*Ribes grossularia*

A berry much esteemed in the kitchen in trifles, sauces, puddings, pies and chutneys and as a corrective of rich foods. Leaves were often used in salads.

GRISKIN

The lean part of the loin of a bacon pig.

GROATS
Coarse meal, husked oats or wheat.

GUM ARABIC
A gum that exudes from certain species of acacia.

GUM DRAGON
See Tragacanth.

HARSLETT
'Harslet', properly haslet; liver, lights, etc., usually of a pig, also the griskin.

HARTSHORN
A preparation of shavings or clippings of the horns of the hart; formerly the chief source of ammonia. Spirit of hartshorn is made from a solution of ammonia and water. Salts of hartshorn are made from a solution of impure carbonate of ammonia.

HASTY PUDDING
Flour stirred into milk and the mixture boiled quickly.

HIP
Fruit of the wild rose.

HIPPOCRAS
A wine flavoured with spices, so called because it was passed through a cloth filter known as 'Hippocrates' sleeve'.

HUMBLES
A pie made of 'umbles' or entrails of the deer or occasionally other animals. This is almost certainly the derivation of 'eating humble (umble) pie'.

ICE HOUSE
By the mid-seventeenth century, the British had learned from the French and Italians how to preserve ice and snow during the summer months. The rich learned to build ice houses. These, either sunk in pits or enclosed in earth, had hollow straw-stuffed walls (short barley straw was best) and a double floor with a straw-closed drain. Once filled with snow or ice, the doorway was also strawed, the door tightly closed and the contents left until needed.

ISINGLASS
A gelatinous substance made from the swimming bladder of the sturgeon, cod, and other fish. Used for making jellies and glue.

JOHN APPLES
A good keeping variety. (Mentioned by Falstaff in Shakespeare's *Henry IV*, part ii.)

JUNIPER BERRY—*Juniperus communis* and other species
Sweet and aromatically-scented berry from the juniper bush. It exhales a pine-like scent. Used as a spice pickle for hams, as a conserve and as a flavouring. Used also medicinally as a stimulant for kidneys. Used to flavour gins and other spirits.

[327]

KEEL

To stir the pot, sometimes specifically to cool the contents or prevent it boiling over. ' . . . and greasy Joan doth *keel* the pot.' (Shakespeare, *Love's Labours Lost.*)

LEEK—*Allium porrum*

Regarded both as a vegetable and as a flavouring. Said to have been brought to Britain by the Romans. Leeks baked under hot embers were claimed by Parkinson to be a remedy against a surfeit of mushrooms.

LEMON—*Citrus limonum*

A native of south-east Asia. There seems to be some confusion in ancient writings about lemons and citrons. Lemon juice was often used to replace vinegar in salads.

LIFT OF BEEF

Often the upper part of a round of beef cut lengthways. The precise application varies according to locality.

MACE—*Myristica fragrans*

Aril of the nutmeg, pressed flat and dried. Its native habitat was Indonesia and the Philippines. Used in cakes and sweet dishes and many other confections which call for 'a blade of mace'.

MAIDENHAIR FERN—*Asplenium trichomanes*

The common maidenhair fern when boiled with water and sugar forms the syrup caoillaire. It forms a kind of jelly with a characteristic taste.

MALIGO SACK

Probably sack from Malaga.

MANGO

Evergreen tree of the family *Anacardiaceae*, a native of the East Indies. The fruit first became known in Europe in chutneys and preserves. Efforts were made to emulate its delicate and exotic flavour by growing melons (*Cucurbitacaae*) which were introduced into Britain from Asia in 1570. Rebecca often refers to mangoes, but almost certainly means melons.

MARCHPANE

'Massepain', now marzipan. A confection of almonds, sugar and white of egg. Often made into small cakes and coloured to resemble fruit, flowers or animals. Rebecca used to make 'egg and bacon' of marchpane to please her grandchildren.

MARIGOLD—*Calendula officinalis*

A flower much esteemed in domestic medicine. In Holland the flowers were used in broth. In Britain the marigold was used both as a pot-herb and as a salad herb.

MARJORAM—*Origanum majorana*

The sweet marjoram, the winter marjoram and the pot marjoram are all cultivated for their use in the kitchen, but the wild marjoram, *O*

[328]

vulgarex, whence the others stem is the only one used in medicine. The word marjoram may derive from the Greek word meaning 'joy of the mountain'. It is used for stuffing meat and poultry and makes a good flavouring for soups. The fresh leaves of the sweet marjoram are excellent in salads.

According to Gerard's *Herball*; 'Bastard Marjerome of Candy hath many threddy roots; from which rise up divers weake and feeble branches trailing upon the ground, set with faire greene leaves, not unlike those of Penny Royall, but broader and shorter; at the top of those branches stand scalie or chaffie ears of a purple colour. The whole plant is of a most pleasant sweet smell. Bastard Marjerome is called in shops, Origanum Hispanicum, Spanish Organy.'

MEAD

A fermented liquor made from honey, water and spices.

METHEGLIN

A variety of mead which originated in Wales.

MINT—*Mentha viridis*

Introduced into England during the Roman conquest. There are a great variety of species of mint, mostly native to western Asia and to the Mediterranean. In Britain, the species most useful in cookery are the round leaved apple mint, Bowles mint and pineapple mint.

MOUNTPELIER

Montpelier. A popular spa in France much frequented by British exiles during the Civil War. One of its chief industries was the manufacture of tallow and soap, so it is not unreasonable to suppose that Roger Price, the tallow chandler, combined business with pleasure when he visited this town with Rebecca. Montpelier's women were supposed to be as 'fayre' as its water.

MULBERRY—genus *Morus*

Any tree of the genus *Morus* bearing a collective fruit like a large blackberry. There are two kinds, black and white. According to herbalist Culpepper, 'the juice of the leaves of the Mulberry is a remedy against snakebite'. Parkinson states that the fruit was not much eaten because it stained the lips and fingers but it had an astringent quality and was good for sore mouths and throats and a syrup was made from it for this purpose.

MULL

To warm (wine, beer, etc.), sweeten and flavour with spices.

MUSHROOM—*family Agaricineae*

Wild fungi have always been eaten all over the world. They are important both as a food and a flavouring. Mushrooms were first cultivated in France around 1700, first as a garden crop and then in caves. In a menu for a royal repast in 1689 there is mention of 'Morelles' truffles, and asparagus and 'Hartichokes'.

[329]

MUSK

Dried secretion from certain glands of the male musk deer. Its natural purpose appears to be for the attraction of the female. It was long esteemed as a medicine, and as a flavouring. Its major use today is as a fixative in the manufacturing of perfume. Musk with rosewater was in common use in French and English kitchens in Shakespeare's time.

NASTURTIUM—*Tropaeolum majus*

A member of the cress family used in salads, the seeds of which, while green, were sometimes pickled as capers. This is the variety commonly grown today in gardens as a flower.

NEATS TONGUE

Tongue (ox or other). Neatherd: a cowherd.

NUTMEG—*Myristica officinalis* or *Myristica fragrans*

A native of the Moluccas and the islands of the Dutch East Indies, this spice was extremely popular in English kitchens from the seventeenth century onwards.

ONION—*Allium cepa,* variety *Aggregatum*

The onion is the basis of nearly all good cookery, especially French cookery. Its ancestor was probably a native of central Asia. It has been known and used for more than four thousand years. The onion has the power of absorbing poison, and in Latin countries a string of onions is hung outside and inside cottage doors to protect the inmates from infectious diseases.

ORANGE—Bitter: *Citrus vulgaris,* variety Bigaradia

Sweet: *Citrus Aurantium,* variety Dulcis

The orange came to us from India. It was unknown to the Spaniards until the sixteenth century. The China orange contains the most juice, but the bitter, Seville orange is more prized medicinally. The oil extracted from orange flowers is called 'oil of neroli', and is used in perfumery. Orange flower water is made from the flowers once the oil has been extracted. Orange peel was candied, crystallized and used as a flavouring in puddings, sweetmeats and confectionery. The first orange trees appear to have been brought to Britain by the Carew family, who had them grown in tubs in orangeries. By the reign of Charles II they were cried about the streets of London and sold in the theatres.

ORRIS—*Iris florentina, Iris germanica, Iris pallida*

Closely related varieties of iris, also known as fleur-de-luce (fleur-de-lys). Now very rare. The fragrant roots of these plants were extensively used in perfumery and medicine.

OYSTER

Edible bivalve mollusc of the genus *ostreidae,* found in salt or brackish water and eaten as food. Until the present century they were obtainable

[330]

in large quantities extremely cheaply and therefore constituted a staple item of diet. Oysters were widely used in cookery in the seventeenth century, being baked, fried, boiled and roasted, and pickled and often used as stuffing or sauce for meat and poultry.

PACK THREAD
Thick, strong thread for sewing or tying up parcels.

PALLETT
Tongue.

PEAR—*Pyrus communis* and allied species
Among the varieties of pears quoted by John Evelyn are 'bon chretien of winter', 'winter popling' and 'little dagobert'. These and others would have been known to Rebecca.

PENNYROYAL—*Mentha pulegium*
The popular pennyroyal is a variety of mint, used in domestic medicine as a remedy against coughs and colds. Virgil recounts that wounded deer seek it out as a cure. Used by Rebecca and her contemporaries in infusions, salads and jellies. Gerard, in his *Herball*, wrote of pennyroyal: 'it groweth naturally wild in moist and overglown places, as in the Common neere London called Miles End, about the holes and ponds thereof in sundry places, from whence poore women bring plenty to sell in London markets; and it groweth in sundry othern Commons neere London likewise. A Garland of Pennie Royall make and worne about the head is of great force against the swimming in the head, and the paines and giddinesse thereof.'

PEPPER—species of *piper* and related species
One of the most important of all spices since the days of the Romans. It was the main cause of the search for the Route to the East. There are many kinds of pepper including vine pepper which produces black and white peppercorns. Black pepper is prepared from the berries dried when not quite ripe and white pepper from the berries dried when fully ripe.

PICKLING SPICE
Generally devised by housewives to suit their individual tastes. The basic formula seems to have been made up of coriander seeds, mustard seeds, all spice berries, tiny hot chillies, bayleaves and minute pieces of dry ginger root.

PIPPIN
Generic name for several varieties of apple raised from seed.

PISTACHIO—*Pistacea vera*
Pistachio nuts came originally from Turkestan and were cultivated in the Mediterranean and Middle Eastern countries for three or four thousand years. See Genesis 43. Delicate of flavour, these nuts were included in certain meat and game recipes in the sixteenth and seventeenth centuries. They were also made into a delicacy called 'pistachio butter'.

PLUM

The fleshy drupaceous fruit of *Prunus domestica* or other trees of the same genus. Parkinson in 1629 listed no fewer than sixty-one varieties of plum many of which had been newly introduced by John Tradescant the Elder.

PORRINGER

Altered from the earlier 'potager'. A small basin or bowl out of which soup, broth, etc. was eaten.

POSNET

Corrupted from *poconet*, diminutive of *pocon* in Old French—a pot. A small pot or basin used for boiling.

POSSET

A drink made of curdled cream and eggs with ale or wine. It was used on social and convivial occasions and was served hot in a silver or 'cheney' basin.

POTATO—*Solanum tuberosum*

It would appear that the potato was brought to Europe by the Spaniards between 1580 and 1585. Sir Walter Raleigh also brought it back from the New World *circa* 1586. It was first found in a wild state only in Chile, but it is probable that before the arrival of the Spaniards in America, the plant had been spread by cultivation into Peru and New Granada. From thence it was most likely introduced in the latter half of the sixteenth century into that part of the USA now known as Virginia and North Carolina where it was discovered by Raleigh.

PURSELANE—*Portulace oleracea* (green purselane)
Portulace sativa (golden purselane)

Salad herbs, rather like samphire. The young shoots of either the green or golden variety are succulent and the seeds can also be eaten.

QUINCE—*Pyrus cydonia*

Native habitat: Cydonia, Crete. A hard yellow fruit belonging to the pear family used for flavouring and preserves. They were often preserved whole in sugar and served at banquets.

RASPBERRY (Raspes)—*Rubus idaeus* and related species

It was a 'pilgrim' plant and the homesick Crusaders, plodding along to Jerusalem, wrote that 'the way is very hard and stoney and maketh pilgrims very boney, but raspberries grow by the way with pleasure you may assay'. Its country name was 'bramble of Mount Ida' whence the raspberry came. It was also known as 'hindberry' and 'raspis'. Raspberry vinegar was considered invaluable for sore throats. Raspberries were made into jam, used in tarts, were preserved and eaten raw with clouted cream.

RATAFIA

A liqueur or cordial flavoured with cherry kernels, or the kernels of peach,

[332]

almond or other kinds of fruit. Also the name given to a sweet biscuit eaten with the liqueur.

RENNET

A preparation of enzymes from the calf's stomach used to 'turn' milk to make junkets and cottage cheese.

ROSE—various species of the genus *Rosa*

Roses came to Britain from Persia. A flourishing trade was carried on by the Persians in water distilled from roses in the eighth and ninth centuries. Juleps and conserves of roses were made in Provence in the thirteenth century and soon became popular in England. Housewives like Rebecca used dried rose leaves for their potpourri and scented bags; for candying, flavouring and for making into honey of roses, claret of roses and even into rose butter.

ROSEMARY—*Rosemarinus officinalis*

Hardy evergreen shrub, member of the family Labiatae. It is a native of southern Europe whence it was introduced into Britain in 1548. The leaves yield a valuable oil, one of the chief constituents of eau de cologne. Used abundantly in cookery and in salads. Has a distinctive and delicious scent.

SAGO—*Metroxylon laevis*, *Metroxylon rumphii* and related species

The soft inner portion of the trunk of several species of palms or cycads, the starch of which is separated and used as food.

SALT—sodium chloride

This was obtained by evaporating seawater in pans. Salprunella is a chemical variant of Saltpetre. Bay salt came originally from Portugal.

SALTPETRE—potassium nitrate

Salt of the rock potassium nitrate. Minute quantities were used in salting down meat, game, etc.

SAMPHIRE—*Crithmum maritimum*

'Herbe de St Pierre' known as 'sea fennel'. It is a plant of sea cliffs with a strong aromatic and salty taste. Used mainly for pickling but was also used fresh in salads or cooked in butter and cream as a vegetable.

SAVORY—*Satureia hortensis* (summer)
> *Satureia montana* (winter)

This plant (both summer and winter varieties) is aromatic and tasty in salads. It was made into conserves and syrups and the Romans mixed savory leaves with vinegar to make a sauce like mint sauce. The plant had a reputation for preserving sight and hearing.

SCURVYGRACE—*Cochlearia officinalis*

An anti-scrofulous plant, also known as scurvygrass. Its country name was Spoonwort on account of its hollow or spoon-shaped leaves. The succulent leaves were eaten in salads and the juice was added to beer and also made into a syrup. It grows on the sea coast of northern and western Europe. Scurvygrass ale was usually recommended in the spring.

SCUTENEEL—*Coccus cacti*

Variously spelt, but usually known as 'cochineal'. A carmine dye and colouring agent, used in cookery. Made from the dried bodies of the female cochineal insect.

SEARCE

A sieve or strainer.

SHILLING—New

This refers to the new milled coinage introduced in the reign of Charles II, as opposed to the earlier, hammered coinage which it replaced. It would have been a little smaller than a modern 10p piece.

SILLABUB POT

A small glass pot with spout, cover and two handles, similar in form to a teapot.

SIPPET

Small piece of toast.

SLIPCOTE CHEESE

One of the oldest and best of English cream cheeses. Originating in Rutland, it was traditionally ripened in cabbage leaves. Its name 'slipcote' comes from the fact that it has a loose skin which slips off when the cheese is ripe.

SORREL—*Rumex acetosa* and related species

Country name: 'o cuckoo's meate'. The sorrels belong to the same family as the docks and share their cooling virtues. There are many varieties of sorrel, e.g., mountain sorrel, wood sorrel, sheep's sorrel. It grows everywhere in the fields and meadows and flowers in May. The leaves have a sharp, sour taste and were much used for sauces.

SPICE

The term spice can be loosely applied to three groups of produce; herbs such as sage, rosemary, thyme; aromatic seeds like aniseed, fennel, carraway; and spices such as pepper, ginger and nutmeg.

Spices are mentioned in the Old and New Testament on many occasions. Fennel seed, aniseed, coriander seed, sage and thyme and many other sweet-smelling herbs were grown in Persia, Mesopotamia and Syria, and carried through Palestine to Egypt by Arab camel caravans.

It had been discovered that the leaves of the herbs, when dried in the hot sun, retained their flavour and aroma. After being ground, probably between two stones, they were mixed with oils and ointments and used for dressing wounds, for embalming bodies, as perfumes and for the flavouring and garnishing of certain dishes.

At the entrance to the Persian Gulf is the Island of Hormuz, which

[334]

was used as an entrepot by the Arabs. As time passed new spices were marketed abroad; pepper, cardamoms and ginger came from India. From Hormuz, cargoes were taken overland to Trebizond for Constantinople and also up the Red Sea for Alexandria.

SPINACH—*Spinacea oleracea*

Originally came from Persia. Sometimes used for colouring. It was also used in salads; or cooked without additional moisture, but with butter and spice added, as a vegetable. Robert May in his *Accomplish't Cook* (1685 edition) gives an elaborate recipe for a spinage tart in three colours.

STONES

Lamb's testicles, or testicles generally.

STORAX—*Styrax officinalis* and *Liquidamber orientale*

Gum from bark and branches. Two distinct substances under the name of storax have been known since the sixth century. One is the resin of the *Styrax officinalis*, a solid resin. The other is the liquid storax which has the consistency of honey. Used as an ingredient in potpourri and incense.

STRAYNER

Strainer. Rebecca often makes mention of a 'cotton' strayner, and of a 'haire' strayner.

SUGAR

In the seventeenth century sugar was the most important of the many commodities to become available in ever-increasing quantities from the New World. In the Middle Ages sugar loaves from India and Arabia had cost up to 2s. a pound, but first Canary sugar, and then in the seventeenth century Caribbean sugar, brought the price tumbling down so that it was selling at around 4d. per pound by the 1680s when Rebecca was writing.

It seems likely that the sugar-cane—the original source of sugar—came from Polynesia in the Pacific. From there, several thousand years before Christ, the wild reed and the secret of extracting its sweetness were carried up to India, to the north of Bengal, and from there to Western China.

. In the first century AD one can find the word 'saccharum' in the writings of Pliny the Elder. Sugar beet as a plant was still unknown, although some later Roman writers mention a wild plant (*Beta maritima*) found on the sea shore which had a sweet taste. Only the white beet (*Beta cicla*) was already being eaten as a vegetable by the Romans.

In 1099 the Crusaders discovered sugar-cane in Syria and the sugar that came from it. They could hardly wait to make this information known in Britain. Here the new commodity brought back by the Crusaders was sold by apothecaries at very high prices. In 1319 one single

[335]

cargo fetched a million pounds of today's money! There was a great variety of forms of sugar obtainable in medieval times.

Sugarloaf, also called sugarstone or sugarrock, was a refined sugar, hard and white, milled in conical shapes resembling actual loaves.

Caffetin or palm sugar owed its name to its country of origin, the Genoese colony of Caffa, a town of the Crimea, and to its appearance. It was wrapped in mats plaited from palm-leaves (in Arabic—*caffa*).

Casson sugar or broken loaf sugar was a soft sugar which broke easily in the course of the extensive handling it received. This in the sixteenth century was known as cassonade (probably from the French *casser*—to break) or cask sugar.

Lump sugar was more breakable. It came from the sugar mills reduced to a fine dust and was the forerunner of our powdered sugar. The mills of Cyprus, Syria and Babylon were known according to their various particular qualities.

Muscarrat sugar was perfumed with musk. Its name was derived from the word *muchera*, an Arab word meaning 'improved by cooking over and over again'.

Candi sugar differed from other forms, as today, by the shape of its large crystals. At the end of the fifteenth century, five sorts of candi would be found in any good apothecary shop: simple candi, rose candi, violet candi, lemon candi, red gooseberry candi (all these candies were extracts of syrups).

Other sugars obtainable were Barbary sugar, Madeira sugar (from Portugal) and Montreal mill sugar which came from a town in Syria, situated south of the Dead Sea.

SYLLABUB

A popular drink at the end of the seventeenth century and the eighteenth century when it became the fashionable drink for ladies at evening functions. It was made with cream fresh from the cow, to which was added sack seasoned with ratafia and spices. It was served in straight-sided glasses similar to jelly glasses.

TANSY

The earlier tansies (of the tenth to fourteenth centuries) seem to have been a hot, purgative porridge, made of worts (tansy), rough grains (barley or bran) and fats (marrow or suet). This was taken while fasting and was followed by drinking a hot herb tea. Later, the tansy became a kind of flan, much used in conjunction with apples. Tansy is also a herb —Tanacetum vulgare—used as a flavouring. In the seventeenth century it was beaten with eggs and fried into cakes known as 'tansies' which were eaten in Lent.

TEA—*Camellia sinensis*

Term applied specifically to the leaves of the tea-plant. The Chinese

[336]

name is *cha*. The Chinese may have used tea medicinally as early as the third or fourth century AD, but seemingly not as a beverage until the sixth century. By the ninth century when it was introduced into Japan, tea had become the staple Chinese drink. It is said that Christopher Borough, who had been on a trading expedition into Persia, first introduced *cha* into England in 1579. Tea came to England at about the same time as coffee; the first supplies being brought from China by the Dutch East India merchants. Some of it reached the London market where it was sold for the remarkable price of £3 10s. per pound. The price dropped to about £2 in nine or ten years when, according to Rugge's *Diurnal*, 'coffee, chocolate and a new kind of drink called Tea was sold in every coffee-house'. By the end of the seventeenth century good supplies were being brought in by the East India Company and, in spite of the heavy tax imposed in 1689, it could be bought for little more than 20s. a pound.

THYME—*Thymus vulgaris*

Thyme will grow wherever lavender and rosemary thrive. The wild thyme, which is called serpyllum because of its creeping habit, grows best on light soil. Garden thyme provides us with the antiseptic oil known as Thymol. There are many varieties of thyme, all sweet-scented. It is used in cooking as a flavouring.

TIFFANY

A kind of thin, silk-like gauze. Was sometimes used as a strainer.

TINMOULD

A vessel used for shaping puddings, etc.

TRAGACANTH

A gum from several species of *Astragulus*, a low-growing spiny shrub found in Persia, and from *Sterculia tragacantha* of west Africa.

TRUFFLE

Fleshy fungus from the genus *Tuber* used for seasonings. Until the early years of this century, the truffle-hunter with his dog gathered a satisfactory harvest of this fungus under the beech trees on the chalk downs. A rare delicacy now, and very expensive.

TURKEY

First discovered in Mexico and brought by the Spaniards to Europe in 1530. They became popular in the second half of the seventeenth century. They were bred in Norfolk and Suffolk and were walked to London in droves of up to a thousand, being then fattened for the market artificially by the poulterers.

VEGETABLES

It was only in the reign of Charles II that certain vegetables as we know them today became regular items of diet—cauliflower, broccoli, kale, French beans and artichokes were all novelties introduced to English

[337]

gardeners from abroad, as well as greatly improved carrots, turnips, onions and cabbages from Dutch gardeners. Potatoes were, however, extremely rare, except in Lancashire, until about 1700. Vegetables were (like fruit) extremely expensive, cabbages and cauliflowers costing up to 4d. each. The only cheap vegetables were peas and beans, commonly used as fodder.

VERJUICE

This is a sharp cider and is not a vinegar. Made from crab apples and unripe grapes, etc.

VERMICELLI

A wheaten paste in the form of long slender tubes or threads, like macaroni. Derived from *vermicillo*, a dimunitive of *verme*, worm.

VIOLET—*Viola odorata*

The Romans used violets in making wine. Leaves and flowers were popular in salads. Violets give their flavour and colour to liqueurs and conserves. Violet pate, or violet sugar, was popular in the reign of Charles II, and violet vinegar was much in demand for headaches. Leaves and flowers used to decorate or garnish meat dishes. Violet flowers were preserved in sugar as crystallized violets, and used mainly for decoration, but they were sometimes crushed as a flavouring.

VIPER'S BUGLOSS—*Echium vulgare*

Used for the same purposes as borage. A cordial herb much esteemed in domestic medicine, and decorative in wine cups and summer drinks. Gentlewomen candied the flowers for comfits.

WASSAIL OR LAMB'S WOOL BOWLS

Used in the sixteenth and seventeenth centuries. These bowls are almost exclusively of the hard and dense-grained wood of the West Indian tree known as the guaicum tree, much held in repute for its supposed medicinal properties, and for this reason called *lignum vitae* or the tree of life. This tree is indigenous to Brazil. Wassail bowls were often used to contain a large quantity of hot liquid, so it was essential that the wood from which they were made should be durable and dense-grained. The word 'wassail' derives from the old English word 'waes hael' meaning 'be whole' or 'be well'.

The custom of wassailing obtained not only in lay but in monastic houses in the Middle Ages; in the monasteries the bowl was known as *poculum caritatas*—the cup of charity.

WESTPHALIA HAM

Named after its country of origin.

WIGGS

A pudding, still made in the north country.

WINES

Some came from Bordeaux ('Burdeaux') such as Gascoigne, Anguella,

Rochelle; and there were Rhenish wines of two sorts: Elstertune and Brabant. Sack was imported from various countries, though the best came from Xeres in Spain. Muscadine and Malmsey were well liked.

WOOD SORREL—*Oxalis acetosella*

A low-growing woodland plant, excellent for purifying the blood. See also SORREL.

WOODWARD

An officer appointed to look after plantations of trees.

XERES

Also known as 'sherry' sack. Made in Bristol and known as 'Bristol milk' because it was the first moisture to wet an infant's lips. Xeres is now known as Jerez de la Frontera, in Spain.

BIOGRAPHICAL NOTES

BEECH, Mrs—probably one of the Beeches of Redbourne, Hertfordshire. (Rebecca's younger daughter Rebecca married Thomas Beech of Redbourne.)

CHAPMAN, Simon—Roger Price's woodward. Roger Price left him ten pounds in his will.

CHAPMAN, Mrs—wife of Simon.

CHARLTON, Mrs—probably Mary Charlton, the wife of Nicholas Charlton, one of Roger Price's executors. Sir Joseph Sheldon left her his silver teapot in his will dated July 1681. There was a Nicholas Charlton of St Michael, Cornhill, woollen draper, citizen and merchant taylor—Warden 1697.

CLERKE, first cousin—see notes on Rye and Franklin below.

CLERKE, second cousin—see notes on Rye and Franklin below.

DANVERS (Danvis), Lady—the Danvers family had property in Culworth, Northamptonshire. Sir Samuel Danvers (died 1683) had a wife, Anne, daughter of Sir William Pope of Wrexton, Oxfordshire (died 1678).

DUNCOMBE, Mrs—presumably one of the Duncombes of Great Brickhill, Ivinghoe, Aston or East Claydon, Buckinghamshire. Rebecca's granddaughter Ann married a William Duncombe, attorney at Chalgrave, Buckinghamshire, in 1753, possibly a descendant.

FLETCHER (ffletcher), Mr William—servant of Rebecca's elder sister Anne and her first husband John Warner. He later went into partnership with Anne's nephew John Warner, apothecary. She left the same William Fletcher the sum of twenty pounds in her will dated 8 April 1728.

FRANKLIN (ffranckline), Aunt—this was no doubt the Mrs Ann Franklin, widow, buried at Westbury in 1683. Rebecca's father, Roger Price, in his will dated 1678, left a legacy 'unto each of the five sons of my aunt Francklin'. She was probably related in some way to the Franklins of Maverne and Bolnhurst in Bedfordshire as to which see following entry.

FRANKLIN, Lady—probably Dorothy, the second wife of Sir John Franklin (died 1707) of Bolnhurst, Bedfordshire. She was born in 1657, the daughter of George Clerke (c. 1626–89), son of Sir George Clerke of Watford, Northamptonshire, and died 7 October 1707.

GREEN, Mrs—probably the wife of the Rev. Francis Green, vicar of East Claydon, Buckinghamshire.

HOWE, Lady (my Lady How)—probably the wife of Scrope Howe, first Viscount Howe (1648-1712), Whig politician. She was Lady Anne Manners, sixth daughter of John, eighth Earl of Rutland.

JONES, Lady Mary—wife of Sir Samuel Jones of Courtenhall, Northamptonshire.

KERSTEMAN, Mrs Anne (sister Kersteman)—Rebecca Price's elder sister (1658–1728). She married, first, John Warner, citizen of London, and, second, Mr William Kersteman. She lived at Camberwell in Surrey, in a large brick house surrounded by orchards. It is clear from her will dated 8 April 1728 that she was a woman of some substance. She left numerous bequests of jewellery, money, clothes and furniture. It is clear that Anne and Rebecca must have remained very close to each other throughout their lives as Anne appointed Rebecca the sole executrix of her will and they are buried next to each other under handsome black marble slabs in the chancel of Houghton Regis church.

LEECH, Mrs Anne—servant to Roger Price, Rebecca's father. It is clear she was either the cook or housekeeper at Westbury. Roger left ten pounds to her son Richard in his will.

MASON, Mrs (Mrs Mason of Stratford)—wife of John Mason, rector of Water Stratford, Buckinghamshire, who was presented to the living in 1674. He was noted for his extraordinary piety and had visions during which he believed he was a second Elias.

NAPIER, Lady—probably the wife of Sir Richard Napier, MA, of Great Linford, Buckinghamshire.

NEWTON—Rebecca's cook at Houghton Regis.

PENN (Pen), Jos.—probably one of the Penns of Penn in Buckinghamshire from which family William Penn who founded Pennsylvania was descended.

POWIS, Lady—Lady Elizabeth Somerset, wife of William Herbert, first Marquis and Earl of Powis.

PRICE, Anne (my mother)—wife of Roger Price of Westbury and Rebecca's mother. Little is known of her except that she was buried at Westbury in 1670 when Rebecca would have been ten years old, and that her maiden name was Ingham—this we learn from the tomb of one of her sons, Ingham Price, who is there described as having been baptized by his mother's maiden name.

PRICE, Roger (my father)—squire of Westbury, Buckinghamshire. His father had purchased the Manor of Westbury in Buckinghamshire from Dame Catherine Lyttleton, the widow of a well-known Royalist, Sir Thomas Lyttleton, in 1650. He had seven sons, the eldest of whom, another Roger, was elected MP for Buckingham in 1702 in succession to Sir Edmund Verney, and three daughters of whom Rebecca, born in 1660, was the middle one. It is clear from Roger Price's will that he was a man of considerable wealth and position. He leaves portions of £1,500 to each of his six younger sons and his three daughters, a great sum in the values of that time, together with extensive property in London as well as his property at Westbury. He numbered among his closest friends, Sir William Dolben (Dalbin), Recorder of London, and Justice of the King's Bench, Sir John Moore and Sir Joseph Sheldon, both of whom were Lord Mayors of London in their time. He died at Bilbao in Spain in 1677.

RYE, Aunt—almost certainly a Rye of Culworth in Northamptonshire. There was a John Rye whose wife Mary made a will in 1681. Her son, George Rye, c. 1637–77, was at Trinity College, Oxford, in 1654 and a student at Lincoln's Inn in 1656. This George married Elizabeth Tipping, the daughter of Sir Thomas Tipping, in 1661, when she was aged sixteen (another of the donors of recipes to Rebecca is a Mrs Frances Typing which supports this connection between the Ryes, the Tippings and the Prices). Mary Rye's will also mentions a grandchild called Judith Clerke who was to be kept by her cousin Anne Rye one of the six daughters of George Rye, until she was eighteen or married. This clue to the identity of 'first and second cousen Clerke', mentioned by Rebecca as donors of many of the recipes, can be followed up in the 1681 Heralds Visitation of Northamptonshire, published by the Harleian Society, where on page 51 will be found the statement that John Clerke of Guilsborough, Councellor at Law, christened in 1625 at Willoughby, Warwickshire, married Judith 'wife of John Rye of Culworth'. This must be an error for daughter and shows the connection of the Clerkes of Guilsborough with the Ryes.

SHELDON, Sir Joseph—nephew and heir of Dr Gilbert Sheldon, Archbishop of Canterbury. He was the son of Ralph Sheldon of Stanton in Staffordshire and married as his second wife Margaret Rose, daughter of George Rose. It is this Lady Sheldon who is the donor of so many of the receipts. Sir Joseph was apprenticed to Rebecca's grandfather in 1657 and became her father's great friend. Like him he was a member of the Tallow Chandlers' Company, and was later translated to the Drapers' Company. He was an alderman of the City of London (1666–81) and was Lord Mayor in 1675. He died 16 August 1681. Roger Price was godfather to Sir Joseph's daughter, Elizabeth (this Elizabeth married Sir John Cotton, Bart., of Lanwade and Maddingly Hall, Cambridgeshire, at Westminster Abbey on 14 January 1679 and their son Sir John Hynde Cotton (died 1752) was the famous Jacobite politician), to whom he left his silver warming-pan in his will; and Sir Joseph in turn acted as one of Roger Price's executors. Sir Joseph's sister Katherine married John Dolben, Bishop of Rochester and brother of Sir William Dolben, Justice of the King's Bench and Recorder of London and another of Rebecca's father's friends and executors. The Sheldons had a town house called 'The Drum' in Drury Lane where no doubt Rebecca often stayed and where as Lord Mayor and alderman Sir Joseph would have entertained lavishly, using many of the receipts given to Rebecca by Lady Sheldon.

[342]

SHELDON, Lady Margaret (Lady Sheldon)—wife of Sir Joseph Sheldon. She was Margaret Rose, daughter of George Rose.

SHELDON, Mr Daniel—brother of Sir Joseph Sheldon. He lived at Ham in Surrey.

SILL, Mrs—no doubt one of the Wellesborne Sills of Westbury, Buckinghamshire. The advowson was held by Wellesborne Sill in 1634 and by his widow, Philippa Sill, in 1646.

SWANNELL—probably Rebecca's housekeeper or cook at Houghton Regis.

TIPPING (Typing), Mrs Frances—almost certainly one of the Tipping family of Wheatfield in Oxfordshire (see note on Rye above).

TOOTH, Mary—Rebecca Price's cousin. It is not known exactly how she was related but she is described as such by both Rebecca's father and her sister, Anne Kersteman, in their wills.

WHEATLY, Cousin—this must be the Mrs Ann Franklin who married John Wheatley at Westbury in 1680. Presumably she was the daughter of the widow Ann Franklin who was buried in Westbury in 1683 (see note on Aunt Franklin above).

APPENDIX I

Rebecca's Will

In the name of God Amen, I REBECCA BRANDRETH of HOUGHTON REGIS in the County of Bedfordshire Widow being in good health of body and of sound and disposing mind memory and understanding for which I bless God do make and ordain this my last Will and Testament in manner and form following (that is to say) ffirst and principally I commend my Soul unto Almighty God my Creator assuredly beleiving That I shall receive full pardon and Remission of all my Sins and be saved by the precious death and Merits of my Blessed Saviour and Redeemer Jesus Christ and my Body I commit to the Earth desireing it may be decently buried in the Chancell of the Parish Church of Houghton afforesaid by my Daughter Alice Brandreth according to a paper of directions for that purpose which I shall leave written and signed by me with my own hand and entituled Directions about my ffunerall and it is my desire to be buried out of the best hall in the ffront of the Mansion house of Houghton were I *now dwell faceing the Green* and I also desire that the family pew in the said Church be put into Mourning for twelve Months next after my decease in like manner as it was for my late Husband Nehemiah Brandreth Esquire deceased and I likewise desire that the Pulpit and Desk may be put into Mourning and so continue for one year next after my decease in like manner as it did for my said late Husband and as for such Worldly Estate as it hath pleased God to bless me with I give and dispose thereof in manner following (that is to say) ffirst I will that all such Debts as I shall justly owe at the time of my decease and my ffunerall Charges be in the first place paid by my Executrix hereinafter named Item I give to my Son Nehemiah Brandreth the sum of Ten Pounds for

[344]

Mourning Item I give to my Daughter in Law Mary Brandreth late Wife to my Son Henry Brandreth deceased the sum of Ten Pounds for Mourning Item I give to my Son in Law Mr Thomas Beech and his Wife the sum of Ten Pounds a peice for Mourning Item I give to each of my Grand Children a Ring of the value of Twenty Shillings Item I give to the poor of Houghton Regis aforesaid the Sum of Ten Pounds to be distributed amongst them by my Executrix as she shall think fitt after the expiration of one Month next after my decease Item I give to my Servant Richard Arnott the sum of Twenty Pounds to be paid him within Six Months next after my decease Item I give and Bequeath unto my Daughter Alice Brandreth for her own Sole and proper use and benefitt and to dispose of as she shall think fitt my black Cabinett and inlaid Chest of Drawers with the Appurtenances thereunto belonging and my inlaid dressing Box lined with Silk standing and being in my dressing Room within my Bed Chamber where I now lye and my hanging press by my Bedside in my Bedchamber with all the things whatsoever within them or any of them and also my Chest of Drawers Bed which stands in my said Bed Chamber with the bed and Bedding belonging to it and also all the Mohair Bed wherein I now lye with the feather Bed Bolster pillows and all the quilts and Blankets belonging to it and I give to my said Daughter Alice Brandreth all my wearing Cloaths and Apparell of all sorts or kinds whatsoever and all my wearing Linnen Table Linnen Sheets pillowbears and Towells of all sort and kinds whatsoever and wheresoever and all my books *except my two receipt Books in folio written by myself* and hereinafter bequeathed And I also give unto my said Daughter Alice Brandreth my two Charriots with the Appurtenances belonging to each and every of them and I also give unto my said Daughter all such Horses and Geldings which I shall die possessed of and also all my China and China Ware of what sort and kind soever I also give to my said Daughter Alice Brandreth all my Pewter Brase Iron Tin Earthen Ware and Wooden Ware and I also give unto my said Daughter one of my Silver Chaffen Dishes such as she shall make choice of with a Silver Lamp thereunto belonging my two dozen of hafted Silver knives and forkes with the two Cases thereunto belonging Item I give and Bequeath to my said Daughter Alice Brandreth her Executors and Administrators the Picture of my late ffather set in Gold and my two receipt Books in folio written by my self one of which said Books being for Surgery and physick and the other for Cookery and Preserves both of the said Books being bound with Leather and on the inside of the Lidds of each of them is mentioned that they were written in the year 1681 by Rebecca Price (that being my Maiden name) and written by myself And I doe alsoe give and Bequeath to my said Daughter Alice Brandreth her Executors and Administrators my Gold Strikeing Watch with the Amithyst Seale sett in Gold hanging to it And also all the severall peices or parcells of plate hereinafter particularly mentioned and discribed (that is to say) One large Silver Bason on which is engraved a Coat of Arms of three Escollop shells and three Cornish Chaffs the said Basson weighing sixty ffive Ounces and a Quater or thereabouts One Silver Tankard weighing Thirty ffive Ounces and a Quarter or thereabouts my Silver Coffeepott weighing Twenty Eight Ounces and a Quarter or thereabouts my two Silver Salvers weighing together thirty nine Ounces or thereabouts my three Silver Castors with a small Silver Spoon belonging to them weighing together Twenty ffour Ounces or thereabouts my Silver Chaffendish and a Silver Lamp thereunto belonging weighing together one and Twenty Ounces or thereabouts upon all which said severall peices of plate are engraven the said Coat of Arms as are upon the said Bason And also my two Silver Pottingers on which are engraven the same Coat of Arms upon the handles weighing together fourteen Ounces and one Quarter or thereabouts and a small Silver Pottinger with the Letters N.R.B. on the handles thereof weighing ffour Ounces or thereabouts my Silver Cup with a Spoutt Silver Cover and Chain to it the said Cup being marked with the Letters N.B. and weighing together Eight Ounces and an half or thereabouts and my Silver Mugg weighing twelve Ounces or thereabouts four Silver Salts weighing together Eight Ounces or thereabouts Twelve Silver Spoons with flat Handles and one with a Scoope handle weighing together twenty ffive Ounces or thereabouts my Silver Ladle weighing Six Ounces and an half or thereabouts upon all which last mentioned severall peices of plate except the said Spoon with a large Scoopehandle are engraven the same arms as are upon the aforesaid Bason my Six small Silver Tea Spoons which said Spoons weigh near three Ounces or thereabouts Six gilt Small Silver Tea Spoons and one small gilt Silver Spoon with holes in it belonging to the said Tea Spoones and a Small pair of Silver Tea Tongues Gilt which said small gilt Spoones and tongues weigh altogether three Ounces or thereabouts and my mind and Will is and I do hereby declare that the said Picture and Two Receipt Books and also the said Watch and Seal and the said Severall peices or parcells of Plate are and were so by me given and Bequeathed to my said Daughter Alice Brandreth her Executors or Administrators upon this Speciall Trust and confidents that the said Alice Brandreth her Executors or Administrators do and shall deliver the said Picture Receipts Books and Watch and Seal and peices or parcells of Plate to my Grandson Henry Brandreth Son of my said late Son Henry Brandreth by Mary his Wife when he shall attain his age of one and Twenty years to and for his own use and benefit and in case my said Grandson Henry Brandreth shall depart such life before such age Then my mind and Will is that my said Daughter Alice Brandreth shall have and I do hereby give and Bequeath to her the said Picture Receipts Books and Watch and Seal and also the said Severall peices or parcells of plate to and for her own use and benefit absolutely and my mind and Will further is that my said Daughter Alice Brandreth shall be at liberty to make use of the said Picture Receipt Books Watch and Seal and peices or parcells of Plate at her own Will and pleasure untill the time herein before appointed for her delivering the same . . . all my ffurniture and other things mentioned in the Schedule or Inventory hereunto annexed and which I have Signed with my name and which Goods and ffurniture and other things are standing and being in and about my Bedchamber Dressing Room Dineing Room and other places in Houghton Regis aforsaid I Give and Bequeath the same Goods ffurniture and other things to my said Grandson at the age of Twenty one years and in case my said Grandson Henry Brandreth shall die before the age of twenty one Then I Give and Bequeath the same Goods and ffurniture and other things unto my said Daughter Alice Brandreth to and for her own use and benefitt Item as to all the rest and residue of my Estate whatsoever and wheresoever both reall and personall not otherwise by this my Will given or disposed of (after payment of my Debts and ffunerall Expences and the severall Legacies hereinbefore by me given and Bequeathed) I give and Bequeath the same and every part thereof unto my said Daughter Alice Brandreth her Heirs Executors and Administrators and Assigns respectively to and for her and their own use and benefit absolutely And I do hereby make ordain constitute and appoint my said Daughter Alice Brandreth Sole Executrix of this my last Will and Testament And I do hereby revoke all former and other Wills by me at any time heretofore made and do declare this present Writing to be and contain my only last Will and Testament In Witness whereof I the said Rebecca Brandreth the Testatrix have hereunto set my hand and seal the tenth day of Aprill in the year of Our Lord 1740 and in the thirteenth yeare of the Reigne of Our Sovereigne Lord George the Second by the Grace of God of Great Britain ffrance and Ireland King Defender of the faith Exd. Rebecca Brandreth.

This Writing was Signed and Sealed by the Testatrix Rebecca Brandreth and published and declared by her as and for her last Will and Testament in our presence who have likewise in her presence subscribed our names as Witnesses thereto (the Interlineations between the 8th and 9th and 16th and 17th lines first appearing) Amb: Reddell ffrancis Collyer Daniel Burr Exd.

THE SCHEDULE referred to by the annext Will IN my Bed Chamber Six yellow Stuff Window Curtains with Valence and Rods to them Six yellow Mohair Cushions and One peice of Tapestry Hangings a Great easy Chair and Cushion covered with a blew Gold and Silver Stuff Six Cane Wallnutree Chairs a Peir or long Looking Glass in a Gilt fframe between the Windows and a Buroe Wallnutree Dressing Table and a Wallnutree Card Table and a Wallnuttree plate Case with two Glass Doors to it a Gilt leather Screen with two leaves an Iron back to the Chimney and an Iron Hearth and Tongs Shovel Hand Irons and Bellows Two Glass Sconces over the Chimney and a Copper Warming Pann in my Dressing Room Six Chairs covered with yellow Mohair and four peices of yellow Mohair Hangings Six yellow Stuff Window Curtains with Valence and Rods to them a large looking Glass the fframe thereof inlaid, placed between the Windows, a large Table inlaid standing underneath the said Glass also a hanging Dressing Glass in an inlaid fframe, and a Comb box two Powder boxes two Patch boxes and two small Brushes all inlaid a Round Cane Walnuttree Stool a low Wallnutree Stand a Copper Tea Kettle with a Copper Lamp to it and a High brass Stand a Small Japan Teapott and a Lamp to it a Silk Toilet flowered red and white laced round with fflanders Lace and a deep fflanders Laced Table Cloth Within the light Closett in my Bed Chamber a little Oak Table with a Drawer to it and a low Cane Chair In the dark Closett in my Bed Chamber a Sweetmeat Cupboard large and high with Six Shellow boxes therein and in the said Closett is a Small Oak Table with two leaves and alsoe a Close Stool of Oak, In my Dineing Room a great easy Chair and Cushion covered with red and white figured Velvet two Square Stools covered with the like and Six Cushions of the same Velvet Six Cane Chairs made of Cherrytree a peir or long looking Glass in a Black fframe between the Windows, a black Card table the top whereof covered with Crimson Velvet, one of the best painted Dutch Tables a large Japan Tea Table a Japan Corner Cupboard four red Stuff Window Curtains with Valence and Rods to them an Iron Back to the Chimney Tongues Shovel, hand Irons and a pair of Bellows, ffour Glass Sconces and a Corner Cupboard of Oak that is in the entry by my said dineing Room the ffeather Bed and Bolster with two pillows that my Daughter Alice Brandreth now Lyeth on in the Room over my aforesaid Bed Chamber and which said Bedding I removed since I became a Widow out of the Room now called a Dineing Room being heretofore a Bed Chamber and in which my Sons used to lye And a ffeather Bed and Bolster on which my Servant Richard Arnott lyeth Rebecca Brandreth Signed by the Testator Rebecca Brandreth in Our presence who have likewise in her presence subscribed our names as Witnesses thereto Amb: Reddall ffrancis Colyer Daniel Burr. Exd.

APPENDIX II

Extract from an Inventory of the Contents of the Manor House at Houghton Regis taken 23 May 1740 by John Smith and Ambrose Cooke

In the kitchen

(Pewter) 37 dishes, 79 plates, 2 water plates, 1 pasty pann, one ditto plate, 7 cheese plates, a mazarine and waiters,[1] one bason, 2 porringers, a plate ring, one chamber pott, one cistern and cock, one bottle cistern.
(Copper) one boyler, and cover, one bottle cistern, three sausepans, two

[1] A large deep dish containing smaller dishes for the setting out of ragouts or fricassees.

tea kittles, two drinking potts, one chocolate pott, one coffee pott, two preserving pans and one stewpan, two bellmettle potts with brass and copper lidds, two . . . one boyleing pott, three kittles, one skillett, one small pan, one skimmer, a pudding pan without a bottom, eight candle sticks, a snuffer stand and pepper box.

(Iron) a range of grates, a chocks[1] keeper fender fire shovell, Tongs and poker, one iron back, two pott hangers, one chaffin dish, ten iron sconcers and frame, a hand cleaver, a chopping knife, a pigiron,[2] a pair standing spitt racks, a wind-up jack compleat, three spitts, two bird spitts, one frame, three candle sticks, one hussiff, a plate warmer, and pr. snuffers, a flesh fork, a pair bellows, three boxirons, five pads and two rests, a pair stilliards.[3]

(Tin) a candle box, a breadgrater, a dish and plate covers, a drudger, a half pint pott, two sconces.

(Wood) a napkin press, a square table, six chairs, one stool, a bacon rack, a salt box, a marble morter (broke) and wooden pestle, eleven knives, twelve forks (ivory handled) twelve odd knives, and forks, one kitchen knife, four pr. window curtains and rods, two payls, a plate rack, three bowles, one flour tubb, nine trenchers, and dishes and meat screen.

Valued at £22. 4s. od.

In the Pastrey, Pantrey, Bacon Room and Lobb Hall

(Pastrey) One large ovell table, two dough troughs, two cupboards, two tosting irons, with tin pans, a nursing candlestick and saucepan, a parcel tin patty pans, a Pye peele, an ironing board, cloaths baskett, three basketts, one cage, two voiders,[4] one plate baskett, one lawn sive.

(Pantrey) Three tin cake hoops, one pudding pan, a safe cupboard, two forms, one box, an old wyer scive.

(Bacon Room) Three sacks and three bags with feathers, a parcel of loose feathers in a cupboard at stairhead.

Lobb Hall

A tin kittle and cover, a double cupboard, a square table, one form, corner shelves, and some earthenware about the severall places.

Valued at £2. 7s. od.

[1] Logs for burning.

[2] An iron plate hung between the meat and the fire when the latter is too hot.

[3] Steelyards.

[4] Large wicker baskets for holding soiled clothes, dishes or scraps.

In the Washhouse and Launders

One copper and ironwork only half belonging to the estate, a washstand, a kiver and one form, two cupboards, two wooden bottles, a powdering tubb and cover, two forms, a chopping block, a stone bottle, seven pieces red earthenware.

In the Brewhouse

A copper and ironwork, an old mash tun and under back a lead pump and cistern from under back to copper, a lead pipe from yard pump to copper, two working tubbs, two coolers, a jett a mashridder, a trimoll, a rich kittle and marking irons.

Valued at £12

In the Cellars

(Further Cellar)
One hogshead, three beerstalders,[1] one stoole.
(Hither Cellar)
Two hogsheads, one kilderkin, three firkins, three half anchors, one two gallon bottle, three drink stalders, two brass cocks.
(Small beer cellar)
One hogshead, one kilderkin, two tapp tubbs, about thirty dozen quart glass bottles and one dozen and a half pint bottles in severall places and lumber about the house.

Valued at £4. 2s. 6d

Linnin

4 pr. Holland sheets, 14 pair flaxen ditto, 3 pr. Hempen ditto, and 3 pr. and a half ditto, very old, 3 Damask table cloths, 3 sideboard cloths and thirty four knapkins, two new Damask table cloths (just made) twelve Diaper table cloths, two and twenty knapkins six Huckerback tablecloths, six very old tablecloths, fifteen diaper towels, eight flaxen ditto, three round ditto, four pair Holland pillow beirs, fourteen ditto very old, six pr. flaxen ditto.

Valued at £18. 16s. 0d.

[1] A stalder is a frame for casks to stand in.

Milkhouse

A powdering tub and cover, two trussells, and two slabs, four wooden
bottles, a cheese press, and three vatts, two butter boards, two forms, one
pair butter scales, one pound lead weight, a strainer, sciming dish, one
round baskett, one stone bottle, thirteen pieces earthenware, 14 quart glass
bottles, a cheese curd rack, a pair milk tongs, one sheet.
                    Valued at £1. 0s. 6d.

BIBLIOGRAPHY

Background reading

AITKEN, J. (ed.), *English Diaries of the Sixteenth, Seventeenth and Eighteenth Centuries*, Harmondsworth, Penguin Books, 1941

BARING-GOULD, S., *Old Country Life*, London, Methuen, 1890

BATSFORD, H. and FRY, C., *Homes and Gardens of England*, London, Batsford, 1932

CECIL, E., *A History of Gardening in England*, London, Quaritch, 1895

CHAPMAN, H., *The Tragedy of Charles II in the Years 1630–1660*, London, Cape, 1964

CHARLES, C. J., *Elizabethan Interiors*, New York, Greenfield, 1912

CLARK, A., *Working Life of Women in the Seventeenth Century*, London, Routledge, 1919

CLARK, G., *The Later Stuarts 1660–1714*, Oxford, Clarendon Press, 1934

COATE, M., *Social Life in Stuart England*, London, Methuen, 1924

COGAN, T., *The Haven of Health*, 1584

CULPEPER, N., *The English Physitian Enlarged*, London, Cole, 1663

DAVIS, D., *History of Shopping*, London, Routledge, 1966

DEFOE, D., *Journal of the Plague Year*, London, 1722

DITCHFIELD, P. H., *The Old English Country Squire*, London, Methuen, 1912

DUTTON, R., *The English Country House*, London, Batsford, 1935

DUTTON, R., *The English Interior 1500–1900*, London, Batsford, 1948

EMMISON, F. G., *Tudor Food and Pastimes*, London, Benn, 1964

EVELYN, J., *The Diary*, Oxford, Clarendon Press, 1955

GERARD, J., *The Herball*, London, 1597

GODFREY, E., *Home Life under the Stuarts 1603–1649*, London, Paul, 1925 (revised ed.)

GODFREY, E., *Social Life under the Stuarts*, London, Grant Richards, 1904

HARRISON, G. B., *A Jacobean Journal 1603–1606*, London, Routledge, 1941

HARTLEY, D. and ELIOT, M., *Life and Works of the People of England*, 6 vols, London, Batsford, 1925–31

HOWARD, W., *Selections from the Household Books of Lord William Howard of Naworth Castle*, Surtees Society, 1878

JEKYLL, G., *Old English Household Life*, London, Batsford, 1925

KENYON, J. P., *The Stuarts—a study of English kinship*, London, Batsford, 1958

LE GRAND, P. J. B., *L'Histoire de la Vie Privée des Français*, Part 1, 3 vols, Paris, 1782

MEAGER, L., *The English Gardener*, London, 1670

MISSION, *Mission's Memoirs*, trans. Mr Ozell, 1719

MORRIS, C. (ed.), *The Journeys of Celia Fiennes*, London, Cresset Press, 1949

OGG, D., *England in the Reign of King Charles II*, Oxford, Clarendon Press, 1934.

OGG, D., *Europe in the Seventeenth Century*, London, Black, 1954 (revised ed.)

PEPYS, S., *The Diary of Samuel Pepys*, edited with additions by H. B. Wheatley, 8 vols, London, Bell, 1904–5

PEVSNER, N. (ed.), *The Cities of London and Westminster*, vol. 1, London, Penguin (The Buildings of England Series)

PHILLIPS, H., *History of Cultivated Vegetables*, 2 vols, London, Colburn, 1822 (2nd ed.)

PLATT, H., *The Jewell House of Art and Nature*, 1594

PONSONBY, A., *English Diaries*, London, Methuen, 1923

PYNE, W. H., *The History of the Royal Residences*, London, 1819

QUENNELL, M. and QUENNELL, C. H. B., *A History of Everyday Things in England*, vol. 2, 1500–1799, London, Batsford, 1937

ROGERS, J. E. T., *History of Agriculture and Prices in England 1259–1793*, 7 vols, Oxford, Clarendon Press, 1866–1902

ROHDE, E. S., *The Old English Gardening Books*, London, Hopkinson, 1924

STEER, F. W., *Farm and Cottage Inventories of Mid-Essex 1635–1749*, Phillimore, Chichester, 1969

STUART, D. M., *The English Abigail*, London, Macmillan, 1946

SUMMERSON, J., *Architecture in Britain 1530–1830*, London, Penguin, 1953

THOMAS, O. E., *Domestic Utensils of Wood*, London, Evan-Thomas, 1932

TREVELYAN, G. M., *England under Queen Anne*, London, Longmans, 1930

TREVELYAN, G. M., *England under the Stuarts*, London, Methuen, 1904

TREVELYAN, G. M., *Illustrated English Social History*, vols 1 and 2, London, Longmans, 1949

VERNEY, M., *Memoirs of the Verney Family*, 1892

WEDGWOOD, C. V., *Seventeenth-Century English Literature*, London, O.U.P., 1950

WEST, V. S., *Knole and the Sackvilles*, London, Heinemann, 1922

Local history

ELAND, G. (ed.), *The Purefoy Letters*, vol. 2, London, Sidgwick & Jackson, 1931

LE BRETON MARTIN, E., *History of Westbury. Buckinghamshire*, London, Acorn Press, 1928

LIPSCOMBE, *History and Antiquities of the County of Buckinghamshire*, London, Robins, 1847

Cookery and recipe books

ALLDE, E., *The Good House-wives Treasurie*, London, 1588

ALLDE, E., *The Books of Cookerie—otherwise called; the good huswives handmaid for the kitchen*, London, 1597

BOORDE, A., *The Dietary of Health, a Compendyous Regyment or a Dyetary of Healthe made in Mountpyllyer*, London, 1542

BUDGE, E. W., *The Divine Origin of the Craft of the Herbalist*, Society of Herbalists, 1928

DIGBY, K., *The Closet of Sir Kenelm Digby Opened*, 1677 (3rd ed.). Later edition ed. A. MacDonell, London, Warne, 1910

EVELYN, J., *Acetaria—A Discourse on Sallets*, London, 1699

HARTLEY, D., *Food in England*, London, Macdonald, 1954

LEYEL, H. W. W., *Herbal Delights*, London, Faber, 1937

MARKHAM, G., *The English Housewife*, London, 1615

PARSONS, M., *The Lady's Cabinet Opened*, 1639

PLATT, H., *The Garden of Eden*, London, 1615

SALMON, W., *The Family-Dictionary; or, household companion*, London, 1696

STOBART, T., *The International Wine and Food Societies' Guide to Herbs, Spices and Flavourings*, Newton Abbot, David & Charles, 1970

VARENNE, F. P. DE LA, *Le Patissier françois*, Amsterdam, 1655

Dyet's dry dinner, London, 1599

Other sources

London marriage licences

Boyd's *Citizens of London*

The Visitation of London for 1634

WILLIAMS, M. F., *History of the Tallow Chandlers' Company*, London, Chiswick Press, Charles Wittingham & Co., 1897

CULINARY INDEX

Ale: in cake, 195; in fish sauce, 65, 110; in meat sauce, 81, 86–7, 89; in posset, 167–9

Almond, 58, 80; butter, 174–5; in cakes, 191, 193, 198; caundle, 296; in confectionery, 258, 262–7; cream, 45, 161–2; in desserts, 162, 165, 168–9, 171, 174–5; in puddings, 126–7, 132–3; tart, 150

Ambergris: in cakes, 190–4, 198–9; in confectionery, 255, 259, 262, 276–7; in desserts, 148, 155, 158, 161, 165, 168; in jam, 215, 218; in perfume, 315; in wine, 305, 307

Anchovy: in fish sauce, 62–7, 108–10; in meat sauce, 79–82, 85–7, 89, 92–7, 102, 111–15

Angelica: cakes, 258; candied, 283

Aniseed, 261, 276

Apple, 273; baked, 172; cakes, 270–1; cider, 292–5; cream, 159–60; dried, 278–9, 281; flan, 177; fritters, 178–9; jam, 215; jelly, 217–19; juice, 307; pie, 148; pudding, 44, 130; with quince, 272; stewed, 172–3; tart, 148–9; water, 214, 216, 221, 225, 228

Apricot, 270; cake, 258, 266–9, 271; dried, 278–81; jam, 213; jumbell, 261; paste, 272; preserve, 220–1; pudding, 131–2; puff, 263; syrup, 166; tart, 149; wine, 298, 301

Artichoke, 145–7

Bacon: gravy, 114; mock, 255–6; with turkey, 80

Barbel, roast, 62

Barberry jelly, 219, 225–6

Barley: cream, 155; pudding, 127; in soup, 58

Beans: in beer, 295; blanched, 57

Beef: baked, 102; coller, 43, 97; dried, 98; fried, 181; gravy, 113–14; potted, 102; roast, 86; salt, 98–9; in soup, 54, 56–8; stewed, 86–7, 90

Beer, 69, 295–6

Biscuit, 42, 274–7; cream, 165; pudding, 133

Blackberry syrup, 235

Blackcurrrant, see Redcurrant

Brandy: cherry, 305; in wine, 305–6

Bread: baking methods, 184–5; in desserts, 121, 128–9, 133, 150, 157; in dumplings, 120–1; sauce, 113

Buns, 185

Butter: almond, 174–5; burnt, 114; cheese, 207; clarified, 115; orange, 174; pistachio, 174–5; salted, 204

Buttermilk, 204

Cabbage: pudding, 121; in soup, 58

Cake, 41–2; fruit, 190–4, 198; plum, 194–5; seed, 195–8; short, 198

Calf: foot, 144, 162; head, 82, 90; liver, 93

Caraway seeds, 195–8, 256, 276

Carp, 63–4, 109

Carrot pudding, 43, 121

Caudle, 66, 146–7, 157, 296

Cauliflower, 79; pickle, 244–5

Cheese, 42; butter, 207; with cream, 169; egg, 206; hard, 205–6; sage, 207; slipcote, 204–5; water, 206

Cheesecake, 139, 173–4

Cherry: brandy, 305; cream, 161; dried, 281; jam, 213; preserve, 223; wine, 297, 299–300

Chicken: boiled, 80; fricassee, 94–5; fried, 82; hash, 92; pie, 142–3; sauce for, 110–11; in soup, 54–7; stew, 90, 95

Chocolate: cream, 171–2; hot, 308–9

Cider, 292–5; see also Verjuce

Cinnamon, 147, 314

Citron: in cake, 191, 193, 196–7; dried, 278–9; in jam, 215; jelly, 217–18; pudding, 132; syrup of, 291, 296, 301, 304

Claret: in fish sauce, 62, 64, 108–10; in meat sauce, 81, 91, 93, 95, 97, 102, 112–14; in soup, 54

Clove gilly flower: pickle, 250; syrup, 171, 232–3; wine, 303–4

Cochineal, 148, 226, 293

Cod, sauce for, 110

Colouring: agents, 171, 255–7, 261, 273–5, 285; preservation of, 278

Frontiniac, 305; gooseberry, 298; grape, 303; in mead, 291; in meat sauce, 80, 90, 92–7; mulberry, 301; orange, 301; plum, 300; posset, 167; in preserves, 222; quince, 300–1; raisin, 302; raspberry, 297–9; red-currant, 296–8; sage, 304–5; sieving, 296; spiced, 306–7; strawberry, 298; in syrups, 236; vinegar, 242–50

Yeast: in bread, 184–5; in cake, 41–2, 190–8; in wine, 301, 304, 305